THE UNIVERSITY OF WINCHESTER

Martial Rose Library
Tel: 01962 827306

To be returned on or before the day marked above, subject to recall.

The Contemporary Political Play

Rethinking Dramaturgical Structure

SARAH GROCHALA

Bloomsbury Academic
An imprint of Bloomsbury Publishing Plc

B L O O M S B U R Y
LONDON · OXFORD · NEW YORK · NEW DELHI · SYDNEY

Bloomsbury Methuen Drama

An imprint of Bloomsbury Publishing Plc

50 Bedford Square   1385 Broadway
London   New York
WC1B 3DP   NY 10018
UK   USA

www.bloomsbury.com

**BLOOMSBURY, METHUEN DRAMA and the Diana logo are trademarks of
Bloomsbury Publishing Plc**

First published 2017

British Library Cataloguing-in-Publication Data
A catalogue record for this book is available from the British Library.

ISBN: HB: 978-1-4725-8847-0
       PB: 978-1-4725-8846-3
       ePDF: 978-1-4725-8849-4
       ePub: 978-1-4725-8848-7

Library of Congress Cataloging-in-Publication Data
A catalog record for this book is available from the Library of Congress.

Cover design: Eleanor Rose
Cover image: 4.48 PSYCHOSIS by Sarah Kane; Daniel Evans, Jo McInnes,
Madelaine Potter; Directed by James Macdonald; at the Royal Court Theatre,
London, UK; June 2000 © Pete Jones / ArenaPAL

Typeset by Fakenham Prepress Solutions, Fakenham, Norfolk NR21 8NN
Printed and bound in Great Britain

To find out more about our authors and books visit www.bloomsbury.com. Here
you will find extracts, author interviews, details of forthcoming events and the
option to sign up for our newsletters.

For Gile.

Thanks for hanging in there.

CONTENTS

ACKNOWLEDGEMENTS

With extra special thanks to Michael McKinnie, Maria Delgado, Tony Fisher, Gilli Bush-Bailey, Catherine Silverstone and Nadia Davids for all their help and support during the development of this research.

With special thanks to Henny Finch, Jeremy Herrin and everyone at Headlong and to everyone in the research office at the Royal Central School of Speech and Drama for enabling me to take the time I needed to prepare this book. Also to the London Library Trust for making it possible for me to have access to the library during the research and writing of this book.

With thanks to Julia Böll, Stephen Bottoms, Deborah Dooley and Bob Cooper, Melissa Dunne, Rupert Goold, Andrew Haydon, Margherita Laera, Maria Millsavjevic, Martin Middke, Gwendolen Morgan, Cuong Nguyen, Monika Pietrzak-Franger, Sam Potter, Ben Power, Dan Rebellato, Trish Reid, Nick Ridout, Daniel Swift, Ben Tan, Julia Tyrrell, Eckart Voigts-Virchow, Clare Wallace, Ellen Wiles, Penelope Woods and to all my very extended family.

The initial development of this research was supported by a PhD studentship from Queen Mary, University of London. This research was also supported by the German Society for Contemporary Drama for English through their PhD Forum. The PhD on which this book is based was joint runner up for the CDE Award in 2014.

Introduction

We need to find new questions, which may help us answer the old ones or make them unimportant, and this means new subjects and new form.

CHURCHILL 1960: 446

This book explores the role that particular dramaturgies play in our understanding of what is and what is not a political play within the context of post-Thatcher British theatre. The idea for this book was originally sparked by an argument between British theatre critic Michael Billington and Scottish playwright Anthony Neilson. In June 2008, two new plays dealing with the issue of child abuse opened in London: Australian playwright Anthony Weigh's *2000 Feet Away* (Bush, London 2008) and Neilson's *Relocated* (Royal Court, London 2008). Billington reviewed both plays for one of the UK's leading newspapers, the *Guardian*. Both plays share similar themes but Billington delivered opposing verdicts, judging one to be a politically productive piece of theatre and the other to be politically irresponsible.

Weigh's *2000 Feet Away* is based on real events. In 2005, the state of Iowa passed a law banning sex offenders from living within 2,000 feet of places where children might gather, such as a school or a playground. Weigh's play centres around a doughnut-loving deputy sheriff from a small Iowa town who is charged with enforcing the new law. As there is no place in his town that is more than 2,000 feet from somewhere children might gather, the town's sex offenders end up stranded in a remote motel off the highway. The sheriff, who states that he would 'cut his hands off' if he thought he might ever make sexual advances towards a child, finds himself developing some sympathy for one of the sex offenders, A.G. (Weigh 2008: 103). When the motel is burnt down, at the climax of the play's action, the deputy gets in his car with A.G. and takes him to Chicago where he releases him back into the wild.

Neilson's *Relocated* is also inspired by real events. In 2002, Maxine Carr, a classroom assistant working in the English town of Soham, provided her boyfriend, Ian Huntley, with a false alibi after he murdered two of her pupils. Carr was convicted of perverting the course of justice and granted anonymity for life on her release from jail for her own protection. The story of *Relocated*'s protagonist, Connie, echoes that of Carr. Connie is a classroom assistant, whose ex-boyfriend, Liam, murdered children in their bathroom. Connie, like Carr, is given new identities to protect her, Marjorie Charles and Kerry Balfour. Three different actresses play Connie's three different identities. At the beginning of the play, Marjorie collapses while vacuuming: 'she clutches her chest and falls to her knees, then pitches forward face-down onto the floor' (Neilson 2008b: 1). At the end, the play returns to Marjorie lying motionless on the floor. The action of the play can be read as a hallucination Marjorie has, as she hovers between life and death. Marjorie is visited by a policeman who tells her it is time to move on again and take on another new identity. She becomes Kerry Balfour, moves to a new flat and takes up a new position at a new school. She also starts a relationship with John Nickleson, an art teacher. Her new neighbour, Marj, gives her a strange picture of children playing in the schoolyard at midnight. Kerry discovers that the artist, an eight-year-old girl called Molly Cairns, went missing two years earlier and is presumed dead. Kerry becomes convinced that Molly has been kidnapped by a notorious German criminal, Johon Schinkel, who imprisoned his daughter in a basement for many years and fathered children with her (echoing the real-life story of the Austrian criminal Josef Fritzl). Kerry becomes determined to track down Schinkel and rescue Molly. John Nickleson, however, is revealed to be Johon Schinkel. He kidnaps Kerry and locks her in his basement, where she finds Molly. Kerry, Molly and Johon become a happy family. Kerry warns Molly never to reveal that they were actually happy together if she is ever released from captivity.

While the two plays share similar subject matter, they employ very different dramaturgies. Billington's verdict on the plays' different political characters is rooted in the different nature of these dramaturgical structures. Billington argues that Weigh's play is politically productive on the basis of his use of a specific dramatic form. Weigh's play has a political thesis at its heart: 'whether America has the right answers in demonizing adult-child relationships, taking refuge in religious sloganizing and relentlessly commercializing sex'. This thesis is framed within the context of a realist dramaturgy that provides the audience with a 'rigorous portrait of a community filled with a superstitious ignorance'. On the basis of these structural elements, Billington rules that *2000 Feet Away* is a 'serious play' (Billington 2008a).

In contrast, Billington sees *Relocated* as politically irresponsible. His main objection to the play is its lack of a 'general thesis' on child abuse. Billington's language also, however, betrays a level of moral alarm around the relationship between the political content of the play and its dramaturgy. There is a 'disjunction between its content and style' (Billington 2008c). In *Relocated*, Neilson employs a dramaturgy of '*disorientation*' and '*claustrophobia*' (Neilson 2008b: 1). The play's sense of time and space is disrupted, the narrative fragmented and the characters fractured. Billington views the use of these dramaturgical structures as 'hideously inappropriate', producing a 'Gothic thriller' that offers 'titillation without illumination' (Billington 2008c).

Neilson responded publicly to Billington's assessment of *Relocated*, claiming that his play was being judged against an inappropriate set of criteria. Billington and he, Neilson observes, 'disagree utterly on what it is a play should do'. Neilson argues that the idea of a 'play-as-thesis is by nature reductive, an attempt to bring order to the unruliness of existence' (Neilson 2008a). He states that, as he does not believe in a world where there are permanent truths, it would be dishonest of him to put forward a coherent thesis about the world, even if the presentation of a coherent thesis is the criterion on which his plays will be judged. Instead, he claims that *Relocated* is 'an entirely subjective piece, taking place in the mind of the central character'. The play expresses 'a state of mind, not the "state of things"' (Billington 2008b).

I saw both plays back in 2008 and, as an audience member, I found *Relocated* the more affecting of the two. I would identify this as a direct result of the discordant relationship Neilson creates between the play's content and its dramaturgy. I agreed with theatre critic Kate Bassett, who pinpointed the importance of this discordant relationship in producing a political impact on the spectator in her review of both plays in the major UK newspaper the *Independent on Sunday*: '[i]t's not morally comfortable, yet that is surely the point. *Relocated* taps into the profound permeating terror such atrocities generate, as well as raising disturbing questions about the morbid fascination they exert' (Bassett 2008a). As I followed the debate between Billington and Neilson, I became curious about both Billington's sense that there was an appropriate and serious dramaturgy for dealing with political issues and Neilson's observation that Billington and he were judging the value of a play using different sets of criteria. This book, born out of this curiosity, is an investigation into the reasons *why* certain dramaturgical structures are commonly associated with the idea of a political play and an exploration into the political potential of alternative dramaturgical approaches currently in use in British theatre. I will argue that these alternative dramaturgical structures highlight the importance of considering the ways in which a play operates politically through its form, as well as through its content.

Politics and political theatre

What is a 'political play'? It seems a straightforward question but there are a number of commonly held assumptions about what a political play is and what a political play does that need closer examination. Is it literally a play about politics? A play about the processes and workings of government? Or is it a play about a political issue? Or a play that does something political either by attempting to alter the audience's beliefs about the world or rallying them to take political action?

First, in considering this question, it is necessary for me to define what I mean by the term 'politics'. Following literary theorist Stefan Collini, I take politics to essentially mean: 'the important, inescapable, and difficult attempt to determine relations of power in a given space' (Collini 2004: 67). Performance scholar Joe Kelleher identifies this definition of politics as particularly useful because it conveys the idea that politics is not a static thing in and of itself but a dynamic social process: 'power – or powerlessness – is nothing in itself and only ever meaningful in terms of the distribution of power across social relations, among different groups or classes or interests that make up, however momentarily, a social body' (Kelleher 2009: 3). Politics can take on a range of different political characters depending on the types of power relations it supports. It can be seen as democratic or authoritarian in terms of the distribution of power. It can be seen as socialist, communist, feudalist, capitalist or even fascist in terms of the economic system associated with it. It can be thought of as liberal or collective in terms of whether it prioritizes the rights of the individual or the rights of the group. It can be thought of as progressive or reactionary depending on whether it seeks to challenge or uphold the values of the existing social order.

In Britain, politics is habitually thought of as broadly divided into a left wing and a right wing, having predominantly socialist or conservative values respectively. Technically, socialism is a political system run on the basis of the social ownership of the means of production and co-operative management of the economy. At its fullest extent, socialism is commonly thought of as communism. Whereas capitalism is an economic system based on the private ownership of the means of production, which are used to generate profit within a competitive marketplace, communism is a classless society based on the common ownership of the means of production. Within a British context, socialism tends to take a softer form, a type of managed capitalism in which the state puts limits on the market in order to curb the worst of its excesses and essential industries such as power, water and transport are owned by the state and are non-profit-making. It is associated with the maintenance of a welfare state that supports people in times of need and is thought of as a progressive form of politics whose aim is to create a fairer society by trying to address inequalities between the advantaged and the disadvantaged. It is liberal in its outlook, in that it campaigns for the freedom of the individual in terms of their basic human rights. This form of politics is characterized as progressive as it seeks to change the current social order.

In contrast, right-wing or conservative politics is associated with liberal capitalism and campaigns for a free market, uncontrolled by government regulations, offering the individual the greatest opportunity to capitalize on the forces of the market and improve their own circumstances. It is based on the idea of a meritocracy in which people are rewarded in line with their ability to take advantage of their talents. It is liberal in terms of its belief in the right of the individual to determine their own destiny. It thinks of the market as self-regulating, controlled by eighteenth-century philosopher Adam Smith's concept of the 'invisible hand'. The rich, he argues, 'are led by an invisible hand to make nearly the same distribution of the necessities of life, which would have been made, had the earth been divided into equal portions among all its inhabitants, and thus without intending it, without knowing it, advance the interest of the society' (Smith 1817: 296). Right-wing politics is associated with conservatism because it seeks to uphold traditional values associated with ideas of family, religion and patriotism. As a result of this, it is usually characterized as a reactionary rather than a progressive form of politics. At its most extreme, right-wing politics is associated with fascism. Fascism is an economic system based on the private ownership of the means of production on the condition that these are run in the interests of the state. The free market is abolished. Prices and wages are set by the government. The means of production are implicitly as opposed to explicitly nationalized. The state's interests are imposed by authoritarian control. Fascism is the point where the values of the right wing and the left wing meet. In theory, however, it differs fundamentally from both socialism and conservatism in that it is a political system based on authoritarianism as opposed to democracy.

A political play is commonly thought of as a play about a political issue. A play that, as theatre scholar Amelia Howe Kritzer observes, 'presents or constructs a political issue or comments on what is already perceived as a political issue' (Kritzer 2008: 10). A political play, however, is not simply a question of political content; it is also a question of political intention. Writer and scholar Graham Holderness argues that a political play is a play that attempts to 're-shape the world along particular lines of development' (Holderness 1992: 2). As Kelleher points out, a political play 'does not just happen of its own accord but is put together in a particular way for our benefit, which means also put together to "work" on us in particular ways' (Kelleher 2009: 8). There is a political intention behind its creation.

The concept of artistic intention has currently fallen out of fashion. Intentionality was discredited as a decisive factor in establishing a particular reading of a text by literary theorist W. K. Wimsatt and philosopher Monroe Beardsley in the 1940s.

Wimsatt and Beardsley argue that it is impossible to determine authorial intention purely from a text and therefore the worth of a text cannot be judged on the basis of whether it fulfils its author's supposed intentions (Wimsatt and Beardsley 1970: 3). In the context of political theatre, I would argue that the author's intentions can be considered if they have been explicitly stated by the author. In this case, as literary theorist Linda Hutcheon argues, 'these statements can and must be confronted with actual textual results' (Hutcheon 2012: 109). To intend something is, of course, not the same thing as achieving it; however, if politics is, as Collini thinks of it, an 'attempt' then intention should be considered political. To intend to have a political impact is a political act, regardless of ultimate success or failure. After all, if political theatre were defined exclusively in terms of theatre that can be empirically proven to have had a direct political impact, the field of study would be very small indeed.

Sometimes a political act can be unintentional. As literary theorist Roland Barthes argues, the meaning of a text can be determined by the reader's interpretation as opposed to the writer's intentions (Barthes 1977: 148). A political act is a political act because we perceive it to be one, regardless of whether it was intended as one. In 2010, the Polish president Lech Kaczyński was killed in a plane crash. Before his death, he had been an unpopular figure in the eyes of a large section of Polish society. After his death, he was controversially raised to the status of national hero. This controversy coincided with an unfortunate advertising campaign for Lech beer. Posters appeared around Poland advertising the joys of a 'cold Lech' (Anon 2010). While the intention behind the poster was to sell beer, it was read as publicly ridiculing the president's memory and incited political outrage. Despite having no ostensible political intentions, the poster was ultimately seen as a political act. Politics is a question of function as well as of intention.

Context also plays a role in whether a play is perceived as being political. English playwright Lucy Prebble had the idea for her play *ENRON* (Headlong/Chichester Festival Theatre/Royal Court, London 2009), about the rise and fall of the American energy giant, long before the financial crisis of 2008. At the point of inspiration, the collapse of Enron looked like 'an isolated scandal' (Adams 2009). By the time the play was produced in 2009, however, 'the system of belief' that led to one company's downfall had become emblematic of a worldwide economic crisis (Prebble quoted in Adams 2009). Although Prebble claims she did not set out to write 'the "story of our times"', the timing of the play's production meant it was widely read by British theatre critics as a play that 'crystallises the mood of its age' (Spencer 2009). When a play's themes chime with current events, it takes on a political character, regardless of its author's original intentions.

In the context of British theatre, a play is generally only considered political if it has a specific political character: that of a socialist and progressive viewpoint. As theatre scholar Michael Patterson argues, the political play usually 'implies the possibility of radical change on socialist lines: the removal of injustice and autocracy and their replacement by fairer distribution of wealth and more democratic systems' (Patterson 2003: 4). Holderness claims that there is no political theatre of the right: '[i]t seems that political theatre can be progressive, but not regressive; socialist but not conservative; subversive but not conformist or radically reactionary' (Holderness 1992: 3). As a rare example of right-wing drama, he cites English dramatist Ian Curteis's television play *The Falklands Play* (BBC 2002), which portrays British Conservative prime minister Margaret Thatcher as a heroic leader moulded in the style of English renaissance playwright William Shakespeare's *Henry V*. According to film, theatre and television scholar Derek Paget, the BBC withdrew *The Falklands Play* from broadcast in the late eighties on the basis that it was not only, in their view, badly written, but also 'out of synch' with the times (Paget 1992: 167). The ultimate irony of this was that, when the play was finally broadcast, it was clear it 'might well have provoked more turbulence – simply by presenting uncensored the authentic self-congratulatory odour of Thatcherian righteousness' than the left-wing drama *Tumbledown* (BBC 1988), which replaced it, did (Paget 1992: 178).

The idea that political drama is always left-wing drama, as I will argue in the first chapter of this book, has a basis in the origins of the dramaturgical structures that are commonly identified with the idea of a political play in Britain. It is not a universal truth. As someone of dual cultural heritage, I can attest to the existence of a prominent strand of right-wing drama in contemporary Poland. The form of this drama, a type of heroic historical tragedy termed 'Polish romanticism', is very different from the form that is thought of as political drama in Britain. It focuses either on significant historical events within Polish cultural memory (e.g. Katyń, the Warsaw Uprising) and/or specific historical figures whose actions are recognized as heroic (e.g. the martyred priest Jerzy Popiełuszko, the leader of the Solidarity movement Lech Wałęsa). Drawing on moments of collective trauma and/or national pride, these dramas actively promote right-wing values, including nationalism and religious conservatism, through exploiting and, at times, rewriting cultural memory. The form can be accused of attempting to 'manipulate the viewer's emotions and play on patriotic sentiment' (Etkind et al. 2012: 48) and so being a form of 'patriotic blackmail' (Kot 2007).

Rather than arguing the right-wing political play does not exist, it is more accurate to say right-wing drama takes a different form to left-wing drama, one that may not be instantly recognized as political. Kritzer points out that the non-political play can be considered to have a right-wing – or, more accurately, reactionary – political character as it can be read as supporting the prevailing social order simply because it fails to actively challenge it: '[t]heatre that does not draw its audience into a dialogue about politics may serve the existing power structure by contributing to apathy and disengagement' (Kritzer 2008: 12–13). Theatre scholar David Ian Rabey identifies Anglo-Czech playwright Tom Stoppard as a 'right-wing dramatist' on this basis (Rabey 2003: 93). He argues that Stoppard's *The Real Thing* (Strand Theatre, London 1982), a comedy about a love affair between a playwright and actress and the illusive nature of reality, reconfirms the conservative values of its audience through its seeming lack of political engagement: 'the pseudo-neutrality of its elevation of language and traditional institutionally-approved style above other alternative values or claims of politics, justice or relevance' (Rabey 2003: 94).

English dramatist and theatre scholar Dan Rebellato has identified certain forms of theatre as having a right-wing or, more accurately, a capitalist politics, as a result of the mode of their production. He observes that global mega-musicals, such as *Les Misérables* (Palais des Sports, Paris 1981), *Mamma Mia* (Prince Edward Theatre, London 1999) or *Wicked* (George Gershwin Theatre, New York 2003), are a form of mass-industrialized theatre, which he terms 'McTheatre' (Rebellato 2009: 40). On any one night, these musicals are playing in a number of different theatres around the world and the audiences in each theatre are seeing an exact reproduction of the same show. The sets are the same. The costumes are the same. Rather than making the characters their own, the actors are part of a production line, tasked with recreating the performances of the original company down to reproducing identical gestures and line readings. McTheatre articulates a capitalist politics because it demonstrates 'the ruthless inventiveness of global capitalism for transforming everything into a way of making money' (Rebellato 2009: 48). From this perspective, a play in production can be considered to have a political character based on the economic mode through which it is produced.

American playwright, theatre critic and theatre scholar Elinor Fuchs critiques the politics of site-specific immersive performances, such as *TAMARA* (Strachan House, Toronto 1981) and *Tony and Tina's Wedding* (American Legion Hall, New York 1985), on the basis that they, too, reproduce capitalist structures, in this case in their form as opposed to their mode of production. Rather than articulating a politics of democracy and freedom in allowing their audience free rein to explore the performance space and determine the nature of their experience by creating their own narrative, Fuchs argues that this type of performance is the equivalent of 'a theatrical shopping mall' (Fuchs 1996: 132): 'a new kind of theater that mimics in its underlying structures of presentation and reception the fundamental culture of contemporary capitalism' (Fuchs 1996: 129). As a consumer in a capitalist society, the social subject is encouraged to relentlessly pursue the accumulation of desirable commodities, the acquisition of which, they are told, will increase the pleasure they take in life. In a similar way, site-specific immersive theatre encourages the audience into a relentless pursuit of theatrical commodities: 'I must make choices, weigh my interests, and achieve them through actual physical pursuit, occasionally at a run. My attention is acute, looking for advantages – of place, storyline, and more material consumables in the form of food and drink' (Fuchs 1996: 132). Form can therefore be considered political on the basis of the political character of the structures it reproduces in its structures.

Another common understanding of political theatre is the idea that it challenges its audience's beliefs. The opposite, however, is equally, if not more frequently, true. Political theatre works to unite and confirm people in their common beliefs. As theatre scholar Erika Fischer-Lichte observes, theatre can be used to 'confirm a sense of community, to renew the emotional bond between its members' (Fischer-Lichte 2009: 13). What performance scholar Baz Kershaw argues is true of community theatre is true of political theatre more generally: 'the intention of community theatre is to strengthen the self-determination of the community, to contribute to the empowerment of the community, and through that to augment the ideological survival of the community within – or against the dominant socio-political order' (Kershaw 1992: 66). This has wider political implications when thought about in terms of a community's relationship to the prevailing social order. A performance can potentially 'unite a range of different groups and communities in a common project in order to make them into an ideological force operating for or against the status quo' (Kershaw 1992: 36).

Ultimately, from the perspective of Marxist theory, all theatre is political. The prevailing social reality in any society at any time is predicated on the dominance of a set of social structures. Culture either reproduces and confirms the dominant social structures of the society within which it was produced or challenges those social structures by identifying them as constructed or reordering them to present a vision of a world predicated on a different set of social structures. As social and cultural theorists Jonathan Dollimore and Alan Sinfield note: '[c]ulture does not (cannot) transcend the material forces and relations of production. Culture is not simply a reflection of the economic and political system, but nor can it be independent of it' (Dollimore and Sinfield 1994: viii). All culture consciously or unconsciously carries political meanings. Culture can consciously carry one political meaning at the level of its content, while unconsciously carrying contradictory political meanings at the level of its structure. There can be a discord between the ostensible political content of a play and the political character of the dramaturgy through which it is articulated.

This book starts from the assumption that all plays are political and function politically on a number of different levels: their ostensible political content; their creator's political intentions; their political function; the political context of their production; the politics of their mode of production; by challenging or confirming their audience's beliefs; and the politics of the structures that make up their form. Although it considers all these levels, it focuses predominantly on the final aspect: the politics of form. The first two chapters of this book investigate the political character of the dramaturgical structures commonly identified with the idea of a political play in Britain, both in terms of their origins within the political context of the late-nineteenth century and their continued use in contemporary British theatre. The final four chapters explore the political character of a range of alternative dramaturgical structures currently in use in contemporary British playwriting. This book will argue that in order to determine the political character of a play, it is necessary to consider the politics of its form, alongside the politics of its content.

Political plays

This book argues that there is a specific dramatic form commonly recognized as political within contemporary British theatre. As performing arts scholar and theatre practitioner Mary Luckhurst observes, despite the fact that British theatre embraces a wide range of different forms, from musicals to physical theatre, from live art to stand-up comedy, '[p]lays written after the fashion of the late-nineteenth century realists such as Ibsen, Shaw and Granville Barker are still critically privileged' (Luckhurst 2002: 82). Theatre scholar Ruby Cohn identifies these plays as employing a specific form of realism whose dramaturgical features she summarizes as follows:

> Mimetic at both ends, the realistic play is embedded in the contemporary scene. The heir of the well-made play, it too is well made in linking cause and effect within a plot. The characters behave with sociological and psychological credibility; [...] Often rooted in the stock types of melodrama – innocent ingénue, beleaguered hero, benign older man, eccentric older woman, and (modified) nefarious villain – the character can wind away from its roots, but will nevertheless remain psychologically coherent from first to last [...] Even when the character's change is at the heart of the drama [...] it is traced with credible gradualism that is expressed in a discursive dialogue [...] the coherence of realistic dialogue parallels that of plot and character. [...] people speak grammatically in complete sentences [...] connect one sentence logically to

another; they answer pointed questions, they swear meaningful oaths [...] stage realism may be recognized as a code of conventions – picture frame proscenium bounding a room furnished with three-dimensional objects [...] Today, the realistic frame may be more flexible [...] Token objects may suffice to convey the milieu, and atmospheric lighting colors the mood.

(Cohn 1991: 3)

Within the frame of this realist dramaturgy, a pressing political issue is either discussed by the characters and/or embodied by the characters themselves, whose narrative journeys represent different perspectives on the issue in question. As American playwright Keith Urban observes of British political playwriting:

For an issue to be represented properly within this dominant theatrical model, one side must be confronted with its opposing viewpoint and through conversation lies the hope that dialectical reconciliation may be achieved. An individual character serves as a stand in for a political ideology, a symbolic 'talking head', and the dramatic form best suited for this forum of ideas was, hands down, a realistic linear narrative.

(Urban 2001: 39)

The political play continues to be commonly thought of as a play that yokes together the dialectical discussion of a political issue with a realist dramaturgy in a way that is considered to produce political efficacy.

This form of British political theatre, which I will term 'serious drama' for reasons that will be explored in the first chapter, is strongly associated with the single-authored play to the point of being conflated with it. As theatre scholar and dramaturg Duska Radosavljević argues, there is a tendency within British theatre culture to make a sharp division between text-based and non-text-based performance as if they were discrete, diametrically opposed forms of theatre. Non-text-based performance is often characterized as using processes that attempt to resist the structures and modes of production of serious drama. The character of this work is commonly understood as progressively avant-garde, produced through collaborative devising processes and privileging visual over textual dramaturgy. Text-based theatre is, in comparison, thought to be conservative and reactionary in its form and mode of production. Radosavljević points out that these distinctions are far too simplistic. In practice, the processes behind the creation of both text-based and non-text-based theatre 'resist neat categorization within those respective traditions by blurring the distinctions between them' (Radosavljević 2013: 5). On the one hand, non-text-based companies such as the Belgian theatre collective Ontroerend Goed script their work (albeit with space for improvisation) and employ structures traditionally associated with text-based work such as the neo-classical unities and three-act structure. On the other hand, playwrights such as Tim Crouch explicitly use conceptual framing strategies more often associated with non-text-based performance, such as experimenting with the spatial relationship between the spectator and performer. There is a false assumption that text-based performance, usually thought of as the single-authored play, always takes the form of serious drama, despite the use of scripts or scores in other types of performance and the existence of many plays whose structures lie outside of this form. As Luckhurst observes, there is a 'gap between the actual multiformity of theatrical styles and practices and the reported constructions of those styles and practices' (Luckhurst 2002: 77).

Serious drama's domination of the idea of the political play and of playwriting itself has not gone uncontested. As early as 1923, the English theatre reformer William Archer noted that 'various attempts' had been made to 'dethrone' serious drama from its 'ascendant' position (Archer 1929: 269). Throughout the twentieth century, serious drama's claim to be representative of both the political play and the single-authored play has been repeatedly challenged by the existence of a range of divergent playwriting practices within British theatre, many with their own claims to political efficacy: the agitprop plays of the 1930s Workers' Theatre Movement by writers such as Montagu Slater and Ewan MacColl; the socially committed popular drama produced by Joan Littlewood's Theatre Workshop and by playwrights including John Arden, Margaretta D'Arcy and John McGrath; community plays as pioneered by Ann Jellicoe in the 1970s; J. B. Priestley's experiments with time in the 1930s;[1] the verse dramas of T. S. Eliot, Christopher

---

[1]For a discussion of Priestley's representation of time in *Time and the Conways*, see pp. 96–9.

Fry, Tony Harrison, Benjamin Zephaniah, Stephen Berkoff and, more recently, Kate Tempest; the absurd plays of N. F. Simpson; the poetic existentialism of Samuel Beckett; Harold Pinter's theatre of menace; Peter Brook's theatre of cruelty; Edward Bond's 'rational' theatre; the farces of Joe Orton; the Brechtian theatre of Howard Brenton, Caryl Churchill and Trevor Griffiths; Howard Barker's theatre of catastrophe; and factual/verbatim theatre as exemplified by the Living Newspapers of the 1930s and work of writers such as Eric Bentley, Nicholas Kent, Gillian Slovo, Robin Soans and Alecky Blythe. This list of alternative playwriting practices within British theatre is indicative rather than exhaustive. There are many other British playwrights and theatre practitioners whose work can be thought of as transcending the boundaries of serious drama.

As there is not enough space in this short book to investigate all the divergent playwriting practices mentioned above, I will confine myself to a single area of investigation in my exploration into the political potential of alternative dramaturgical approaches in British theatre. The plays analysed in this book are predominantly drawn from the post-Thatcher period. They are characterized by disrupted dramatic structures and, although I will argue that these plays are political, they frequently lack any engagement with explicitly political issues in their content.

Kritzer observes that there has been a significant shift in approaches to political playwriting post-Thatcher. She claims that post-Thatcher playwrights are responding to a major shift in the nature of the British political landscape, arguing that the rise of New Labour in the 1990s brought a more monologic form of politics into being in Britain, which forced playwrights to reimagine the nature of the political play: '[p]olitical convergence and the breakdown of ideological identity have reoriented political theatre' (Kritzer 2008: 7).

While Kritzer's observations about shifts in the British political landscape hold, I would argue that these shifts are not a singular cause. They are symptomatic of a wider set of global shifts in social, economic and political structures since the 1970s, which have forced a re-evaluation of both politics and the nature of political action. Sociologist Zigmunt Bauman argues that these shifts are the result of a shift in the relationship between power and politics caused by increasing globalization under the pressures of post-industrial capitalism. As the world becomes more interconnected, its networks of power become more complex and transcend the boundaries of the nation-state. There is a dislocation between power and politics: 'power (that is, the ability to do things) has been separated from politics (that is, the ability to decide which things need to be done and given priority)' (Bauman 2012: viii). Global problems have global causes and global solutions. On 'a planet integrated by a dense web of interdependencies', it becomes difficult to know not only what to do, but who should do it (Bauman 2012: xiv). As a consequence, Bauman claims that post-industrial capitalist societies are currently experiencing 'a time of "interregnum" – when the old ways of doing no longer work [...] but when the new ways of tackling the challenges and new modes of life better suited to the new conditions have not as yet been invented' (Bauman 2012: vii). He classes this phase as 'liquid modernity' (Bauman 2012: xii). I will argue that it is to these wider shifts in social structures that the plays, whose disrupted or 'liquid' dramaturgical structures are discussed in the final four chapters of this book, are fundamentally responding.

Serious drama is born out of a phase Bauman terms 'solid' modernity which is synonymous with the dominance of indus-trial capitalism in Britain. Solid modernity is characterized by a common belief in the idea of rational positive progress: 'the modern ambition to subdue, harness and colonize the future in order to replace chaos with order and contingency with a predictable (and so controllable) sequence of events' (Bauman 2012: 137). Change appears to be purposeful: 'a movement towards the splendid vision on the horizon' (Bauman 2012: xi). Society offers the individual a plan of action: 'clear patterns, codes and rules to which one could conform' (Bauman 2012: 7). The social subject is imagined as a 'citizen' who seeks to secure their own welfare through uniting with others in a 'common cause' (Bauman 2012: 36). Serious drama reflects this belief in rational positive progress in the solidity of its dramaturgical structures.

In contrast, the liquid phase of modernity offers no sense of direction for either the individual or society as a whole: 'we don't have a clear image of a "destination" towards which we seem to be moving' (Bauman 2012: vii). It is a phase characterized by insecurity, uncertainty and unsafety. Its social structures are in a state of flux; they 'can no longer (and are not expected to) keep their shape for long, because they decompose and melt faster than the time it takes to cast them'. They can no longer 'serve as frames of reference for human actions and long-term life strategies because of their short life expectation' (Bauman 2007: 1). Agency becomes weak or absent as structures in which 'thinking, planning and acting could be inscribed' disappear (Bauman 2007: 3). There is little sense of collective purpose because human bonds become as fragile and short-lived as the social structures that support them. The individualized social subject lives in a perpetual state of indeterminacy plagued by existential anxiety: 'forever becoming, avoiding completion, staying undefined' (Bauman 2012: viii).

Bauman argues that this shift from a solid to a liquid phase of modernity calls for a comparative shift in narrative structures: '[t]he remoteness and unreachability of systemic structure, coupled with the unstructured, fluid state of the immediate setting of life-politics […] call for a rethinking of old concepts that used to frame its narratives' (Bauman 2012: 8). The post-Thatcher plays whose dramaturgies are explored in the final four chapters of this book are political because their dramaturgical structures reflect and attempt to negotiate this shift: temporal dramaturgies shift from a successive towards a more simultaneous understanding of time; spatial dramaturgies become less concrete and more virtual; plot structures question linear mechanical and socio-psychological models of causation; the focalization of the social subject moves from an objective to subjective viewpoint. Through their liquid dramaturgical structures, these plays tackle the question of how to have agency within a society made up of ever-shifting social structures, offering ways of rethinking how 'to act, to plan actions, to calculate the expected gains and losses of the actions and to evaluate their outcomes under conditions of endemic uncertainty' (Bauman 2007: 4). They offer an alternative model of political theatre to serious drama, one that operates predominantly through a politics of form as opposed to a politics of content.

The structure of this book

This book is split into two main sections. The first two chapters are an investigation into the reasons why the dramaturgical structures of serious drama came to be associated with the idea of the political play in Britain, as well as the political character of those structures. The final four chapters are an exploration of the political potential of some of the more liquid dramaturgical approaches currently in use in British theatre and the implications of such structures for a rethinking of what constitutes 'the political'.

The first chapter, 'Serious Drama', examines the political character of serious drama in terms of its origins, its content and its claim to articulate a progressive socialist politics. It traces the historical genesis of serious drama, locating its roots in eighteenth-century domestic tragedy. It argues that contemporary serious drama is not simply a matter of political content. Serious drama articulates a set of specific dramaturgical structures, which frame its serious content in a way thought of as having political efficacy. It locates the origins of these dramaturgical structures in Irish-born playwright George Bernard Shaw's campaign for the creation of a serious socialist theatre in Britain in the late-nineteenth century. It examines serious drama's claim to a progressive socialist politics, concluding that this claim holds when the dramaturgical structures of serious drama are considered purely in terms of their dialectical discussion of a political issue. Conversely, however, it argues that this claim is troubled when it is considered in light of the form's origins in a class conflict between the working-class audiences of melodrama and middle-class theatre reformers. The chapter illustrates its argument through the analysis of plays by George Lillo, George Bernard Shaw and John Walker.

The second chapter, 'The Politics of Structure', examines the political character of serious drama in terms of its form. The idea that a play articulates political messages through its form is not a new idea, but it is an undertheorized one. Cohn argues that many British plays employ non-realist form or elements of non-realism and that these plays are in some way involved in a political battle over the representation of reality (Cohn 1991: 1–4). Patterson goes further and divides post-war British political plays into two different types that he argues employ two different formal modes: the reflectionist and the interventionist. The reflectionist mode of political theatre 'asserts that the main function of art and indeed theatre is to hold up a mirror to nature and to reflect reality as accurately as possible'. In contrast, the interventionist mode 'asserts that, even if it were possible to reflect reality accurately, the task is futile, since it is the task of the artist and playwright to interpret reality and to challenge our perception of it' (Patterson 2003: 15). Patterson sees the reflectionist mode of playwriting as descended from Ibsen and the interventionist mode as descended from Brecht. Patterson's definitions are useful because they identify playwrights as using different formal strategies in order to produce political efficacy. He presents these two different strategies, however, as two distinct modes in binary opposition to each other. This limits their usefulness as a critical framework because, as Patterson acknowledges, many plays do not neatly sit in one category or the other but seem to combine elements of both. Instead, I propose something simpler. The plays Patterson identifies as working in a reflectionist mode predominantly articulate their politics at the level of content. The plays he identifies as interventionist are predominantly attempting to articulate a politics of form by challenging accepted social structures through subverting them in their dramaturgy. If, instead, a play is analysed in terms of how it articulates its politics at both the level of its content and its form, it is possible to account for some of the anomalies that Patterson notes.

The second chapter provides an introduction to the theoretical basis on which it is possible to analyse a play's form for its political character. The chapter explains why social reality can be thought of as constructed of a range of social structures and the relationship between these structures and the exercise of power. It considers the ways in which plays can be thought to act politically by reproducing or reordering these social structures through their dramaturgical structures. It illustrates these ideas with an analysis of Sam Holcroft's *Edgar and Annabel* (National Theatre, London 2011). The chapter then moves on to consider the politics of serious drama's form. It argues that, while serious drama can be argued to articulate a progressive and effective politics of form within the historical context of the solid modernity of the late-nineteenth century, its structures are insufficient to capture 'the complex mechanisms' of contemporary liquid modernity (Bauman 2012: 23). This claim is supported with a comparative analysis of Charlotte Jones's *Humble Boy* (National Theatre, London 2001) and Caryl Churchill's *Love and Information* (Royal Court, London 2012).

The following four chapters explore the political potential of some of the more liquid dramaturgical structures currently in use in British theatre. This exploration begins with time, as time is both the backbone of dramatic structure and the initiating 'factor of disruption' in the movement from solid to liquid modernity (Bauman 2012: 111). The third chapter, 'Time', examines the nature of dramatic time and observes that the dramaturgical structures of serious drama are predominantly organized on the temporal axis of succession. It argues that liquid dramaturgical approaches attempt to reflect shifts in the social structures of contemporary social reality towards liquid modernity by shifting the temporal emphasis from the axis of succession to the axis of simultaneity. The chapter concludes with analyses of four plays, by J. B. Priestley, Nick Payne, Caryl Churchill and David Eldridge, that attempt to present a liquid experience of time as simultaneous through their temporal structures.

Shifts in the representation of time necessarily cause shifts in the representation of space and so the fourth chapter deals with 'Space'. It begins by examining the nature of dramatic space and the spatial codes that underlie it. It argues that, while serious drama predominantly thinks of space in terms of concrete settings, liquid dramaturgies present space as virtual, fluid and multi-layered. The chapter contains analyses of four plays, by Tim Crouch, Harold Pinter, Sarah Kane and David Greig, that explore a more virtual and fluid understanding of space and attempt to communicate meaning through their layering of different spaces.

As plots are plotted through time and space, shifts in spatio-temporal structures inevitably cause shifts in plot structures. The first half of the fifth chapter examines the causal structures that shape 'Plot'. It argues that serious drama's plot structure employs mechanical linear causation and is driven by desire. As such, its political character can be seen as both determinist, capitalist and reflective of solid modernity's belief in progress as 'a road with an *a priori*, pre-ordained finishing line' (Bauman 2012: xi). Through the analysis of plays by Mike Bartlett, debbie tucker green and Rupert Goold and Ben Power, this chapter explores alternative causal models for plot structure that are more liquid in their indeterminacy, presenting the world instead as 'an infinite collection of possibilities' (Bauman 2012: 61). The second half explores a shift in the traditional Aristotelian relationship between plot and story through an exploration of plays by Martin Crimp and Mark Ravenhill. It concludes by examining the ways in which these plays challenge the idea of socio-psychological causation.

If socio-psychological causation is in question, then this automatically has an effect on how character is constructed. The final chapter explores 'Character' and begins by examining the structural role character plays in drama. It puts forward the idea that character is a lens through which the social subject imagines themselves and their role within society and explores some of the different ways the social subject has imagined themselves through character over the course of history. It argues that, in liquid dramaturgies, the focalization of character shifts from an objective to a subjective viewpoint through analyses of plays by Anthony Neilson, Simon Stephens and Mark Ravenhill. This shift in focalization reflects the idea that liquid modernity is 'a powerful *individualizing* force' and raises questions about the nature of community in a globalized world (Bauman 2012: 148).

Together, these four final chapters explore the idea that, since the early 1990s, a range of contemporary British playwrights have attempted to address a gap between dominant representations of social structures as solid and our lived experience of them as liquid through the dramaturgy of their plays. Following Bauman, I will argue that our understandings of social structures are vital to our understanding of how to act and so have agency in the world as they are 'complex mechanisms which connect our moves with their results and decide their outcomes' (Bauman 2012: 23). Therefore, any rethinking of these structures through art that better enables us to understand how to have agency is a political act.

The book concludes that the political character of serious drama within the context of contemporary British society is questionable as its structures seem insufficient to articulate the complex mechanisms that underlie our lived experience of liquid modernity. In comparison, the more liquid dramaturgies of the plays discussed in this book have political potential because they offer an attempt to understand, negotiate, critique and reimagine the social structures that define contemporary lived experience.

The study in this book is limited to Britain. This is the theatre culture I know intimately well as a practitioner, teacher and scholar. This book is the result of thoughts generated not only by studying British theatre, but through years of teaching playwriting within a British context, watching British plays and working within the British theatre industry, first as an actress, and later as a playwright and dramaturg. The plays chosen for this study are not oddities, but have been selected from the heart of the British new writing mainstream. They premiered on major stages, including those of the National Theatre, the Royal Court and the Edinburgh International Festival. These British plays are analysed within the context of the work of European and American theorists. The theoretical frameworks used are drawn not only from dramatic theory, but from critical theory, philosophy, sociology, economics, geography and linguistics. The practice of playwriting is a practice in which ideas have frequently crossed both time periods and borders. The history discussed within this book alone offers many concrete examples of this. Roman playwrights draw heavily on Aristotle, as do many European playwrights from the Renaissance onwards. The French playwright and philosopher Denis Diderot draws on the work of the English playwright George Lillo. Shaw and his contemporaries draw heavily on the work of the Norwegian playwright Henrik Ibsen. To ignore these international influences and transnational currents would be to paint a disjointed picture of playwriting practices in Britain. At times, the work of some international playwrights will be discussed or used as exemplars of particular dramatic structures. For example, as Ibsen was a major influence on Shaw, *Hedda Gabler* is used as an example of both the realist and non-realist nature of naturalistic dramaturgies.

Finally, many of the plays discussed in this book may, at first glance, appear metaphysical rather than political in terms of their content. This is a result of the particular understanding of how art functions politically that I will advance in this book. For me, a political play is not necessarily a play that addresses a political issue; rather, it is a play that opens the audience's eyes to how the world could be different. Concrete shifts in the political nature of society involve a shift in the social structures that underlie it – for example, from liberalism to socialism to neo-liberalism. In order to create political change, the social subject needs to be able to imagine how their social reality could be structured differently. A play that articulates a politics of form, reimagining the structure of social reality through its structures, allows the social subject to access a vision of a world structured on fundamentally different principles. As the philosopher Theodor W. Adorno puts it, it is 'an analogy of that other condition which should be' (Adorno 2007: 194).

This book is primarily aimed at theatre practitioners, at playwrights and at students studying the craft of playwriting. It offers a critical investigation into the dramaturgical structures that underlie playwriting as a craft and which are too often presented as an ahistorical and universal set of rules. At the same time, by breaking down and articulating the structures of plays that successfully eschew these so-called rules of playwriting, I hope to offer both a method for thinking unconventionally about dramatic structure and some models to inspire the building of new dramaturgical structures. In addition to this, it asks playwrights to consider more carefully the political character of the structures on which they build their plays. As a result of this, this book does not assume any prior scholarly knowledge of areas such as critical theory.

For a scholarly audience, this book offers a new and valuable approach to reading and studying plays. Contemporary scholarly readings of plays often remain rooted in the text, identifying a singular coherent meaning in a play's themes, in what the characters say about those themes and in a reading of the politics of the character's actions from a socio-psychological viewpoint. As Fuchs observes, there is 'an immediate (and crippling) leap to character and normative psychology that underwrites much dramatic criticism' (Fuchs 2004: 5). This book outlines a different approach to reading a play and critically evaluating its meaning. It asks scholars to think more like playwrights. To focus, in reading a play, more on the dramaturgical structures that form the building blocks of a play and articulate political messages through their dialectical relationship to social structures in the world outside the theatre doors, in order to be able to better unpick how a play delivers a set of potentially contradictory meanings. It asks scholars to examine the words on the page of the playtext, not purely for their literal content, but for the ways in which these patterns of words articulate structures that are brought into being during performance. As theatre scholar Marc Robinson argues, a whole new world of meaning is brought into being when plays are considered as three-dimensional objects that are 'sculpted, scored, or built' as opposed to merely words 'spilt onto the page or stage' (Robinson 1997: 3). More discussion of the craft and structures of playwriting in contemporary scholarship will allow for more nuanced and complex understandings of the plays it produces and the relationship of these plays to contemporary society.

This book offers a new and unconventional way of analysing plays for their political meaning through their structures, but one, I hope, that is ultimately both productive and provocative.

1

Serious Drama

*[A] certain kind of social realism has been understood
as quintessentially English and promoted as the national
drama – a campaign so successful that practically
everyone has come to believe it.*

LUCKHURST 2002: 3

The first two chapters of this book examine how the dramaturgical structures of serious drama came to be associated with the idea of the political play in Britain and the political character of those structures. This chapter begins this investigation by exploring the political character of serious drama in terms of its origins, its content and its claim to articulate a progressive socialist politics. It examines the history of the term 'serious drama' and traces the roots of the contemporary form that is thought of as serious drama in Britain today back to eighteenth-century domestic tragedy. Contemporary serious drama, it argues, is a matter of form as well as content. A set of specific dramaturgical structures is identified as associated with serious drama. These dramaturgical structures are thought to frame serious drama's serious content in a way that is felt to have political efficacy. The origins of these dramaturgical structures are located in Shaw and Archer's campaign for the creation of a serious socialist/literary theatre in Britain in the 1890s. The continued use of these structures by contemporary political playwrights, as exemplified in the work of English playwrights David Edgar and David Hare, is explored.

The second half of the chapter interrogates serious drama's claim to a progressive socialist politics through the use of the first two of literary theorist Frederic Jameson's three levels of textual analysis: that of a politics of content and a politics of class origins. It concludes that serious drama's claim to a socialist politics holds when its dramaturgical structures are considered purely in terms of their dialectical discussion of a political issue. Conversely, however, it argues that its claims to a progressive socialist politics are troubled when they are considered in the light of the form's origins in a late-nineteenth-century class conflict between the working-class audiences of melodrama and middle-class theatre reformers. The chapter illustrates its argument as it progresses through analyses of three plays: Lillo's 1731 domestic tragedy *The London Merchant*; Shaw's 1892 serious drama *Widowers' Houses*; and British playwright John Walker's 1832 melodrama *The Factory Lad*.

Serious drama

So what is 'serious drama'? The simple answer is that it is drama people consider to be 'serious'. According to the *Oxford English Dictionary*, the adjective 'serious' can describe something 'thoughtful, earnest, sober, sedate, responsible, not reckless or given to trifling', something 'not merely for amusement' or something 'concerned with religion or ethics'. It describes something of high value: something 'important, demanding consideration' (Allen 1990: 1106). The term 'serious drama' links the forms of drama it is applied to with these ideas of responsibility, utility and value. The term is not thought of as holding critical weight. Film and television scholar John Caughie, however, justifies his own use of it on the basis that, although 'it is not a term which anyone would own up to or defend seriously', it is in regular common usage. The term has 'a long history in formal and informal criticism and in everyday conversation, referring to forms of drama which are approved by "serious" critics or "serious" people' (Caughie 2000: 3).

The term originates with the Ancient Greek philosopher Aristotle and his definition of tragedy. Tragedy, he states, is 'a representation of an action, which is serious' (Aristotle 1987: 37). Classical scholar and literary theorist F. L. Lucas argues that the problem of understanding what tragedy or serious drama is lies in the very simplicity of Aristotle's original definition. The Greek word translated as 'serious' more accurately means 'that matters' or 'is worth troubling about' (Lucas 1927: 17). Our sense of what it is that matters, however, is not fixed. It changes over time, is different in different cultures, and within the same culture it can differ from person to person. As a result of this constant shift in our understanding of what it is that matters or is serious, there is a constant shift in our understanding of the parameters of what is and what is not serious drama.

Serious drama is not a specific form of drama. Rather, it is a floating term used to validate particular forms of drama at particular moments in time: '"serious drama" operates to mark off a legitimate cultural territory'. Our understanding of the term is vague precisely because of this legitimizing function: 'the territory of "serious drama" is undefined because it does not need to be defined: it is the shared currency of those who own the cultural capital [...] a code understood by like-minded people, signalling a sense of worth which is assumed to be shared but which there never seems to be enough time or need to elaborate' (Caughie 2000: 3).

Many theatrical campaigners have used the term 'serious drama' to attempt to legitimize certain forms of drama at particular moments in time. In Britain, during the Restoration, the term was associated with a form that is very different from our contemporary understanding of serious drama, heroic tragedy. In his 1668 'An Essay on Dramatick Poesie', English playwright and poet John Dryden uses the term to campaign for the cultural value of heroic tragedy. He draws on the authority of Aristotle's original definition of tragedy as serious drama to justify his use of the term: 'The end of Tragedies or serious Playes, sayes Aristotle, is to beget admiration, compassion or concernment' (Dryden 1971: 35). Serious plays are plays in which the 'subject and characters are great, and the Plot unmix'd with mirth, which might allay or divert these concernments which are produc'd' (Dryden 1971: 68). The serious play demands a heightened form: ''tis Nature wrought up to a higher pitch. The Plot, the Characters, the Wit, the Passions, the Descriptions, are all exalted above the level of common converse, as high as the imagination of the poet can carry them'. This heightened form requires heightened expression in heroic verse: 'Tragedy we know is wont to image to us the minds and fortunes of noble persons, and to portray these exactly, Heroick Rhime is nearest Nature, as being the noblest kind of modern verse' (Dryden 1971: 74). Unsurprisingly, Dryden's description of serious drama perfectly fits the form of his own heroic tragedies, such as *All for Love* (Drury Lane, London 1677).

Our understanding of what serious drama is shifts but the term's legitimizing function remains consistent. It is a term that excludes other forms' claims to legitimacy without clearly defining its own. Everything that is not serious drama must be non-serious drama and therefore of lesser worth.

George Lillo and *The London Merchant*

The origins of contemporary British serious drama can be traced back to the early eighteenth century and the rise of domestic tragedy. In 1731, the English actor-manager Theophilus Cibber produced a new play, *The London Merchant*, by the relatively unknown playwright George Lillo at Drury Lane in London. Cibber presented Lillo's play as a radical change in direction for British theatre: 'almost a new species of tragedy, wrote on an uncommon subject' (Cibber 1968: 339). *The London Merchant* is an adaptation of a popular ballad about a London apprentice, George Barnwell, 'who was undone by a strumpet [...] having thrice robbed his master, and murdered his uncle in *Ludlow*' (Anonymous 1658). The ballad is supposedly based on a set of true events. In Lillo's version, the strumpet, Sarah Millwood, seduces Barnwell and persuades him to steal money from his master, the merchant Thorowgood. When Barnwell realizes his crime will be discovered, he runs away to be with Millwood, but she rejects him, as he no longer offers her a source of income. Barnwell reveals that he has a wealthy uncle and Millwood convinces him to rob and murder him. Barnwell murders his uncle but cannot bring himself to steal his uncle's goods. Millwood, furious with him for returning empty-handed, reports the murder. Barnwell and Millwood are arrested and sentenced to death. Barnwell repents of his actions and goes heroically to his execution.

In his dedication to *The London Merchant*, Lillo challenges Dryden's definition of serious drama as heroic tragedy. He claims a need to 'enlarge the province of the graver kind of poetry' (Lillo 1965: 4) from a narrow focus on 'scenes of royal woe' to the 'tale of private woe' (Lillo 1965: 8). Lillo sees tragedy as 'a most useful kind of writing' whose purpose is 'the exciting of passions in order to the correcting of such of them as are criminal'. He argues for a shift in subject matter on the basis that tragedy will have greater moral utility if it is directly relevant to the lives of a wider audience: 'tragedy is so far from losing its dignity by being accommodated to the circumstances of the generality of mankind that it is more truly august in proportion to the extent of its influence and the numbers that are properly affected by it' (Lillo 1965: 3). Lillo also challenges Dryden's prescription that tragedy should be written in heroic rhyming verse by writing his tragedy predominantly in prose.

Lillo's choice of subject matter and use of prose is revolutionary but his play follows many of the conventions of Dryden's heroic tragedy, relocating them to the domestic sphere of a middle-class household rather than challenging them. Although the setting, the characters and the use of prose are more characteristic of comedy than tragedy, the play takes its subject matter seriously from beginning to end. It does not contain a single joke or comic situation. The action is unified. There are no subplots. The play can be read, not as an attempt to lower theatre to the level of the middle class, but rather to raise the status of the middle class to the level of the heroic. Discussing 'men of the greatest rank', the merchant Thorowgood and his daughter, Maria, conclude that 'high birth and titles don't recommend the man who owns them', not unless 'his merit recommends him more' (Lillo 1965: 14). At moments of high drama, the play's middle-class characters are placed on a par with men of the greatest rank as they are allowed to express their emotions in the heroic verse conventionally reserved for noble characters.

The play encourages its audience to feel the same tragic emotions of admiration and compassion for its middle-class characters that Dryden's heroic tragedy attempts to arouse for its noble characters. In his gallows speech, Barnwell positions the audience as feeling compassion for him, while his stoical attitude elicits admiration:

If any youth, like you, in future times
Shall mourn my fate, though he abhors my crimes,
Or tender maid, like you my tale shall hear

And to my sorrows give a pitying tear,
To such a melting eye and throbbing heart,
Would gracious heaven this benefit impart:
Never to know my guilt, nor feel my pain.
Then must you own you ought not to complain,
Since you nor weep, nor shall I die in vain.

(Lillo 1965: 78)

Cibber testifies to the strong emotional affect the play had on
its original audience: 'the play, spoke so much to the heart, they
were drawn in to drop their ballads, and pull out their handker-
chiefs' (Cibber 1968: 339). The play aims at moral instruction
through emotional affect as opposed to intellectual understanding.
It was considered so effective in its time that it was employed as
a cautionary tale for young apprentices for over eighty years: 'It
was often acted in the Christmas and Easter holidays, and judged
a proper entertainment for the apprentices, &c as being a more
instructive, moral and cautionary drama than many pieces that had
been usually exhibited on those days' (Cibber 1968: 340).

The London Merchant was seen as a piece of effective moral
instruction, but what are the morals it teaches? The play's central
message concerns the uses and abuses of capitalism. The merchant
of the play's title, Thorowgood, stands at one extreme, as a model
of benevolent capitalism:

I would not have you only learn the method of merchandise
and practice hereafter merely as a means of getting wealth.
'Twill be well worth your pains to study it as a science, see
how it is founded in reason and the nature of things, how it
has promoted humanity as it has opened and yet keeps up an
intercourse between nations far remote from one another in
situation, customs and religion; promoting arts, industry, peace,
and plenty; by mutual benefits diffusing love from pole to pole.

(Lillo 1965: 40)

At the other end of the capitalist moral spectrum is Millwood,
who sees men purely in terms of their financial value. Her aim is
to strip them of their assets and then drive them to destruction
in the quest to accumulate more riches for her: 'I would have my
conquests complete, like those of the Spaniards in the New World,

who first plundered the natives of all the wealth they had and then condemned the wretches to the mines for life to work for more' (Lillo 1965: 16). Barnwell vacillates between these two moral extremes, initially driven to ruin through his relationship with Millwood but ultimately choosing redemption through siding with Thorowgood and the morals of benevolent capitalism.

Diderot and the *genre sérieux*

In 1757, inspired in part by Lillo's *The London Merchant*, the French philosopher and playwright Denis Diderot wrote a domestic tragedy of his own, *Le Fils naturel* (Court of the Duke of Ayen, Saint-Germain-de-Laye 1757). He prefaces the published version of the play with three dialogues in which he makes an extensive case for this new form of drama – which he terms the *genre sérieux* ('serious drama'):

> any dramatic composition where the subject matter is important, where the author assumes the tone used in dealing with serious matters, and where the dramatic action is driven by perplexity and obstacles. It seems to me that since these are the most common actions in real life, the genre that depicts them must be the most useful and the most wide-ranging. I will call this the *genre sérieux*.
>
> (Diderot 1991a: 51)

Diderot follows Lillo in his description of the main features of the *genre sérieux*. The *genre sérieux* focuses on the domestic life of the middle classes: 'men of letters, philosophers, shopkeepers, judges, lawyers, politicians, citizens, magistrates, tax-collectors, aristocrats, stewards' (Diderot 1991a: 56). Consequently, it is more relevant to its audience than neo-classical tragedy, because it takes their everyday concerns as its subject: 'The subject should be important. The plot should be simple, deal with domestic matters, and be modelled on real life' (Diderot 1991a: 52).

Diderot takes Lillo's innovations one step further. The *genre sérieux* not only deals with everyday reality as its subject; it also aims to reproduce everyday reality in its dramaturgy. Diderot advises the playwright to 'get as close to real life as you can' (Diderot 1991a: 53). He argues that characters should be detailed studies of human nature – 'the human being must always be recognizable' (Diderot 1991a: 51) – and develop over the course of the play's action: 'a character that develops gradually until it can finally be seen in all its power' (Diderot 1991b: 60). Character dialogue should reflect how people express themselves in real life: '[t]he artist must find exactly what everyone would say in the same situation, so that all who hear it will immediately recognize it within themselves' (Diderot 1991a: 42). For example, in moments of strong emotion, the dialogue should be 'broken into dislocated syllables, the speaker dart[ing] from one idea to another, beginning many different speeches, without finishing any' (Diderot 1991a: 43). The acting style should be naturalistic and, to encourage this style of performance, Diderot introduces the idea of an invisible fourth wall between the stage and the audience: 'take no more thought for the spectator than if he did not exist. Imagine, at the edge of the stage, a great wall separating you from the audience' (Diderot 1991b: 65). The stage settings for the *genre sérieux* should be exact replicas of real-life places: a 'drawing-room exactly as it is' (Diderot 1991a: 45).

Diderot's *genre sérieux* has moral instruction at its heart: 'Let the moral import of your play be universal and clear' (Diderot 1991a: 52). It promotes 'the love of virtue and the horror of vice' (Diderot 1991a: 55). He sees the *genre sérieux*'s combination of contemporary social issues and realistic dramaturgy as a highly effective strategy for achieving this:

> Can you not imagine the effect that would be created by realistic scenery and costumes, words that are in keeping with actions, simple plots, and dangers as real as those that must at some time have threatened your relatives, your friends, or yourself? An abrupt change of fortune, the fear of public humiliation, the effects of poverty, a passion that leads to moral or financial ruin, from ruin to despair, from despair to violent death – these are not uncommon occurrences.
>
> (Diderot 1991a: 53)

Diderot thinks of the *genre sérieux* as having political efficacy because it encourages its audience to reflect on their actions and the possible consequences of them in response to the familiar situations they see represented on stage.

Diderot's *genre sérieux* initially made little progress on the French stage. The eighteenth-century German playwright and dramaturg Gotthold Ephraim Lessing, a fan of the form, observes that 'no matter how much their Diderots and Marmontels preach this to the French, it does not seem as though domestic tragedies are coming into vogue among them' (Lessing 1962: 39). He does, however, find strong advocates for his ideas among other playwrights. The French playwright Pierre Beaumarchais, for example, praises the form in his 1767 'Essay on the Serious Genre of Drama' and expands on Diderot's thinking (Beaumarchais 1991). Diderot's ideas only really began to take hold in the nineteenth century through the work of naturalist playwrights. The French novelist and playwright Émile Zola openly acknowledges the influence of Diderot on his work: 'it is understood that Diderot supported the same ideas as me, he also believed in the need to bring the truth to the theatre; it is understood that naturalism is not an invention of my brain, but an occasional argument I use for the defence of my own work. Naturalism was bequeathed to us by the eighteenth century' (Zola 1968b: 389, my translation). While critics, including Brian Johnston (Johnston 1992: 269–71) and Toril Moi (Moi 2006: 113–16), have argued for Diderot's influence on Ibsen's work, Ibsen himself has nothing to say about Diderot or his *genre sérieux*. Ibsen, however, rarely acknowledges outside influences. For example, his few comments about Zola tend towards contempt: 'Zola descends into the sewer to bathe in it; I, to cleanse it' (quoted in Meyer 1971: 299). Ibsen may deny the influence of French writers on his work, but Zola sees the situation differently. When asked about Ibsen's influence on naturalism, Zola is rumoured to have stated that 'the ideas which were supposed to rain on Paris from the North were in reality French ones which had been disseminated by French writers and had come back to their place of origin' (Vizetelly 1904: 389). Diderot's *genre sérieux* lays the foundations for contemporary serious drama. It does not, however, fully describe the form. It is missing one vital ingredient: dialectical debate.

George Bernard Shaw and the dialectic

In the 1880s, William Archer declared British theatre to be in a terrible state. Though British drama, he admits, 'exists and flourishes' (Archer 1882: 3–4) on the melodramatic stage, it 'falls short of any literary merit' (Archer 1882: 4). He lays the blame for this deficiency with the theatre audience. The theatre, he argues, 'is supported mainly by people who have no taste or thought whatever' (Archer 1882: 9). They regard the stage as 'a vehicle for mere amusement' (Archer 1886: 266) and will 'laugh always, cry sometimes, shudder now and then, but think – never' (Archer 1882: 9). As a result of this, British theatre is stuck in a vicious circle from which it cannot escape: 'A frivolous public calls for frivolous plays, and frivolous plays breed a frivolous public' (Archer 1882: 17).

In an effort to lift British theatre out of the terrible rut into which he felt it had fallen, Archer launched a campaign for the creation of a 'literary drama' dealing predominantly with 'moral, social, political' issues and characterized by an element of 'seriousness' (Archer 1882: 4–5). Archer took on the task of writing such a 'serious play' himself. Unfortunately, although he was a 'born constructor', he soon discovered he 'could not write dialogue a bit' (Shaw 1993: 8). The solution to this problem came in the form of George Bernard Shaw, whom Archer first encountered in 1884, sitting in the British Library 'day after day, poring over Karl Marx's *Das Kapital*' (Archer 1931: 119). Together, the men embarked on the writing of a serious play entitled *Rhinegold*. Archer provided Shaw with a plot and Shaw went away to write the dialogue.

Archer and Shaw's writing partnership soon broke down, however, because they had fundamentally different visions of what a serious play was. Archer was primarily interested in reforming the theatre, so his focus was on the construction of plays that would have a claim to the title of literature. Shaw was primarily a social reformer, whose socialist aims included the nationalization of land and industry, better rights for children, political equality for women, a liberal education for all and an end to a system that divides society 'into hostile classes with large appetites and no dinners at one extreme and large dinners and no appetites at the other' (Shaw 1884: 1). Shaw was initially drawn to the theatre because he believed that it could be reconfigured as a vehicle for radical social change.

Shaw sees theatre's potential as an agent of social reform as rooted in the use of dialectical structure. Within the work of Ibsen, he claims to have identified an innovative new element of dramatic structure, which he terms 'discussion'. Discussion takes the form of 'a conflict of unsettled ideals' (Shaw 1986: 165). Shaw attributes a specific meaning to the term 'ideal'. Central to his thought is a distinction between an idealist and a realist approach to the world. Shaw divides human beings into philistines, idealists and realists. If you take a community of a thousand people and analyse their attitudes to a social institution such as marriage, Shaw postulates that 700 of them will find marriage to be a good enough arrangement for them and not question it. These people Shaw classifies as philistines. Another 299 will experience marriage as being a failure. These 299, however, seeing the contented 700 and lacking the courage to face the idea that they themselves are failures, will try to persuade themselves that marriage is an ideal institution no matter what the actual reality of their own marriage might be. Shaw classifies these people as idealists. Idealists are more dangerous than philistines because they take an unsatisfactory social institution and reposition it as an ideal. They create 'a mask for reality, which in its nakedness is intolerable to them'. In order to strengthen this mask they require others to confirm it. They instigate 'the policy of forcing individuals to act on the assumption that all ideals are real, and to recognize and accept such action as standard moral conduct, absolutely valid under all circumstances, contrary conduct or any advocacy of it being discountenanced and punished as immoral' (Shaw 1986: 49). The single individual left over from Shaw's community of a thousand is the realist. The realist's function is to tear down the ideal the idealists have created and reveal what lies behind it.

For Shaw, discussion is not the presentation of the right and the wrong of a situation. It is a conflict between two differing but equally strong ideals. This idea of opposing ideals is exemplified in *Mrs Warren's Profession* (Stage Society, London 1902), whose main characters embody different idealist perspectives on women's roles. Vivie idealizes the notion of the overturning of conventional gender roles to the point that, when she discovers her own mother, Mrs Warren, is running high-class brothels, she judges her to be 'a wonderful woman' (Shaw 1946: 251). Mrs Warren, however, for all her apparent unconventionality, espouses conventional Victorian ideals. Using the language of business, she advocates the capitalist system which enabled her to rise out of the gutter through exploiting the only commodity she owned – her body: 'Do you think we were such fools as to let other people trade in our good looks by employing us as shopgirls, or barmaids, or waitresses, when we could trade in them ourselves and get all the profits instead of starvation wages?' (Shaw 1946: 249). Shaw pits these two ideals against each other, forming a dialectic that reveals faults with both positions and so brings his audience 'through contradictory error to relatively greater truth' (Whitman 1977: 195). Drama scholar Robert F. Whitman observes that Shaw understands that the 'essence of the dialectical process as described by Hegel is that its movement is from the less real, because less complete and less self-conscious, to the more real – in other words, from the particular and physical and limited to the more universal and complete' (Whitman 1977: 193). Shaw's dialectic is an open one. He avoids articulating definitive solutions to social problems, using the process of synthesis to approach closer to the truth rather than grasping it. His drama is 'a drama of questioning', not of answers (Shaw 1986: 72).

For Shaw, social progress requires the destruction of ideals 'through the replacement of old institutions by new ones; and since every institution involves the recognition of the duty of conforming to it, progress must involve the repudiation of an established duty at every step' (Shaw 1986: 40). Society, however, cannot cope with the vacuum left by the destruction of an old ideal and immediately creates a new ideal to replace it: 'the replacement of the broken goods will be prompt and certain'. This is still positive progress as each 'new ideal is less of an illusion than the one it has supplanted' (Shaw 1986: 62). The progressive nature of Shaw's dialectic can be seen in his reading of Ibsen's plays, not as single entities, but as a dialectical progression: 'the plays, as they succeed one another, are parts of a continuous discussion; how Mrs Alving is a reply to your hasty remark that Nora Helmer ought to be ashamed of herself for leaving her husband; how Gregers Werle warns you not to be as great a fool in your admiration of Lona Hessel as of Patient Grisel' (Shaw 1986: 173). The synthesis of one play becomes the thesis of the next. The quality of a play's dialectic becomes the benchmark against which the value of a play is judged: 'If the case is uninteresting or stale or badly conducted or obviously trumped up, the play is a bad one. If it is important and novel and convincing, or at least disturbing, the play is a good one. But anyhow the play in which there is no argument and no case no longer counts as serious drama' (Shaw 1986: 164).

Theatre historian Jonas Barish argues that Shaw attempted to turn theatre against itself in order to redeem it. Shaw claims that melodrama corrupts its audience because its characters live by idealist codes it would be foolish for anyone to replicate in real life: '[i]t has fostered a false and unnatural view of the world prompting men to behave falsely and unnaturally themselves' (Barish 1981: 451). Shaw's theatre, Barish argues, is 'a persistent testing of those codes by the canons of common sense, and the exposure of them as gaseous folly' (Barish 1981: 452). While earlier figures, such as ancient Greek philosopher Plato and eighteenth-century French philosopher Jean-Jacques Rousseau, argue that theatre should be banished in order to save the audience from its corrupting influence, Shaw seeks 'not to suppress the theater', but instead to save it from itself: 'for men of good will to seize it and make it serve morality and truth' (Barish 1981: 251). Like Lillo and Diderot, Shaw sees theatre as having a primarily moral function. He repositions the theatre as a school of instruction rather than a place of pleasure, with the dramatist 'teaching and saving' the audience (Shaw 1986: 171).

In order for theatre to act as an agent of moral reform, Shaw argues that discussion must be integral to a play's form as well as its content, 'until it so overspreads and interpenetrates the action that it finally assimilates it, making play and discussion practically identical' (Shaw 1986: 172). For Shaw, there is an organic relationship between the content of a play and its structure: 'Changes in technique follow inevitably from these changes in the subject matter of the play' (Shaw 1986: 170). A shift in content will automatically catalyse a shift in form. Like his predecessors, he argues that, in order for a play to engage an audience, its subject must relate to the everyday problems they experience: 'a play in which problems of conduct and character of personal importance to the audience are raised and suggestively discussed' (Shaw 1986: 162). As the content deals with everyday social reality, the form must work to create a recognizable version of that reality on stage. If the audience can recognize both the onstage world and the problems its characters face as similar to their own, they will empathize with them: 'making the spectators themselves the persons of the drama, and the incidents of their own lives its incidents' (Shaw 1986: 172). Unlike his predecessors, however, Shaw seeks a primarily intellectual rather than emotional engagement from his audience. This is facilitated through the dialectic inserted into this realist dramaturgical frame. The playwright uses the dialectic to mislead the audience into drawing false conclusions: to 'trick the spectator into forming a meanly false judgement, and then convict him of it in the next act' (Shaw 1986: 171). This induces a dialectical thought process in the audience's mind, 'a forensic technique of recrimination, disillusion and penetration through ideals to the truth' (Shaw 1986: 172). The audience is actively forced to question their own assumptions and reconsider the validity of the ideals that society has constructed for them. Shaw's reforms entail not just a change in theatre's content, but the establishment of a relationship between politics, dialectical structure and realist dramaturgy; a relationship that continues to define contemporary understandings of serious drama.

Widowers' Houses

Shaw used *Rhinegold*, the play he started work on with Archer, as the basis for his own play *Widowers' Houses* (Royalty Theatre, London 1892). The finished play is a hybrid mixture of Archer's sentimental marriage plot and Shaw's socialist values. Archer's original plot was drawn from the French playwright Émile Augier's *Ceinture dorée* (Théâtre du Gymnase-Dramatique, Paris 1855). Augier's play concerns an honest young man who calls off an engagement when he discovers that his fiancée's father acquired his fortune by disreputable means. Luckily for the young lovers, the father is then ruined, allowing the marriage to proceed as they had originally hoped. Archer claims Shaw only retained two elements of his plot: the first act's hotel garden setting and 'the bare idea of a young man refusing to marry tainted money' (Archer 1929: 343). Instead, into this initial framework, Shaw grafts a discussion on the social horrors arising from what he sees as the average Englishman's tendency towards avarice and selfishness, a tendency 'to shut his eyes to the most villainous abuses if the remedy threatens to add another penny in the pound to the rates and taxes which he has to be half cheated, half coerced into paying' (Shaw 1946: 26).

The first act appears to be a conventional comedy about love across social barriers. Trench, a young man from a distinguished but impoverished family, falls in love with Blanche, a young girl from a wealthy but disreputable family. Sartorius, Blanche's father, agrees to allow Trench to marry Blanche on the condition that his family agree to accept her into polite society. Shaw leads his audience to expect that the second act will begin with the news that Trench's family have refused to condone his marriage. Instead, Trench's family respond positively. The obstacle the audience is expecting to ruin the lovers' hopes turns out to be no obstacle at all. At this point, Shaw's play departs radically from its original dramaturgical model. Trench discovers that Sartorius is the most ruthless slum landlord in all of London, a man who thinks nothing of pocketing the 'money that ought to have fed starving children' (Shaw 1946: 59–60). The action of the play becomes driven by an exploration of the social problem of slum housing.

Shaw presents the audience with a sequence of theses and antitheses that continually overturn both Trench's and the audience's assumptions by increasing the moral complexity of the issue at the heart of the play. When Trench refuses to accept any money from Sartorius, Sartorius challenges Trench's idealism by arguing that his tenants live in terrible conditions because they have ruined the properties themselves by stealing parts of the fabric of the building for firewood. Repairing the houses only encourages this destructive behaviour. Sartorius also reveals that Trench is actually the mortgage holder for some of his slum properties. In order to pay the high rate of interest that Trench's family charges on the mortgage, Sartorius is forced to be financially ruthless: 'you exact interest from me at the monstrous and exorbitant rate of seven per cent, forcing me to exact the uttermost farthing in my turn from the tenants'. Trench and Sartorius are proven to be equally responsible for the misery of the working classes and equally 'powerless to alter the state of society' (Shaw 1946: 72). The play then returns to the marriage plot momentarily. Horrified by Trench's snobbish behaviour towards her father, Blanche breaks off their engagement.

At the beginning of act three, Lickcheese, a former employee of Sartorius, comes to visit him having developed a new and profitable housing scam he wants Sartorius to invest in. Sartorius initially decides not to invest in the scam as it involves improving the condition of the slum houses and raising the rent. His tenants would then be unable to afford the new rent and become homeless. Sartorius reveals that his understanding of his tenants' needs is founded on first-hand experience, as he comes from a working-class background. Trench decides they should take advantage of Lickcheese's scam. His priorities have changed. He now puts money before compassion. When Sartorius explains that, as the mortgage holder, Trench will be responsible for any financial losses if the scam goes wrong, Trench withdraws his support. Sartorius, reversing his initial position, then threatens to pay off Trench's mortgage completely, so robbing him of his stable income, if he refuses to take part in the scam. If, however, Trench marries into the family, then all these financial matters will be resolved. The discussion concludes with the proposal of marriage as a solution to a financial problem, putting forward the idea that, under capitalism, human beings no longer have feelings but are 'mere calculating machines' (Shaw 1946: 92). Trench rejects this marriage of financial convenience, so appearing to disprove this thesis. In the final scene, however, the play returns to the original marriage plot. Blanche discovers Trench affectionately kissing her portrait. The lovers are reconciled and Trench agrees to support Blanche's father in the compensation scheme.

As Dominic Cavendish, the theatre critic of the leading UK newspaper the *Daily Telegraph*, notes, the dramaturgy of the play is an awkward combination of styles. The first act fails to get to grips with the meat of the play and feels 'circumlocutory', while 'the volte-face actions of the third act seem overly abrupt' (Cavendish 2015). It is, however, in this unsatisfactory combination of marriage plot and social issue-driven drama that the play's dialectical power lies. Though Trench has declared for his heart over his wallet, the motivations for his marriage are unclear. There is a suggested sincerity in his action of kissing Blanche's portrait. The stage directions indicate he thinks he is alone. Shaw notes, however, that '*a cunning expression*' crosses Trench's face once Blanche's reignited passion for him is revealed (Shaw 1946: 94). He sits silently in his chair while Blanche chides him, as if he is waiting for her to fall into his trap. This muddled ending can be read as presenting the audience with a dialectical conclusion. The thesis that love conquers all remains deeply troubled by its antithesis, that the desire for profit is the foundation of all human actions.

Contemporary serious drama

Theatre scholar Christopher Innes observes that: '[i]n claiming a direct social function for this discourse, Shaw not only gave a strong political cast to the mainstream of English drama, but set its stylistic terms' (Innes 1992: 56). The argument that Shavian serious drama continues to dominate British stages is troubled, however, by the commonly accepted narrative of modern British theatre history, which traditionally marks a radical break between the playwriting practices of the Edwardians and contemporary practice in 1956 with the premiere of English playwright John Osborne's *Look Back in Anger* at the Royal Court.

The commonly accepted narrative of modern British theatre history is dominated by the idea of such radical revolutions in practice. David Edgar describes modern British theatre history as 'a kind of three-act drama' (Edgar 1999: 9). Its three acts are associated with the years 1956, 1968 and 1979, each of which delineates a radical shift in the way theatre engages politically with the changing world around it. The beginning of theatre's examination of 'the consequences of working class empowerment' was signalled in 1956 with the premiere of *Look Back in Anger*. The end of censorship in 1968 heralded the birth of more topical and overtly political work, which questioned 'the limits of social democracy and the welfare state'. The third act began with the Thatcher era in 1979, out of which emerged a political theatre focused on articulating the concerns of specific groups within society 'as women, black and gay playwrights confronted the questions of difference and identity which had emerged in the 1960s and 1970s' (Edgar 1999: 5).

Theatre scholar Melissa Dana Gibson challenges the validity of this revolutionary narrative, arguing that it functions to disguise a continuity of practice by dazzling audiences with '"the new" and the ideology of progress through succession' (Gibson 2006: 44). Drama and art critic John Russell Taylor identifies these theatrical revolutions as revolutions in content rather than form; what distinguished the drama of the angry young men and women of the 1950s 'as a decisive break with Rattigan and the older drama was not so much its form as its content: the characters who took part in the drama and the language in which they expressed themselves' (Taylor 1969: 40). Kitchen sink dramas, such as Osborne's *Look Back in Anger*, perpetuate the same serious dramaturgy Shaw advocates, while laying claim to greater realism and a stronger engagement with social and political issues on the basis that their content encompasses characters and concerns from a wider range of social backgrounds than the plays that preceded them. Instead of being a break with Shaw's serious drama, these plays are a reinvigoration of it at a time when even George Devine, the founding artistic director of the Royal Court, was predicting that the much-needed revolution in British theatre would come in the form of a move away from realism; the work of a Beckett as opposed to an Osborne. As theatre scholars Simon Shepherd and Peter Womack note, *Look Back in Anger* can be seen as a renewal of naturalism in the face of the threat of modernism: '*Look Back in Anger* is the point at which English drama of the modern period starts to become both serious and accessible, the moment at which drama starts to say something real again. Osborne returns us to Ibsen' (Shepherd and Womack 1996: 278).

This continuity in form, between the serious drama of Shaw and twenty-first-century political plays, is evident in the way contemporary British playwrights, such as David Edgar and David Hare, theorize the construction of political plays. Both Edgar and Hare's conception of the political play, like Shaw's, connects political content, dialectical structure and realist dramaturgy with political efficacy. Edgar identifies the dialectical discussion of social issues as an essential component of political theatre: 'theatre is a site where important things are being discussed' (quoted in Billingham 2007: 40) through 'a political dialectic of a thesis and an antithesis' (quoted in Billingham 2007: 31). The thesis and antithesis of Edgar's political dialectic are not only discussed, but also embodied in the play's characters. He defines the dialectic of his play *Maydays* (RSC, London 1983) in terms of its characters: 'the argument of the play is that James Grain's kind of politics either turns you into a zealot, or drives you out. And if you leave you may become a zealot in the other direction. That is what happens to Martin Glass' (Edgar quoted in Wu 2000: 118). Hare also thinks of his characters as embodying thesis and antithesis. He describes the dialectic of his play *Pravda* (National Theatre, London 1985 – written with English playwright Howard Brenton) as being embodied by Lambert Le Roux, a right-wing media mogul who 'believes in nothing but who *knows* what he believes in', and a group of committed left-wing journalists 'who don't know what they believe in' (Wu 2000: 172, emphasis in original).

Both Edgar and Hare advocate the framing of this dialectic within a realist dramaturgy. Edgar claims that '[t]he big subjects of this decade appear to lend themselves to traditional mimetic representation' (Edgar 2008). Hare agrees and argues, like Lillo, Diderot and Shaw before him, that the function of such realist dramaturgy is to create 'fictional stories which people recognise as belonging to the public domain or their own lives' (Hare quoted in Wu 2000: 170). Although Edgar and Hare both agree on the importance of realist dramaturgy, their understanding of its nature is subtly different. Hare's plays attempt to reproduce 'real-world' spaces. While working on his National Theatre trilogy – *Racing Demon* (1990), *Murmuring Judges* (1991) and *The Absence of War* (1993) – Hare spent months 'absorbing the details of the real-life world' of the different British institutions (the Church, the justice system and party politics) in which the plays were set. While the details of the institutions Hare depicts in these plays are drawn directly from life, he makes it clear that the characters and their narratives are completely fictional. The attempt to reproduce reality, he argues, should be limited to the reproduction of the world of the play. Any attempt to create characters based on real people and to reproduce real events is a self-defeating task: '[n]o film seeking to explore the psychology of, say, Richard Nixon can do justice to the boundless complexity of the man himself' (Hare 1993a: 4).

Edgar's understanding of a realist dramaturgy is slightly different. He advocates the use of a 'representative fictionalised narrative' within a situation that is a 'generic fictionalised example'. He combines the details of a number of real-life situations to create a fictional narrative set in a fictionalized world built on real-world blueprints. In *The Shape of the Table* (National Theatre, London 1990), Edgar draws on events that he sees as generic to the transition from communism to capitalism in Poland, East Germany, Czechoslovakia, Hungary and Bulgaria to create a narrative that describes a representative version of the process. He sees this as an effective dramaturgical approach because 'setting a play not entirely within but adjacent to observed reality – allows the playwright to explore human processes, freed from the constraints of particular circumstances and personalities' (Edgar 2003). He argues that a realist dramaturgy that aims to photographically reproduce a real-world situation may actually obscure the root of the problem the playwright is aiming to address. Instead, the playwright should paint a picture of reality through which the root of the problem may be revealed: 'the problem with looking in a mirror is that you see what the world sees. Look into a picture, and you may see what you have disguised' (Edgar 2000).

By presenting an audience with a fictional world that repro-duces real-world social structures, Edgar argues that theatre functions as a social laboratory in which 'we can test and confront our darkest impulses under laboratory conditions' (Edgar 2000). It is a place where society's problems can be dissected and examined in order to find possible resolutions. Edgar justifies his sympathetic presentation of fascists in *Destiny* (RSC, Stratford-Upon-Avon 1976) on the basis that it enables the audience to study the way the movement functions: '[t]he reason for making the fascists recognisable, and treating them seriously as human beings, was precisely in order to say to the anti-fascist movement, "You've got to understand these people. You've got to understand how it works – and *this* is how it works"' (Edgar quoted in Wu 2000: 123, emphasis in original). Edgar positions empathy as a vital political tool that helps an audience come to a deeper understanding of such seemingly alien viewpoints by enabling them to see the world through the eyes of others. The playwright invites 'the audience to see the world he creates from competing perspectives' (Edgar 2001).

Like Edgar, Hare envisages political theatre as having the power to change the way people view the world. He hopes that 'people might be moved to change sometimes' by what they see in his plays. He also sees empathy as playing a vital role in this process. For Hare, the audience's change in view is the result of both an intellectual and emotional engagement with the performance: 'good drama is meant to send your head and your heart spinning'. As an example of this, he references the representation of the doctors in English dramatist Trevor Griffiths' television play *Through the Night* (BBC 1975) as having to battle their own feelings of impotence, while treating patients suffering from potentially terminal diseases. By seeing the world from a different perspective, in this case through the eyes of a doctor, Hare argues that theatre acts politically by making 'more sense' of a previously misunderstood 'area of life' (Hare quoted in Wu 2000: 171).

The ultimate function of Edgar's theatre laboratory is to enable the audience to think through the consequences of their actions without having to face those consequences in real life: 'to imagine a series of actions and their consequences and, on the basis of that speculation, to choose between them' (Edgar 2005). By following a character through a series of actions whose consequences lead them to commit 'evil' acts, the audience can become aware of how, under a similar set of circumstances, they too might choose the same path and commit the same acts: a sense of 'there but for the grace of God go I' (Edgar 2000).

While both Edgar and Hare acknowledge that the world has changed significantly within their lifetimes, they both continue to believe in the political efficacy of serious drama. Hare rebukes the idea that the theatrical form he is writing in no longer has any purchase in the context of a more monological politics: 'I believe that this whole idea that politics is finished because there aren't two systems any more is nonsense. I don't believe that the death of socialism means that the question of social justice goes away. The debate about how society should be fair will go on forever' (Hare quoted in Wu 2000: 178). Edgar observes that current literary and philosophical theory should encourage playwrights to 'challenge the linear narrative which is at every genre's core' (Edgar 1999: 29), but he continues to argue for its utility in the real world: 'while the academy has been proclaiming the death of linear narrative, the real world has seen a rush towards it' (Edgar 2008). For both Hare and Edgar, the structures of serious drama continue to define the dramaturgy of the political play.

The politics of serious drama

Serious drama claims to articulate a progressive socialist politics. As a form, it is born out of Shaw's interest in the Marxist dialectic and his desire for 'social progress' (Shaw 1986: 40) in opposition to 'organised robbery and oppression (politely called Capitalism)' (Shaw 1986: 129). With its belief in rational positive progress, Shavian serious drama is very much the child of solid modernity. Through it, Shaw aims to create a fairer world for all; to promote the legislation of 'reason into reality, to reshuffle the stakes in a way that would trigger rational conduct and render all behaviour contrary to reason too costly to contemplate' (Bauman 2012: 47–8). Within the context of contemporary British theatre, Shavian serious drama continues to present itself as an effective vehicle of such social and political change. But how valid is this claim?

Jameson puts forward the idea that if the politics of a text are to be fully considered, they must first be analysed on three different levels. The first is the level of the text's ostensible political content. Does the text address a social contradiction and attempt to resolve it through a dialectical process? The second is the level of the text's class origins. What role does the text play in the social and historical context in which it was originally created, when that social and historical context is considered from a Marxist perspective as a moment of class conflict between a privileged class and an oppressed class? The third and final level is the level of the text's form. The final section of this chapter explores serious drama's claim to a progressive socialist politics on Jameson's first two levels of content and class origins. The question of form will be explored in the next chapter.

On Jameson's first 'narrowly political horizon' of content, a text is read for its dialectic. The text is grasped as 'a symbolic act, whereby real social contradictions, insurmountable in their own terms, find a purely formal resolution in the aesthetic realm' (Jameson 1983: 62). Serious drama can be thought of as articulating a progressive politics on this level. A dialectic is inscribed at the heart of its structure, into which the playwright inserts the specifics of the particular social contradiction they wish to address. The structure is dialectical regardless of the specifics of the social or political issue that constitutes its content. Embodied in realistic characters, the thesis and antithesis fight it out and the resolution of this conflict offers a point of synthesis.

The act of resolution can be read as politically problematic if it produces a closed rather than open dialectic. The resolution of the social contradiction is considered to be more productive if it raises new questions as opposed to offering a definitive solution. Jameson argues, however, that even when the dialectic is closed, it remains politically productive. The solution offered may have been symbolically brought into being in the imagined world of the text but it has not actually been brought into being in the real world: 'a symbolic act is on the one hand affirmed as a genuine *act*, albeit on the symbolic level, while on the other it is registered as an act which is "merely" symbolic, its resolutions imaginary ones that leave the real untouched' (Jameson 1983: 66, emphasis in original). This purely imaginary resolution could be seen as lacking political efficacy because it has no effect in the real world. Jameson argues, however, that it is the very lack of a solution in the real world that is productive in political terms. The contradiction between the unresolved social situation in the world and the imaginary resolution of the social situation inside the theatre is in itself a productive dialectic. This gap provides an impetus to take action to bring the social solution imagined in the performance into actual being. Thus, regardless of whether its resolution offers an open or closed dialectic, on Jameson's first level, serious drama's claim to a progressive politics stands.

When reading the politics of serious drama on Jameson's second level, that of 'social class', serious drama's claim to a progressive socialist politics is troubled (Jameson 1983: 69). On this level, 'the individual utterance or text is grasped as a symbolic move in an essentially polemic and strategic ideological confrontation between classes' (Jameson 1983: 70–1), a class confrontation between 'a dominant and a labouring class' (Jameson 1983: 69). At this level, a text is read as an individual utterance within an antagonistic dialogue between classes, in which their 'two opposing discourses fight it out within the general unity of a shared code' (Jameson 1983: 70). In the case of serious drama, the shared code is theatre.

Serious drama came into being in the late-nineteenth century in opposition to melodrama, which then dominated theatre stages. Serious drama's project consists of the promotion of its own value, combined with an aggressive devaluation of melodrama. Innes argues that contemporary understandings of melodrama as a low form are shaped by 'Shaw's polemics, which successfully created a climate of appreciation for his own work by denigrating his immediate predecessors' (Innes 1992: 9). Archer presents serious drama as theatre's apex, a 'pure and logical art-form' (Archer 1929: 5). In contrast, he presents melodrama as drama's apogee, 'the gradual decline of English drama into something very like inanition and imbecility' (Archer 1929: 252). The success of Shaw and Archer's project can be deduced from the extent to which the word 'melodramatic' has gathered negative connotations in everyday use, implying something sensational, overemotional and crude. This devaluation of melodrama has led to a tendency to lump all of its different genres together into a single, undifferentiated mass and to position all melodramas, as theatre historian Katherine Newey and historian Jeffrey Richards note, 'as symptomatic of the problems of mass culture in the nineteenth century, rather than centrally significant cultural products in their own right' (Newey and Richards 2010: 115).

On one level, the class conflict between melodrama and serious drama can be read as a conflict between a capitalist commercial theatre of melodrama and a socialist subsidized theatre of serious drama. Archer and Shaw both argue that theatre made on a capitalist economic basis is inevitably bad theatre:

> no great art is to be expected while management is a trade, and the theatre is expected not only to pay its way but to yield a handsome interest on capital. A theatre which must make money from day to day and from week to week can do so, they say, only by pandering to 'the giddy Phrygian crowd that hastes not be wise'.
>
> (Archer 1886: 271–2)

Profit and art do not mix. The establishment of both a national theatre and a state-funded cultural sector is a keystone of Archer and Shaw's campaign to reform the theatre.

On another level, however, this conflict can be read as a middle-class struggle for control of a theatre culture dominated by the working classes. Melodrama is a theatrical form whose audiences were predominantly drawn from the working classes of industrial cities. As theatre historian Michael Booth observes, 'rapid industrial expansion [...] created huge urban working classes living in conditions of the utmost drabness and squalor, who demanded entertainment as relief from the long working day' (Booth 1964: 15). The London East End theatres, in particular, attracted a regular local audience, creating a strong sense of community: 'patronised by intensely loyal people whose theatre might have been run for years by the same management, with the same playwrights churning out melodramas and the same actors playing in them' (Booth 1964: 19). These audiences also patronized the patent theatres, Drury Lane and Covent Garden, which included melodrama in their repertoires because it delivered large box-office receipts. Booth argues that melodrama's invasion of the patent theatres, bringing with it lower-class audiences, was one of the reasons for the abandonment of theatre-going as a social habit on the part of the upper classes. Although Booth is a strong advocate for the cultural value of melodrama, he perpetuates Archer and Shaw's association between a lower-class audience and a lower-quality form: '[t]he absence of the upper classes from the popular theatre was one of a complex of factors contributing to the poor artistic quality of nineteenth century drama' (Booth 1964: 16).

Serious drama is predominantly a theatre of the intellectual middle classes. Shaw, Archer and their contemporaries reconfigure the theatre as a form of literature and of moral improvement. They argue that plays should be published, as well as performed. They distance theatre from the idea of entertainment. Theatre, like church or school, becomes something you attend because it is good for you. Pleasing the audience is no longer the theatre's role. Instead, the audience must now be made fit for the theatre. Archer aims 'to create a new class of serious playgoers' who would form a suitable audience for serious plays (Archer 1929: 339). This process of embourgeoisement is mirrored, Shepherd and Womack argue, in the narrative of English playwright Arthur Wing Pinero's play *Trelawny of the Wells* (Court Theatre, London 1898). The play's protagonist, a working-class actress, Rose Trelawny, rises in class through her marriage to an aristocrat. When she then returns to the melodramatic stage, she finds it impossible to act the way she used to. She has lost her vulgarity. Her acting is now only suitable for a new, serious kind of drama. Rose has risen in social rank and become respectable, just as the theatre has through serious drama (Shepherd and Womack 1996: 249–53).

Not every Victorian theatre reformer carried the same poor opinion of melodrama as Archer and Shaw. Newey and Richards claim that the art critic John Ruskin saw melodrama as an effective vehicle for social and moral improvement. They report him as saying: 'I have always held the stage quite among the best and most necessary means of education – moral and intellectual' and argue that his social and aesthetic theories influenced the work of several important British nineteenth-century theatre practitioners, including the actor-manager Henry Irving and the actor-manager and playwright Wilson Barrett (Newey and Richards 2010: 1). In Ruskin's eyes, melodrama's combination of moral purpose, social conscience and stage beauty has the potential to develop its spectator into a 'feeling individual', a process that involves both the intellect and the emotions: '[k]nowledge can only lead to under-standing, argues Ruskin repeatedly, through right thinking. And this is a process of moral cognition which must involve the heart as well as the head' (Newey and Richards 2010: 139). Melodrama's much-criticized emotional intensity is precisely what enables its audience to take its moral content to heart.

Melodrama can also be thought of as having social value in terms of offering its audience a way of navigating the pressures of the newly industrialized world. Theatre and film historian David Mayer argues that melodrama was 'responsive to immediate social circumstances and concerns' of its working-class audience (Mayer 2004: 146). Melodrama is born in 'a period of rapid and profound change. Concomitant with these changes is intense stress' (Mayer 2004: 147). There was a mass movement of people from rural areas to the new expanding industrial cities. This rapid urban growth led to high levels of poverty, ill health and rising crime. Life became more insecure: 'living in the new machine based industries was fraught with uncertainty' as there was a feeling 'that employers were arbitrary in their decisions, that wages and jobs might end abruptly' (Mayer 2004: 151). As the industrial cities expanded, older patterns of social control began to fall apart. Previously, society had been organized through networks of clients, family and friends and focused around the country estates of the aristocracy. Sociologist Craig Calhoun argues that there was a 'breakdown of the structure of hierarchical incorporation which knit local communities into the society as a whole' (Calhoun 1982: 174). There was 'a general concern for establishing new forms of order and discipline' (Lash and Urry 1987: 96). Melodrama responded to a climate in which both traditional ideas of morality and people's understanding of how the world works were in flux. Melodrama reflects this state of uncertainty in its depiction of a world 'where things are seen to go wrong, where ideas of secular and divine justice and recompense are not always met, where suffering is not always acknowledged, and where explanations for wrong, injustice, and suffering are not altogether understandable' (Mayer 2004: 148).

Shepherd and Womack position melodrama as the 'people's drama' (Shepherd and Womack 1996: 236); a theatre of protest that should be recognized not in literary terms 'as a hiatus in the dominant culture of letters', but in theatrical terms as 'a high point in the decentralized culture of working communities' (Shepherd and Womack 1996: 231). Booth observes that melodrama's class attitudes: 'are strongly anti-aristocratic. Villains tend to be wealthy employers and noblemen, heroes workmen and peasants' (Booth 1964: 16). Literary scholar Peter Brooks argues that melodrama envisions a world based on 'merit rather than privilege' in its dramaturgy (Brooks 1985: 44). It expresses its audience's social discontent through the characterization of its protagonist as an 'idealized common man, brave and clever and humane, rebelling against the forces of society' (Booth 1964: 29). Like Lillo's *The London Merchant*, of which melodrama is as much the heir as serious drama, it draws on elements of heroic tragedy in order to raise the status of the actions of its working-class protagonists to the level of the heroic. It aims to produce admiration and pity in its audience through its depiction of heroism in a time of undeserved crisis as 'constantly tensed to surpass itself, to reach a point of self-mastery and self-renunciation which is truly *exemplary*, and which elicits the wonderment and applause, the *admirato*, of characters and spectators alike' (emphasis in original). Its resolution is found in the public recognition of the protagonist's virtue, which, despite many trials, 'goes forth, unscathed, with the blessings of the unvirtuous, who recognize its superior power' (Brooks 1985: 26). Melodrama acts politically through this 'remarkable, public, spectacular homage to virtue' over and above social status (Brooks 1985: 25). Although the recognition of virtue is purely symbolic and confined to the aesthetic realm, melodrama can be seen as articulating a progressive socialist politics on Jameson's first dialectical level of political content as well as his second level of class conflict. The recognition of the virtues of the working class within the aesthetic realm creates a dialectic which calls for their recognition in the real world as well.

The Factory Lad

John Walker's *The Factory Lad* (Surrey Theatre, London 1832) is a domestic melodrama focusing on the plight of factory workers whose jobs are threatened by the introduction of steam-powered machinery. The play's political impact is produced through both an adherence to classical melodramatic form and innovations within that form that confound the audience's expectations of it. The play presents its audience with a conventional opening scene of innocence and bliss. The factory workers – George Allen and his friends – discuss the virtues of their recently deceased master who 'as he became rich by the industry of his men, would not desert them in a time of need, nor prefer steam machinery and other inventions to honest labour' (Walker 1969: 207). The action of melodrama is ignited when the harmonious equilibrium of the initial scene is disturbed by the entrance of the villain. Peter Brooks terms this dramaturgical device 'the violation and spoliation of the space of innocence' (Brooks 1985: 30). The drama moves from a 'presentation of virtue-as-innocence to the introduction of menace or obstacle, which places virtue in a situation of extreme peril' (Brooks 1985: 31).

Westwood, the factory's new owner, informs the workers that their services are no longer required. The factory has fallen behind the times because the old master failed to upgrade the technology. The market is now flooded with cheap, machine-made products and so Westwood needs to reduce his workforce and modernize production: 'A ton of coals will do as much work as fifty men, and for less wages than ten come to' (Walker 1969: 209).

The scene ends with the workers vowing revenge: 'Hard-hearted, vain, pampered thing as thou art, remember, the day will come thou'lt be sorry for this night's work!' (Walker 1969: 210). The vow in melodrama has an important dramaturgical function as it drives the actions of the hero. The vow, once made, is unbreakable.

The workers are led on their unstoppable course of revenge by the character of Will Rushton, an outcast whose life was ruined many years before when he found himself in the same situation as the factory workers now find themselves: 'honest Will Rushton that was once – hard working Will Rushton. You know my fate – torture upon torture, the insult of the proud and the pity of the poor have been my lot for years' (Walker 1969: 223–4). His experiences outline the limited options the workers now have to choose between: starving on the charity of the parish, risking their lives in the Australian colonies or resorting to a life of crime. While machine-breaking is not a practical solution to the workers' situation, it offers a rare opportunity to exercise power over their oppressors: 'to see the palace of the tyrant levelled to the ground – to hear his engines of gain cracking – to hear him call for help, and see the red flame laugh in triumph' (Walker 1969: 225). Both the characters and the audience are offered a brief moment of catharsis in the play's depiction of the workers' violent triumph over oppression. In such moments, melodrama offers its audience a Bakhtinian 'liberation from the prevailing truth and from the established order' (Bakhtin 1984: 10). The social relations that the audience are subjected to in their everyday lives are briefly reversed in the lives of their imaginations. The importance of this moment of triumph is emphasized through a common melodramatic device, the tableau. Brooks describes a tableau as a 'moment when, at a point of crisis, the characters would freeze in a plastic representation of the emotional freight of the situation, each expressing through posture, gesture, and facial expression his or her particular place in the spectrum of reactions'. Tableaux play an important role in the affective communication of meaning, 'melodrama's primordial effort to make its signs forceful and intelligible' (Brooks 1994: 606). At the end of act one, Rushton stands in tableau over the figure of Westwood and '*waves the lighted ember above him in wild triumph*' (Walker 1969: 224). The power structures of everyday social relations are temporarily reversed and the play revels in the momentary triumph of the disenfranchised working class over the pampered rich.

The second act begins with another requisite melodramatic scene, the 'violated banquet'. In this scene, the villain invades the space of the hero's home, signalling 'the triumph of villainy, the fall, eclipse, and even expulsion of virtue' (Brooks 1985: 29). Westwood enters Allen's home to arrest him. At this point, however, there is reversal of traditional form. As the officers seize hold of Allen, Rushton enters and knocks Westwood to the floor, allowing Allen to make his escape. The lighted ember tableau is repeated, marking an overturning of both accepted power structures and narrative conventions. Virtue, instead of being overwhelmed, has unexpectedly triumphed to fight another day.

The workers are eventually caught and brought to trial. The public trial, another stock feature of melodrama, signals the moment in which the hero's virtue is judged and then usually confirmed. Its confirmation, however, depends on the character of the judge and his ability to recognize that the moral crime committed against the hero has greater authority than the official law of the land. In *The Factory Lad*, the official system of justice is shown to be corrupt. The justice who presides over the case is Justice Bias, a man who takes advantage of his position to steal food from the poor inhabitants of the workhouse 'who had no redress but the lash if they dared complain' (Walker 1969: 231). Bias rules in Westwood's favour. The law itself is exposed as a tool of oppression that 'lock[s] the poor man in a gaol, while the rich one goes free' (Walker 1969: 232). The factory workers and Rushton are all sentenced to hang. The play breaks with the conventions of melodrama again at this point. Virtue is punished. Its superior power is not recognized by the unvirtuous. All of melodrama's devices fail. Allen's wife's pleas for mercy, which would normally elicit a Damascian change of heart in the villain, go unheeded. The audience's expectations of a last-minute reprieve as the hero mounts the scaffold are not fulfilled.

If, as Mayer argues, melodrama promises its audience that it 'exacts no toll' and 'good characters emerge unscathed', *The Factory Lad* violates that promise (Mayer 2004: 149). From a dramaturgical point of view, the ending is tragic as opposed to melodramatic in its demand that the hero be sacrificed. This violation of audience expectations creates a productive dialectic. While *The Factory Lad* offers its audience a chance to indulge in a reversal of social relations, it questions the fantasy that virtue always triumphs. If melodrama operates on its audience cathartically, as Brooks argues, by suggesting that if '[v]irtue can finally break through its helplessness, find its name, liberate itself from primal horror, fulfil its desires. We awake from the nightmare', then *The Factory Lad* offers no such reprieve from the nightmare of everyday life (Brooks 1985: 35). Power, not virtue, is triumphant.

On the level of Jameson's first level of analysis, that of political content, melodrama does function politically. Its dramaturgical structure, like that of serious drama, has a dialectic at its heart, albeit one that works through emotional affect as opposed to intellectual discussion: the social contradiction between the idea that moral justice should favour the virtuous and the rule of a political/judicial system that supports the rich and the corrupt in their exploitation of the poor and the innocent. Melodrama can also be read as political on the basis that it both enables its audience to navigate the ever-shifting demands of the newly industrialized world and provides them with a vehicle through which to express their anger at the injustices of liberal capitalism. It is a form clearly allied to the concerns of its working-class audiences.

Contemporary serious drama's origins may lie in eighteenth-century domestic tragedy, but its reinvention as a political form with a progressive socialist character and specific dramaturgical features – dialectical discussion framed within a realist dramaturgy – is rooted in Shaw and Archer's campaign to redeem theatre from the supposed inanity of melodrama in the 1890s. While serious drama's claims to a progressive socialist politics hold on Jameson's first level of content, on Jameson's second level of class origins, the politics of serious drama can be read as reactionary and conservative. Serious drama's claims to a progressive socialist politics are troubled if melodrama is read as a politically engaged form. Rather than redeeming the working class by creating a theatre that campaigned for socialist values, Archer and Shaw's project can be read as an ultimately successful campaign to devalue a form of theatre which was working class both in its concerns and its audiences, replacing it with a theatre that privileged middle-class views and middle-class audiences.

Serious drama can be read as articulating contradictory political messages on the first and second of Jameson's levels of analysis. In the next chapter, serious drama's claim to articulate a progressive socialist politics will be investigated on Jameson's third level of analysis, that of form.

2

The Politics of Structure

[A] play is not a flat work of literature, not a description in poetry of another world, but is in itself another world passing before you in time and space.

FUCHS 2004: 6

This chapter continues the investigation started in the first chapter into the political character of serious drama. Whereas the first chapter explored serious drama's claim to a progressive socialist politics on Jameson's first two levels of analysis – content and class origins – this chapter examines serious drama's claim on Jameson's third level of analysis, that of form.

It begins with an introduction to the theoretical basis on which it is possible to analyse a play's form for its political character, exploring the reasons why social reality can be thought of as constructed of a network of shifting social structures. It examines the relationship between these social structures and the exercise of power, considering the ways in which plays can be thought to act politically by reproducing or reimagining these social structures through their dramaturgical structures. It illustrates these ideas with an analysis of English playwright Sam Holcroft's 2011 play *Edgar and Annabel*.

The chapter then moves on to consider the politics of serious drama's form. The previous chapter concluded that serious drama has a contradictory political character when analysed on the first two of Jameson's levels. This chapter argues that on Jameson's third level of analysis, that of form, serious drama's political character is equally contradictory. While serious drama can be argued to articulate a progressive socialist politics of form within the historical context of late-nineteenth-century Britain, within a contemporary context its politics are more problematic. This claim will be supported with analyses of Charlotte Jones's *Humble Boy* (2001) and Caryl Churchill's *Love and Information* (2012).

The politics of structure

Jameson's third level of textual analysis, the *'ideology of form'*, is concerned with the structural politics of a text. At this level, '"form" is apprehended as content' (Jameson 1983: 84). The structures of a text are thought of as carrying political messages. Some of these structures are the product of conscious authorial choices, but others are unconscious reproductions of the social structures that make up the fabric of the author's social reality. Any one text can carry a range of different structures within it. These different structures carry political messages that may both contradict those of other structures within the text and any explicit political message articulated by the text's content. The text, instead of being seen as articulating a clear and unified political viewpoint, is seen as a network of structures articulating conflicting political messages.

If a text articulates a politics through its representation of structures, then a play can be thought of as a particularly powerful agent for political change. As Fuchs argues, a play is more than its text. It is a tangible, three-dimensional representation of an imagined world with its own networks of social structures. The audience are immersed in this world and the political messages that its structures articulate. They '"see" this other world [...] experience its space-time, its architectonics' (Fuchs 2004: 6). The social structures of these dramatic worlds stand in a relationship to the social structures of social reality, reproducing and reimagining them.

In order to understand how dramaturgical structures reproduce social structures, it is necessary to consider the structure of everyday social reality. The structures of social reality present themselves as the natural order of things. In order to think about a politics of structure, however, they need to be rethought as a construction of human activity. Philosopher John Searle divides the features of social reality into two types. Natural features (e.g. mountains, wood) are 'brute facts', existing independently of human under-standing. Other features are 'institutional facts'. These require the existence of human beings for their existence as facts (Searle 1996: 27). They only *exist relatively to the intentionality of observers, users* (Searle 1996: 9, emphasis in original). A spanner, for example, has features that are brute facts. It is metal. When a spanner is described as a spanner, however, this specifies a 'user or observer relative' feature of the object (Searle 1996: 10). An object is only a spanner if people understand it to be a spanner and use it as a spanner. Human intentionality has imposed a specific identity and function on this object.

Institutional facts depend on 'collective intentionality' for their existence as facts. Collective intentionality is the tendency for human beings to 'share intentional states such as beliefs, desires, and intentions' and engage in 'cooperative behaviour' (Searle 1996: 23). Searle uses the example of a border to illustrate the relationship between institutional facts and collective intention-ality. A tribe builds a wall around its territory to mark its borders and keep intruders out. This wall is not an institutional fact because it performs its functions by virtue of its brute physical properties. One day, the tribe replaces the wall with a line of stones. The tribe and their neighbours continue to recognize the line of stones as a border. It 'counts as' a physical barrier even though it is not one (Searle 1996: 46). The border of stones is an institutional fact because human beings have mutually agreed that it is a border and functions as a border. It depends on collective intentionality for its existence as a fact.

Human institutions, such as language, marriage and religion, are made up of institutional facts that form systems of rules. There are two different types of rule: the 'regulative rule', which regulates a pre-existing activity, and the 'constitutive rule', which not only regulates an activity but brings the very possibility of that activity into being (Searle 1996: 27–8). Marriage is an institution that involves both regulative and constitutive rules. It involves regulative rules that regulate sexual activity by, for example, prohibiting sex outside marriage. These are regulative rules because sex existed as a human activity prior to the existence of marriage. It also includes constitutive rules that define the process of getting married, such as the exchanging of vows. These are constitutive rules because the activity of getting married cannot exist without the institution of marriage. Social reality is a complex network of interconnected human institutions. The institution of marriage implies the institution of family and so on.

Our actions are mediated by these complex, rule-based networks. Searle illustrates this with the example of purchasing a beer from a waiter in a restaurant in Paris and then leaving a tip:

> the scene as described has a huge invisible ontology: the waiter did not actually *own* the beer he *gave* me, but he is employed by the restaurant, which owned it. The restaurant is required to post a list of the prices of all the *boissons*, and even if I never see such a list, I am required to pay only the listed price.
>
> (Searle 1996: 3, emphasis in original)

These social rules are rarely explicitly taught. They are '[b]ackground' (Searle 1996: 129), part of what sociologist and anthropologist Pierre Bourdieu terms the '*habitus*' (Bourdieu 1977: 9, emphasis in original). Over time, the social subject evolves 'a set of dispositions that are sensitive to the rule structure' that surrounds them through a process of trial and error (Searle 1996: 145). They learn to regulate their behaviour on the basis of the positive or negative responses it produces in others. Through this self-regulating process, the social subject develops a '*socially informed body*' (emphasis in original) with certain tastes and distastes, certain compulsions and repulsions. They evolve a set of social senses:

> the sense of necessity and the sense of duty, the sense of direction and the sense of reality, the sense of balance and the sense of beauty, common sense and the sense of the sacred, tactical sense and the sense of responsibility, business sense and the sense of propriety, the sense of humour and the sense of absurdity, moral sense and the sense of practicality, and so on.
>
> (Bourdieu 1977: 124)

They internalize the social structures of their social reality, unconsciously embodying them. Like Aristotle's 'good man', the social subject comes to 'instinctively' understand how to do the right thing 'to the right person, to the right extent, at the right time, with the right motive, and in the right way' (Aristotle 2009: 36).

These social senses also include 'the *sense of limits and of the legitimate transgression of limits*' (Bourdieu 1977: 124, emphasis in original). The social subject not only develops an innate sense of the rule structure but also a sense of when, how and to what extent certain rules can be adapted, bent and broken. There is space for 'regulated' improvisation within the system (Bourdieu 1977: 79). This allows the social subject to adapt to new sets of social circumstances by generating 'an infinity of practices adapted to endlessly changing situations, without those schemes ever being constituted as explicit principles' (Bourdieu 1977: 16). Social reality is a process not a product. The social subject is involved in a continuous process of affirming, refining and pushing the limits of its structures.

Social structures exist and continue to exist because they are used: 'each use of the institution is a renewed expression of the commitment of the users to the institution' (Searle 1996: 57). Bourdieu likens social reality to a map: 'an imaginary representation of all theoretically possible roads and routes, is opposed to the network of beaten tracks, of paths made ever more practicable by constant use' (Bourdieu 1977: 37–8). There are established pathways, but new pathways can be created through collective intentionality. The more a particular pathway is used, the more it is affirmed as an integral part of social reality. Pathways that fall into disuse eventually fade and vanish. The structures of social reality are in a continuous process of production and reproduction, development and renewal.

Cultural representations of social structures play a role in this process. Representations that reproduce accepted social structures reaffirm their validity, helping to maintain the status quo and so have a reactionary political character. Representations that reimagine social structures may support the production of new social structures and can be thought of as politically progressive because they seek to create change.

Power relations

Social structures are political because they determine and maintain the 'structure of power relations' within a particular society (Searle 1996: 94). They confer and remove power. For example, elections confer power on the candidates who win the most votes. As social structures, however, rely on collective intentionality for their continued existence, the relations of power within any particular social reality are fragile as the social structures they rely on are at constant risk of collapse.

Within this fragile system, power relations are maintained through the imposition of discipline. Marxist theorist Antonio Gramsci draws a distinction between hard and soft approaches to maintaining power relations. The hard approach is defined by explicit laws enforced by the threat of physical punishment. The soft approach involves what Gramsci terms 'hegemony', that is '[t]he "spontaneous" consent given by the great masses of the population to the general direction imposed on social life' (Gramsci 1971: 12). It requires a level of collective intentionality.

Philosopher Michel Foucault illustrates the idea of soft discipline with the example of the daily routine of the House of Young Prisoners in Paris in 1838. Instead of suffering physical punishment, these criminals underwent a 'prescription for a possible normalization' (Foucault 1991: 21). They were forced to adhere to a strict daily routine, including nine hours of work, two hours of classes and half an hour of moral instruction. Bourdieu argues that the maintenance of existing power relations depends on the behaviour of the majority of people being 'normal'. Normal behaviour is defined by the idea that certain actions must be performed 'in the proper place at the proper time' (Bourdieu 1977: 162). Abnormal behaviour is characterized by a transgression of these normative spatio-temporal rhythms: '[w]orking while others are resting, staying in the house while others are working in the fields, travelling on deserted roads, wandering around the streets of the village while others are asleep or at the market – these are all suspicious forms of behaviour' (Bourdieu 1977: 161). The prison routine that Foucault describes forces criminals to obey normative spatio-temporal rhythms. It reconditions them to do the right thing at the right time in the right place in line with the spatio-temporal rhythms of the prevailing habitus.

In different societies, the spatio-temporal rhythms of the habitus take different forms creating different senses of normal behaviour that in turn support and maintain different sets of power relations. Based on his studies of the Kabyle of Algeria, Bourdieu argues that temporality in agro-pastoral societies is ordered in a circular structure of 'eternal recurrence' based on the patterns of the agrarian year (Bourdieu 1977: 148). These are societies whose objective is 'simple reproduction'. The community's activities are aimed at maintaining a state of stasis: 'towards the biological reproduction of the group and the production of sufficient goods for its subsistence and biological reproduction' (Bourdieu 1977: 59).

In contrast, capitalist societies are associated with dynamic linear temporalities that mirror the logic of economic accumulation. Sociologist Georges Gurvitch terms this form of temporality, in which the present is perceived as rushing headlong towards the future, 'time pushing forward' (Gurvitch 1964: 139). Bourdieu argues that the movement of an agro-pastoral society towards a capitalist mode of production is accompanied by a transformation of circular temporality into linear temporality. Within Kabyle society actions that disrupt circular temporality, such as rushing, are seen as threatening. Any man who acts as if he is in a 'race with time threatens to drag the whole group into the escalation of diabolic ambition, *thahraymith*, and thus to turn circular time into linear time, simple reproduction into indefinite accumulation' (Bourdieu 1977: 162). His behaviour threatens to disrupt the cyclic nature of the social structures that support and maintain the community in its agro-pastoral form.

Spatial structures also determine and are determined by economic modes of production. Philosopher and sociologist Henri Lefebvre argues that every mode of production produces a particular type of space and is produced by that space: 'the forces of production (nature; labour and the organization of labour; technology and knowledge) and, naturally, the relations of production play a part [...] in the production of space' (Lefebvre 1991: 46). Shifts in the mode of production are accompanied by shifts in spatial structures. The spatial practices of feudal societies were founded on '[m]anors, monasteries, cathedrals – these were the strong points anchoring the network of lanes and main roads to a landscape transformed by peasant communities'. In comparison, the spatial practices of capitalist societies are founded on 'the vast network of banks, business centres and major productive entities, as also on [the] motorways, airports and information lattices' that connect them (Lefebvre 1991: 53).

Different sets of social structures produce different types of social realities. If social reality takes different forms in different places, at different times and across different cultures, then how is it possible for each of these different social realities to seem to be the singular, undisputed natural state of things to those living within them? The social structures that support a particular social reality generate a hegemony, a 'central, effective and dominant system of meanings and values, which are not merely abstract but which are organized and lived'. This produces, as cultural theorist Raymond Williams argues, a mode of perception that constitutes 'a sense of absolute because experienced reality beyond which it is very difficult for most members of the society to move' (Williams 2001: 169). Within this mode of perception, the social structures that define normal behaviour seem to be the natural state of things. They are 'common sense' (Gramsci 1971: 323) or 'established knowledge' (Lefebvre 1991: 90). The social subject reproduces these social structures, reaffirming the naturalness of the hegemony, and the hegemony in turn reaffirms the naturalness of the social structures that support it.

There is a tendency to assume that a hegemony, as Gramsci argues, is imposed on the masses by a 'dominant fundamental group' within society (Gramsci 1971: 12). Philosopher Louis Althusser argues instead that these structures have no single cause. The structure of social reality is caused by the combined effect of all its social structures: 'collectively orchestrated without being the product of orchestrating action of a conductor' (Bourdieu 1977: 72). Althusser terms this phenomenon, in which the nature of a structure is determined by its own *complexity*, 'structural causality' (Althusser and Balibar 2009: 203, emphasis in original).

Althusser identifies three different forms of causality. Mechanical causality is a linear 'billiard-ball' chain of cause and effect (Althusser and Balibar 2009: 201). Expressive causality draws on the Hegelian idea that the ultimate cause of a whole is expressed in each of its individual elements: 'an *inner essence*, of which the elements of the whole are then no more than the phenomenal forms of expression, the inner principle of the essence being present at each point in the whole'. In structural causality, the nature of a structure is produced by the effects of all the structural relationships between its elements: '*the determination of the elements of a structure, and the structural relations between those elements, and all the effects of those relations, by the effectivity of that structure*' (Althusser and Balibar 2009: 205–6, emphasis in original).

To understand clearly what Althusser means by structural causality, it is helpful to think about the system of the human body. From a Christian point of view, the human body is animated by a soul. There is an inner essence that is the ultimate cause of human feeling and thought. A determining presence operates throughout the system, of which every part of the system is an 'expression' (Althusser and Balibar 2009: 206). This view of the human body falls into Althusser's category of expressive causality. From the point of view of contemporary science, however, the human body is made up of interrelated systems of biochemical processes. Human thought and feeling are simply the result of the effects of this network of complex biochemical processes. The nature of this system is determined by the structures that make it up: '*the whole existence of the structure consists of its effects*' (Althusser and Balibar 2009: 209, emphasis in original). There is no single cause. It exhibits structural causality.

Althusser envisages social reality as a dynamic system produced by structural causality. In traditional Marxism, the economic basis of the mode of production ultimately determines the nature of social reality. Althusser argues instead that all the spheres of human activity that make up social reality – the economic, the cultural, the ideological, the juridical (the law) and the political – have an equally determining effect on its nature. Any shift in the nature of any one of these social structures can have an effect on the system itself as a whole, provoking a reordering of structures and so bringing into being a new set of social relations. The reimagining of social structures through a shift in cultural representations of those structures, such as dramaturgical structures, has the potential to create change.

Edgar and Annabel

Sam Holcroft's play *Edgar and Annabel* (National Theatre, London 2011) explores the constructed nature of social reality and the power relations inscribed in the routines of everyday life. The play tells the story of Edgar and Annabel, 'a happily married couple of freelancers', but the life of this middle-class couple is not the simple picture of everyday domesticity that it seems at first (Holcroft 2011: 12).

The regular structure of Edgar and Annabel's daily routine suggests the spatio-temporal rhythms of normal everyday life. The same actions and conversations are repeated over and over again. For example, scenes one, three and eleven all start with a similar sequence of action and dialogue. Edgar or Annabel enters, greets their partner, compliments their cooking and asks what is for dinner: 'Hi, honey, I'm home [...] Something smells good [...] Is that fish?' (Holcroft 2011: 3); 'Hi, honey [...] Something smells delicious. What is it?' (Holcroft 2011: 16); 'Hi, darling [...] Something smells delicious. [...] Is that chicken?' (Holcroft 2011: 59). Sometimes they repeat themselves almost word for word. In scene nine, Edgar apologizes for being late because he got caught in the rain: 'I'm sorry I'm late. But I had to stand in a doorway for ten minutes' (Holcroft 2011: 52). This is an almost exact repetition of the excuse he used previously in scene one: 'I'm sorry I'm late. But I had to stand in a doorway for fifteen minutes' (Holcroft 2011: 4). Edgar and Annabel's daily interactions are so regular and routine that when one of them is lost for words, the other can remind them of what they should be saying. In scene one, Annabel expresses a strong opinion on recycling: 'I hate having to throw all that plastic away' (Holcroft 2011: 6). In an awkward moment of silence in scene nine, Edgar reminds Annabel of her strong opinion on recycling: 'you hate throwing all that plastic away. Yes?' (Holcroft 2011: 52). Edgar and Annabel's daily routine seems too routine.

Edgar and Annabel's everyday life is literally scripted. This is clear from the beginning of the play. Edgar enters with scripts. He *'retrieves two bound documents from his bag'* (Holcroft 2011: 4). Edgar and Annabel then attempt to play out the scene of domestic normality outlined in their scripts. Edgar and Annabel are not real people. Instead, they are a cover for the covert activities of a resistance group, who are trying to overthrow the repressive government of the unnamed country in which they live. Edgar and Annabel's life has to be scripted in order to protect the secret documents and bomb-making materials hidden *'behind false panels and in unexpected places'* inside their house (Holcroft 2011: 7). The state authorities are listening in. Any shifts in Edgar and Annabel's everyday rhythms, 'any deviations from the norm, lack of fluency, shifts in volume, certain words', will alert them to the suspect activity going on inside the house (Holcroft 2011: 11). Edgar and Annabel must stick to the script in order to maintain the consistency of their performance of everyday life and protect the covert activities of the resistance. To break away from the script is extremely dangerous. When Annabel accidentally calls Edgar 'Nick', she is *'paralysed with panic'* (Holcroft 2011: 19). There can be no mistakes and 'no improvising' (Holcroft 2011: 12).

Edgar and Annabel's maintenance of a normal domestic routine is positioned as an act of political resistance as opposed to political conformity. The scripts communicate vital information to resistance members. Domestic details stand in for political activity. A delayed wedding is a metaphor for a delayed bomb attack on a ministry: 'The minister's having dental surgery and so it all depends on when he's recovered' (Holcroft 2011: 35). Domestic objects become political weapons. Bomb-making materials are disguised as *'everyday snacks'* (Holcroft 2011: 33). The domestic routine is literally politicized.

The cover roles of Edgar and Annabel are taken on by a succession of different resistance members. When people are arrested or disappear, they are immediately replaced. Carl and Marianne are the original Edgar and Annabel. Nick replaces Carl, and is in turn replaced by Anthony. Marianne is eventually replaced by Claire. Whenever a new person takes over one of the roles, the script reminds Edgar and Annabel of the merits of domestic recycling. It is essential to their survival: 'Recycling is integral to who they are as a couple and what they tell themselves they stand for' (Holcroft 2011: 56). The reproduction of Edgar and Annabel's daily routine is more important than the individuals who play them.

The characters play their assigned roles, but they remain themselves. There is a dual presence. This creates a dislocation between their words, which are monitored by the authorities, and their actions, which are not. For example, while Edgar and Annabel are growing apart, Nick and Marianne are falling in love. While Edgar storms off to sleep in the spare room after a scripted argument, Nick *'silently takes off his shoes and tiptoes back to [Marianne]. They kiss'* (Holcroft 2011: 44). This dislocation between actions and words highlights a tension between the pressure to conform to the rhythms of everyday life and personal desire. There are points where these tensions cannot be easily reconciled. The play suggests that, at these points, the pressure to conform ultimately suppresses desire. The script of normal behaviour must be upheld even at the cost of personal happiness. When Marianne and Nick attempt to make love, they have to do so in silence so as not to contradict the script. This is, ultimately, too difficult to achieve. Nick and Marianne have to concede '*defeat*' (Holcroft 2011: 44).

In *Edgar and Annabel*, adhering to the rhythms of everyday life is imagined as an act of resistance, but the complete conformity to the script that the resistance ask of Nick and Marianne resembles actual conformity more than political resistance. In assigning Nick and Marianne the roles of Edgar and Annabel, the resistance ask them to imagine themselves as people who 'don't question their choices' (Holcroft 2011: 56). As Nick observes, any form of conformity, even pretended conformity, articulates your agreement with the prevailing system: 'we're sending the message loud and clear, to them and to the rest of the world, "Don't worry, everybody, we're fine, totally fine; in fact we're loving this shitbox of a situation, we can't get enough brutality"' (Holcroft 2011: 26). Marianne has played the role of Annabel for so long that she finds it difficult to tell the difference between Annabel and her real self: 'I'm giving everything I've got, every day, every night of my life, until, until I don't know where she ends and I begin' (Holcroft 2011: 58). Through her performance, political activist Marianne is being transformed into political conformist Annabel.

Ultimately, conformity to the script is positioned as being as potentially damaging as non-conformity. The endless recycling of people becomes unbearable. When Anthony enters to replace Nick, Marianne is so distressed that she '*reaches for a kitchen knife from the sink and, wrapping her fist around it, pulls it clean through her skin*'. She can only express her rage through the code of recycling: 'Recycling is bullshit [...] I think recycling is one of the most wasteful fucking –' (Holcroft 2011: 52–3). Her questioning of the routine and the values it represents is noted by the resistance: 'You'd never have argued about recycling' (Holcroft 2011: 55). Shortly after this act of non-conformity, Marianne herself disappears.

Edgar and Annabel is set in a country with a repressive regime that employs hard forms of discipline, but its scripting of reality points towards softer methods of social control. As English theatre critic and blogger Matt Trueman notes, Edgar and Annabel's scripted reality reflects the methods used to uphold power relations within contemporary British society: '[t]he banality of their script is the very same as that of our lives [...] Holcroft implies that the system, the unchallenged order of things, even the state as a whole, is performed into existence' (Trueman 2011). Holcroft's play highlights the constructed nature of social reality and the ways in which the unquestioning reproduction of the rhythms of normal everyday life reinforces the social structures that support the status quo.

Moral unity

The reproduction of normative social structures can be seen as a political act because it supports prevailing power relations within society. As Williams argues, hegemonies are not fixed structures: their 'internal structures are highly complex, and have continually to be renewed, recreated and defended' (Williams 2001: 168). Plays can be seen as carrying reactionary political messages within their form when they reproduce, rather than reimagine, social structures through their dramaturgical structures.

In order to understand how dramaturgical structures reproduce normative social structures, it is necessary to consider the relationship between the representation of social reality in performance and the audience's lived experience of it. This relationship is rooted in spatio-temporal structures. Lessing argues that two fundamentally different relationships can be created between the spatio-temporal structures of a play and the spatio-temporal structures of lived experience: 'physical unity' and 'moral unity' (Lessing 1962: 138). Physical unity sees dramatic time and space as commensurate with lived time and space if the spatio-temporal structures of a play reflect the audience's lived experience of time and space during its performance. Moral unity sees dramatic time and space as commensurate with lived time and space if the spatio-temporal rhythms of a play reflect the spatio-temporal rhythms of normal everyday behaviour.

Physical unity is traditionally created through a strict adherence to the unities of time and place; or in the parlance of contemporary playwriting, closed time and closed space. Closed time is action in continuous time with no scene breaks: 'the exclusion of all chronological discontinuity'. Closed space is action that takes place in a single location: 'the omission of all changes of locale' (Pfister 1988: 249). The unities of time and place were first articulated in sixteenth-century scholar Lodovico Castelvetro's 1570 (mis)translation of Aristotle's *Poetics*. Castelvetro assumes that dramatic time and space need to physically correspond to the audience's experience of lived time and space during a performance, in order for them to believe in what they are seeing. As English poet Phillip Sidney argues in the late-sixteenth century, 'absurd it is in sense' to ask an audience to give credence to a representation of events happening in many places over many years, when they remain in one place for a few hours (Sidney 1994: 135). If the audience stay seated in a single location, the action of the play must also remain in a single location. If time is continuous and unbroken for the audience, it must be continuous and unbroken onstage. Castelvetro's unity of time imagines an exact correspondence between dramatic time and lived time: 'the time required for the performance of a tragedy equals that which would be required if the tragic action actually occurred in the world' (Castelvetro 1984: 87). Taken in their most literal sense, the unities of time and place imagine an absolute physical correspondence between dramatic time and space and the audience's lived experience of time and space during a performance.

Moral unity, on the other hand, argues for an exact corre-spondence between the spatio-temporal structures of a play and the spatio-temporal rhythms of normal everyday behaviour. Seventeenth-century French playwright Georges de Scudery challenges physical unity on the basis that it compresses human actions into absurdly short timescales:

> in the short time needed to recite 140 lines, the playwright has Rodrigue go home, prepare for the duel, go to the appointed place, fight, overcome and disarm Dom Sanche, return his sword to him, order him to visit Chimène – add to this the time needed for Dom Sanche to reach Chimène's house, and you will see how impossible this is.
>
> (quoted in Howarth 1997: 254)

It also forces actions to take place in inappropriate spaces, as another French playwright Antoine Houdar de la Motte later observes: 'it is not natural for all the parts of an action to take place in the same apartment or in the same place' (La Motte 1754: 38, my translation). Physical unity distorts the spatio-temporal rhythms of normal everyday behaviour to the point that 'events [...] have no air of truth' (La Motte 1754: 40, my translation). Lessing argues that the audience's belief in a performance is more likely to be disrupted by a representation of human behaviour that is at odds with the accepted rhythms of normal everyday life than by jumps in time or shifts in location: 'moral unity must also be considered, whose neglect is felt by every one, while the neglect of the other, though it generally involves an impossibility, is yet not so generally offensive' (Lessing 1962: 138). In order to achieve moral unity, to place actions within the correct timescales and in the correct spaces, La Motte argues for the freedom to use 'a time and scope commensurate with the nature of the subject' (La Motte 1754: 40, my translation), a dramaturgy based on what is now termed open time and open space, which allows the action of a play to freely 'jump in time' and 'shift in locale' (Pfister 1988: 253).

On the third of Jameson's levels of analysis, that of form, serious drama's claim to a progressive politics is problematized by its use of moral unity. Moral unity plays an important role in how serious drama functions politically, as its political efficacy relies on the audience identifying the world of the play as commensurate with their own daily reality, so that the direct relevance of the play's political content to their own lives is clear. In order to do this, as contemporary English playwright Steve Waters notes, serious drama needs to mirror 'the rhythm of lived experience' (Waters 2010: 13). Moral unity is essential to its dramaturgy. Serious drama articulates a reactionary politics because it reproduces normative representations of social structures within its drama-turgy, so reaffirming existing power relations. As Holderness argues: '[a] drama which addresses what is conventionally accepted as the political "reality" of a society may in fact be collusive with that society's ideology. [...] Thus a politics of content cannot guarantee political efficacy' (Holderness 1992: 9).

Representations of normative social structures not only reaffirm existing power relations, but also effect the social subject's ability to have agency. In order to explore this idea, it is necessary to reconsider the nature of social reality in terms of how it is experi-enced, represented and imagined to be. In *The Production of Space*,

Lefebvre juxtaposes three interrelated forms of spatial production within social reality: '[s]*patial practice*', '[r]*epresentations of space*' and '[r]*epresentational spaces*' (Lefebvre 1991: 33, emphasis in original). Spatial practice is the material production of space in terms of the physical environment and the flows that connect its different spaces. Spatial practices include built environments, transport and communications (Harvey 1990: 220). This is space as it is lived and experienced. Representations of space are the conceptualized representations that society produces to define its space. They include 'maps and plans, transport and communications systems, information conveyed by images and signs' (Lefebvre 1991: 233). This is space in terms of how it is represented to be. Representational spaces exist only in the imagination: 'space which the imagination seeks to change and appropriate' (Lefebvre 1991: 39). Representational spaces include artists' sketches, utopias and imaginary landscapes (Harvey 1990: 221). This is space as it can be imagined to be. Lefebvre applies these three categories to space but they can be applied productively to other social structures. For example, time can be thought of in the same terms. The lived experience of time is time as it is viscerally experienced to be in everyday life. Clocks, calendars, timetables, etc. are representations of time. Time can also be imagined in ways that contradict accepted representations. Therefore, social reality can be thought of as made up of these categories in a more general sense: the lived experience of social reality; representations of social reality; and social reality as it can be imagined to be.

Bourdieu argues that most representations of social reality are deceptive. They are 'a collective *mise en scène*' and through their reproduction society 'in a sense lies to itself, producing a truth whose sole meaning and function are to deny a truth known and recognized by all, a lie which would deceive no one, were not everyone determined to deceive *himself*' (Bourdieu 1977: 133, emphasis in original). There is a gap between dominant representations of social reality and lived experience. This makes it difficult to communicate the nature of lived experience effectively, as the representational structures through which lived experience can be communicated are ill-fitted for purpose and limiting. This gap also compromises the social subject's ability to have agency. In order to act politically and create change within social reality, the social subject needs to be able to negotiate its social structures. As Bauman observes: '[t]o work in the world (as distinct from being "worked out and about" by it) one needs to know how the world works' (Bauman 2012: 212). If there is a gap between how the social subject has come to understand social structures to function through society's representations of them and how they actually function in practice, then it is difficult to act effectively to create change. The map of social reality no longer matches the actual landscape.

Humble Boy

English playwright Charlotte Jones's *Humble Boy* (National Theatre, London 2001) is a serious drama about families, beekeeping and the theory of everything. Its protagonist, a theoretical physicist, offers a multidimensional view of the universe. The effective communication of his perspective to an audience, however, is limited by the insufficient nature of the dramaturgical structures available to represent it.

The plot and characters of *Humble Boy* are drawn from Shakespeare's *Hamlet*. Felix Humble (Hamlet) is depressed. His father, James (Old Hamlet), a keen beekeeper, has suddenly died and Felix is now suffering from the physicist's equivalent of writer's block. He returns home to his mother, Flora (Gertrude), who is angry with him for running out of his father's funeral. He is angry with her for killing his father's bees. Mercy (Polonius), an old family friend, tries unsuccessfully to smooth over the situation. Felix encounters his father's ghost in the form of an old gardener tending Flora's garden. He is also reunited with his ex-girlfriend Rosie (Ophelia) and discovers that he is the father of her daughter. Felix's anger with Flora is increased when he discovers that she has been having an affair with Rosie's father, George (Claudius), for years and that George now intends to marry her. Flora, however, discovers that James identified a new species of bee just before his death and named it after her. Touched by this action, she breaks off her engagement to George. James's ghost appears to Flora and they are briefly reunited. Felix is reconciled with his mother and leaves to go back to university.

Structurally, Jones's play falls into the category of serious drama. Time is chronological. Space is concrete. Characters operate with psychological coherence and pursue their personal desires. Each character action leads to a reaction, creating a plot structure based on a linear chain of cause and effect. The play has a clear theme. It examines the idea that there is something rotten in the state of the modern family. The play's characters represent different positions on this issue. Felix is the son who blames his mother for his failures. Flora is the woman who supposedly sacrificed her brilliance to 'rot her life away' for an ungrateful family (Jones 2001: 65). James is the distant father, who neglected his wife in favour of his bees. Rosie, the single mother, offers a vision of a new kind of functional family. George is the man who thinks people should grab love 'by the balls' regardless of the feelings of those around them (Jones 2001: 16). Mercy has no family of her own but sees the value of family and longs for one.

The fragmentation of Felix's family is reflected in the fragmented picture of the universe offered by theoretical physics. Felix's thoughts on theoretical physics are primarily drawn from physicist Brian Greene's book on string theory, *The Elegant Universe*. For example, Felix's use of an analogy of a garden hose (Jones 2001: 25–6) to explain how other dimensions of reality might be hidden from our view repeats Greene's explanation of the same phenomenon (Greene 2000: 186–8). According to string theory, the tiny subatomic particles that form the building blocks of the universe are not solid points in space but microscopic vibrating loops of 'string'. This shift in the understanding of subatomic particles offers the possibility of unifying two previously conflicting areas of physics, relativity and quantum mechanics, so producing a new model of the universe. Relativity is the study of the largest objects in the universe such as stars, galaxies and black holes. Quantum mechanics is the study of the tiniest objects in the universe, such as electrons, quarks and photons. M-theory is the missing link that would enable a quantum theory of gravity (the theory of everything) to be produced, unifying these two conflicting areas. Felix is searching for 'M-theory – trying to unify the various strands of superstring theory' (Jones 2001: 30). He is tortured by the sound of the elusive strings that would make his name as a physicist. At times of stress, their *humming increases to a terrible pitch* (Jones 2001: 25). He is aware of their presence but cannot get a firm enough grasp on their nature: 'the ringing has too many layers. I can't – hold all the notes, all the variables, all the harmonies in my head' (Jones 2001: 31).

Felix's family are like physics. They define their relationships in terms of its concepts. Flora describes the relationship between parents and their children as 'chaos theory': 'I sneezed in public in 1968 and as a result my son found it difficult to connect in social situations for the rest of his life' (Jones 2001: 34). Felix sees Flora and James as being as diametrically opposed as relativity and quantum mechanics. Flora is a 'black hole' that will 'warp you. Pull you out of shape' (Jones 2001: 30). James is 'the little force, fizzing away quietly on a microscopic level' (Jones 2001: 44). These two different approaches to understanding reality do not fit together neatly. Neither do Flora and James. Flora complains that living with James has distorted her, diminished her in scale: 'I've lived my whole life in miniature. And I am not a miniaturist' (Jones 2001: 90). Felix can't understand the 'physics of what attracted them and what kept them together' but he does understand, however, that there is a quantum theory of gravity that would link them (Jones 2001: 44). His search for M-theory is paralleled metaphorically to his search for a way to heal his family.

There is a disjuncture between the complexity of the ideas discussed in the play and the dramaturgy through which they are presented. As Billington observes, the structure of the play 'seems too frail a barque to carry so much intellectual cargo' (Billington 2001b). The understanding of reality put forward by theoretical physics is a point of discussion and provides useful metaphors but it does not infuse the structure of the play. This is problematic, especially in relation to the characterization of Felix.

Felix sees the world differently from the other characters in the play. He views the universe as predicated on a different set of structures. As he admits to Rosie, theoretical physics with its multidimensional perspective on reality has been 'p-percolating my b-brain' (Jones 2001: 43). He does not actually 'know how the world works' any more (Jones 2001: 85). The structures he took for granted have been warped by his new multidimensional understanding of the universe. Solutions based on linear narratives, such as '[h]ow to grieve in twelve easy steps', are no longer sufficient to deal with the scope of his multidimensional problems (Jones 2001: 45).

Felix's multidimensional sense of the world is difficult for an audience to understand because the play offers no visceral way of experiencing the world as he sees it. He talks about the principles of physics that underlie his way of seeing the world in repeated attempts to explain his point of view but it is difficult to understand exactly how these ideas have percolated his brain because the structures of serious drama cannot articulate the multidimensional nature of his perspective on reality. Felix's understanding of the world is only visible from the outside and, from the outside, his behaviour seems sulky or symptomatic of mental illness. To George, he simply seems 'big fat lazy bumbling' (Jones 2001: 92). Flora blames it on the pills Felix is taking. The reasons for Felix's crisis, however, can be read as more complex than this. His crisis is a crisis of representation. It originates in a gap between his lived experience of the world, the way the world has been represented to him and the multidimensional way in which he now senses and imagines it to be. There are no structures that allow Felix to adequately communicate his experience of the world: the 'equations don't exist for what I can already sense' (Jones 2001: 31). This inability to find a form of effective expression for what he feels to be a truth about the universe paralyses Felix. He cannot act, not even to kill himself and put himself out of his misery.

While Felix's perspective can be thought of as specific to theoretical physics, its new multidimensional understanding of the nature of the universe can be argued to be reflective of the shift from solid to liquid modernity; a shift from a solid understanding of the world as built on logical chains of cause and effect to a more liquid understanding of it as 'a matrix of random connections and disconnections and of an essentially infinite volume of possible permutations' (Bauman 2007: 3). There is a need for new representational structures that can support the articulation of such new understandings of the nature of the contemporary social reality.[1]

Solid and liquid modernity in Britain

Humble Boy attempts to represent twenty-first-century understandings of social reality as liquid through the solid dramaturgical structures of nineteenth-century serious drama. This is an impossible

---

[1]For a comparative analysis of a play that uses a liquid dramaturgy to attempt to capture the idea of a multidimensional universe, see the section on Nick Payne's *Constellations*, pp. 100–6.

endeavour. The lived experience of social reality in twenty-first-century Britain is fundamentally different to the lived experience of social reality in Shaw's time. There has been a significant shift in social structures during the period between these two eras. Ultimately, this is a shift from a phase of solid modernity to a phase of liquid modernity, caused by shifts in the nature of capitalism.

The solid social structures of late-nineteenth-century Britain and the liquid social structures of contemporary Britain were both born out of capitalist systems, but these are not identical systems. Sociologists Scott Lash and John Urry split the history of capitalism in Britain into three broad phases. The first phase is liberal capitalism, characterized by liberal beliefs in the freedom of the individual and the free operation of the market. The second phase is organized capitalism, characterized by a movement towards greater state regulation. The final phase is disorganized capitalism, characterized by globalization, deregulation and the rise of neo-liberal politics. Shaw is writing within the context of solid modernity, which in Britain is characterized by a shift from a liberal to a more organized form of industrial capitalism during the nineteenth and early-to-mid-twentieth century. In contrast, contemporary British playwrights are writing within the context of liquid modernity, which is characterized by a shift from an organized form of industrial capitalism towards an increasingly disorganized form of financial capitalism, which began in the 1970s.

Serious drama was born out of the rise of socialist politics in Britain in the nineteenth century and its campaign for a more organized and compassionate form of capitalism. Liberal capitalism, in early-nineteenth-century Britain, was based on pockets of private industry in fierce competition with each other. Initially, working conditions were unchecked. Although there was increasing regulation from 1833 onwards, the workforce remained vulnerable to exploitation. In *Capital*, political economist Karl Marx catalogues the miserable existence of British workers during this period. For example, he tells of children working in the lace industry in Nottingham being 'dragged from their squalid beds at two, three or four o'clock in the morning and compelled to work for a bare subsistence until ten, eleven, or twelve at night' (Marx 2008: 154). Liberal capitalism's ruthless exploitation of the working class provoked growing calls for social change. Shaw was a committed social reformer and an early member of the Fabian Society, which was founded in 1884 to advocate for political reform through social progress as opposed to revolution: 'a peaceful but expeditious path to Socialism' (Shaw 1887: 10). Serious drama was part of Shaw's socialist project. He first discussed his vision of theatre as a vehicle for social progress in an 1890 Fabian Society lecture. Serious drama's form is built around the structure Marx identifies as underlying social progress, the dialectic, whose structure reflects solid modernity's faith in rational positive progress.

It can be argued that solid modernity's faith in the dialectic as an effective tool for creating social change within the historical context of late-nineteenth-century Britain was not misplaced. Ultimately, the British socialist project was a success. As early as 1892, social scientist Friedrich Engels could claim that a more compassionate form of capitalism had already come into being in Britain; the unacceptable level of labour exploitation he witnessed in the 1840s 'belongs to-day, in many respects, to the past' (Engels 1987: 37). There is an optimistic belief within British socialist circles that, as sociologist Max Weber argues, the worst abuses of capitalism will be 'systematically and rationally' eradicated over time as the inevitable result of positive progress (Weber 2011: 88). By the late 1940s, a more organized form of industrial capitalism had come to dominate British society characterized by the Welfare State, Fordist working practices[2] and Keynesian economics.[3] Through its examination of social issues, serious drama can be argued to have played a small role in the transformation of British society into a social democracy. Within its original historical context, it can be seen as articulating an effective, progressive, socialist politics of form.

In contrast, contemporary British playwrights are writing within the context of a shift from an organized form of industrial capitalism towards an increasingly disorganized form of financial

---

[2]American car manufacturer Henry Ford recognized that mass production required the creation of a mass market to consume its goods. He cut the length of the working day and raised his workers' wages, leading to an increase in consumer spending as they had more disposable income and more leisure time to spend it in.
[3]Traditionally, an economic crisis is managed by cutting expenditure and raising taxes. This can, however, lower consumer spending, extending the period of recession. Economist John Maynard Keynes proposed that, in times of economic crisis, governments should instigate policies to increase consumer spending instead, creating an increased demand for commodities, potentially lifting the economy out of recession.

capitalism. Since the 1970s, there have been radical shifts in the social structures that underlie the experience of everyday life in Britain. As a result of improvements in transport and communications, industrial production has been increasingly relocated to regions of the world where labour is cheaper and working conditions are less regulated, leading to a decrease in manufacturing and a shift from an industrial to a financial model of capitalism. Geographer David Harvey notes that, by the 1980s, 'many large non-financial corporations were making more money out of their financial operations than they were out of making things' (Harvey 2010: 23). The growth of the British financial sector has been supported by increasing integration and deregulation of global financial markets. The sector was embraced by New Labour in the 1990s, ushering in a more monologic form of politics, blurring traditional distinctions between left-wing and right-wing.[4] The transition from the social democracy of the 1970s to the liberal democracy of the 1990s was also accompanied by the gradual dismantling of the Welfare State by both right-wing and left-wing parties. This movement within British society, from an organized form of industrial capitalism towards an increasingly disorganized form of financial capitalism, was accompanied by a major shift in the social structures underlying the lived experience of everyday life from a solid to a liquid phase of modernity.

Bauman argues that the shift from solid to liquid modernity is driven by a 'changing relationship between space and time' (Bauman 2012: 8). Harvey describes this changing relationship between time and space as 'time-space compression'. He argues that this change is driven by capitalism's endless desire to facilitate increasingly efficient commodity exchange (Harvey 1990: 147). The foundations for time-space compression were laid during the Enlightenment with its drive to rationalize time and space. Time became mechanized with the invention of the chronometer and subject to objective, universal and precise measurements. Similarly, space became finite and knowable as mathematically accurate maps combined with improvements in navigation allowed the definition of trade and communication routes across the globe. Increasing

---

[4]Old Labour strove to secure common ownership of the means of production, distribution and exchange. New Labour works to create a dynamic economy that produces the opportunity for all to work and prosper.

competition between states and other economic units set the forces of time-space compression in motion. Increasing profit depends on increasing the flow of capital. As society becomes more profit-driven, the 'accumulation of wealth, power and capital bec[omes] linked to personalised knowledge of, and individual command over, space' (Harvey 1990: 244). The ability to traverse large distances in short times becomes an economic advantage. This involves the collapsing of space and speeding up of time: the 'annihilation of space through time' (Harvey 1990: 258) or 'the emancipation of time from space' (Bauman 2012: 112). Improvements in technology enable better transport and communication links, as well as an increased turnover in the actual production of commodities themselves, increasing the speed of the flow of capital. This acceleration has a compressing effect on the lived experience of time and space, 'characterised by speed-up in the pace of life [...] so overcoming spatial barriers that the world sometimes seems to collapse inwards upon us [...] time horizons shorten to the point where the present is all there is' (Harvey 1990: 240).

Harvey argues that, since the shift towards financial capitalism in the 1970s, this acceleration has increased, bringing about 'an intense phase of time-space compression that has had a disorienting and disruptive impact upon political-economic practices, the balance of class power, as well as upon cultural and social life' (Harvey 1990: 284). This acceleration in the speed of life has several causes: an increase in the rate of production facilitated by new organizational structures; improved systems for communication and distribution resulting in an even faster circulation of commodities; and a move towards electronic banking, increasing the rate at which money flows. Post-industrial societies now live in the 'instantaneous time of the software world' (Bauman 2012: 118). These factors are combined with a move from the consumption of material goods to the consumption of ephemeral commodities, such as services and experiences that are instantaneous and instantly disposable. This produces what Alvin Toffler terms 'the throw-away society' (Toffler 1970: 47), in which a throwaway mentality is not only related to the consumption of commodities, a 'decreased duration in man-thing relationships' (Toffler 1970: 50), but also to the turnover of values that underlie social life itself: 'whatever the content of values that arise to replace those of the industrial age, they will be shorter-lived, more ephemeral than the values of the past' (Toffler 1970: 269). In this way, the 'accelerative thrust in the larger society crashes up against the ordinary daily experience of the contemporary individual' (Toffler 1970: 32–3).

These shifts in everyday lived experience have led to what Harvey terms a 'crisis of representation in advanced capitalism' which he describes in terms that reflect Bauman's concept of liquid modernity: '[t]he central value system, to which capitalism has always appealed to validate its actions, is dematerialising and shifting, time horizons are collapsing, and it is hard to tell exactly what space we are in when it comes to assessing causes and effects, meaning or values' (Harvey 1990: 298). Harvey argues that this shift has led to a corresponding shift in cultural forms towards '[f]ragmentation, indeterminacy, and intense distrust of all universal or "totalizing" discourses' (Harvey 1990: 10). There is an increasing gap between the solid rational representation of social reality presented through the structures of serious drama and the liquid nature of contemporary lived experience. There is a need to find new cultural structures through which to articulate this significant shift in the social structures: 'new ways of thinking and feeling have to be created' (Harvey 1990: 322). The plays explored in the rest of this book are read as attempting to respond to this need.

Love and Information

English playwright Caryl Churchill's *Love and Information* (Royal Court, London 2012) attempts to radically reimagine dramatic structure in order to capture the increasingly liquid experience of contemporary social reality. It abandons the structures of serious drama, offering instead a dramaturgy that reflects Bauman's liquid understanding of the structure of contemporary social reality as 'a matrix of random connections and disconnections and of an essentially infinite volume of possible permutations' (Bauman 2007: 3).

The play consists of a network of at least sixty short scenes, featuring over a hundred characters. These scenes are divided into seven acts, each of which revolves around a specific idea about information. The first act raises the question of how to know. A scientist dissects chickens' brains. Two torturers discuss tactics. The second is about not saying things. Someone inadvisably grasses up their friend. A doctor is unable to give a clear prognosis. The third features bad information. Someone gets a dubious message from God. Someone uses a dream to justify having a love affair. The fourth delves into memory. Two exes reminisce about their relationship. Someone has a flashback. The fifth examines meaning. God gives someone's life meaning. Someone tries to work out the meaning of a worrying rash. The sixth focuses on not knowing. A child doesn't know how to be sorry. A censor removes something that must not be known. The final, seventh, act explores how to connect. A manic person connects too much. A bereaved person considers their connection to the person they are grieving. The seven acts are followed by a final scene consisting of facts.

The structure of the play is liquid. It can be played in many possible permutations. Churchill specifies that the 'sections should be played in the order given but the scenes can be played in any order within each section' (Churchill 2012: 2). The text of the play also includes an appendix of random scenes. One of the scenes, 'Depression', is an *essential part of the play*. The other scenes are optional additions. The positioning of the random scenes within the play is open: they *can happen in any section* (Churchill 2012: 74).

The number of possible permutations of the play in performance is further increased by the fact that the exact location of each scene and the exact identity of the speakers are rarely indicated. The scenes change character depending on where they are set. In the original London production, the scene 'Math' was set in a sauna. In the New York production (New York Theater Workshop, 2014), the same scene was set in a taxi cab. A few characters are identified by their social roles, for example doctor, wife, censor. Gender is also sometimes implied. The dialogue, however, is not assigned to specific individuals in the text. The actors and director are left to decide how each character will be embodied onstage.

The number of characters in each scene is also undefined. The dialogue mostly, however, seems to imply two speakers. For example, in 'Savant', the savant remembers while another character questions:

What was the movie?

Godzilla

What happened in it?

You want the whole thing? Shot by shot?

(Churchill 2012: 36)

The next section of dialogue, however, raises questions about who is speaking and how many people are present:

Can you do that?

Let's not do that.

Ok. I remember Godzilla. There's a lizard that's been irradiated by a nuclear explosion

(Churchill 2012: 36)

That the first line belongs to the questioner and the third to the savant is clear, but the second line could be allocated to either speaker, or perhaps more than one person is questioning the savant. The allocation of lines and even the number of characters in the scene is open to interpretation.

The structure of serious drama is rooted in a chain of successive events. *Love and Information* presents a network of possible events instead. In doing so, it mirrors the consumption of information in the contemporary networked world. For me, the experience of watching the play at the Royal Court was like surfing the Web, following a Twitter feed or clicking through YouTube videos. Paul Taylor, the theatre critic of the UK newspaper the *Independent*, argues that the play's structure is 'a calculated and droll example of information-overload' (Taylor 2012). There is so much seemingly unconnected information that it is too difficult to remember everything – as Charles Spencer, the *Daily Telegraph*'s lead critic, observes: 'on my return from the theatre I realized that probably only half a dozen of the many scenes had lodged themselves firmly in my memory' (Spencer 2012). The amount of information available during the performance exceeds the audience's ability to remember it.

In the middle section of the play, Churchill includes a scene called 'Memory House' that attempts to grapple with this problem. One character tries to teach another character how to use the ancient technique of loci in order to help them deal with the 'stacks of information' they need to 'acquire and retain' (Churchill 2012: 39). This memory technique spatializes information. A list of objects is visualized in different locations around a house in a certain order and then recalled by visualizing picking them up one by one in the same order. The objects in the list are unconnected: 'wristwatch', 'elephant', 'poundcoin' (Churchill 2012: 42). The characters encounter two problems with this technique. First, random bits of information inside the house interfere with completing the intended list. One character is stopped in their tracks by a vivid memory of their father. Second, the technique works well for one short list, but does it work for many lists: 'how do we keep the lists separate' (Churchill 2012: 44)? The loci technique is positioned as an inadequate answer for remembering all the information the characters are bombarded with. The technique's spatialization of information, however, is reflective of a tendency to think of the internet metaphorically in spatial terms. Information on the internet is located at 'sites' with 'addresses' that can be 'visited'. The internet itself is like a memory house. It may offer too much information, but it is also the answer to the question of how to store all that information.

Churchill positions information overload as bad for the social subject. It can be bad information, like the messages the schizophrenic receives from the traffic lights. Its documentation of the social subject's life replaces and distorts their memories: 'I can't remember anything about that day that's not on the video not clearly' (Churchill 2012: 35). It bombards the social subject with so much contradictory information that it becomes impossible to make decisions: 'There's things on both sides [...] I'm trying to make a rational decision based on the facts [...] The facts don't add up' (Churchill 2012: 56). At the same time, Churchill suggests that not knowing can be equally bad. The Child Who Didn't Know Pain is constantly hurting themselves. The Child Who Didn't Know Fear gets eaten by a lion.

Billington observes that *Love and Information* conveys 'a deep sense of political and personal unease about a society in which speed of communication replaces human connections' (Billington 2012). In each of the ten segments of the 'Depression' scene that punctuate the play, a speaker tries to engage a depressed person. Each time, the speaker gives up before they have finished their sentence. The depressed person is unresponsive. There is no way to connect with them. The play offers images of people who do not or cannot feel. One person feels nothing for the people who are suffering as a result of an earthquake. She does not even acknowledge the presence of the people in her visualization of what happened: 'That black wave with the cars in it was awesome' (Churchill 2012: 60). People are reduced to pure information, to digital images online. The play's short scenes stress this lack of emotional engagement with others. The audience encounter a character for a few moments and then they are gone forever. There is no opportunity to empathize with them.

At the same time as offering images of characters who seem unable to connect or to feel, the play also offers images of characters who are attempting to connect or who do feel. Every scene in the play implies a relationship. There are always at least two characters. Even in the monologue, 'The Child Who Didn't Know Fear', the presence of a listener is specified. Each scene is an attempt to connect. Characters repeatedly express their ability to feel. The Child Who Can't Feel Pain is split between not feeling and feeling. They don't feel physical pain, but they do feel emotional pain. They have been 'unhappy' (Churchill 2012: 58). Characters who don't feel are partnered with characters who do feel. The other speaker in 'Earthquake' felt the suffering of the victims so much that they cried. For them, the people are more than just information. They feel for them.

The feeling of love is positioned as information, and information is positioned as love. In 'Wife', the wife of someone suffering from dementia describes love as the 'things only we know' (Churchill 2012: 56). In 'Sex', good sex is 'information and also love'. Sex involves an exchange of information in the form of DNA and possibly the creation of new information: 'offspring that's not identical to you' (Churchill 2012: 49). Love generates information and human beings are positioned as made up of information. In 'Fate', human beings are the products of both their DNA and their environment, just like the socio-psychological characters of serious drama: 'there's your genes and everything that's happened to you' and 'if someone could have that information they'd know exactly what you were going to do' (Churchill 2012: 54). Conversely, however, Churchill also suggests that human beings are not information. In 'Shrink', one person refuses to have their meaning reduced to a set of information. When someone describes the person's pain as the product of their experiences, they respond that their pain has meaning in itself: 'It doesn't mean something. There isn't exactly another thing that it means' (Churchill 2012: 52). As another speaker argues, 'red is red and blue is blue' (Churchill 2012: 59).

Love's position as information is questioned in the final scene. In 'Facts', Churchill presents a series of random questions and answers. In among this list of facts, one speaker asks: 'Do you love?' Later, a speaker responds, 'I do yes I do' (Churchill 2012: 71). Love appears to be a fact like the rest of the information given in the scene. The rest of the information, however, is not factual despite its presentation as facts. There is no such battle as the 'battle of Stoneham' and no such dish as 'poulash' (Churchill 2012: 70). This raises a question about the factual nature of love. Is love also a questionable fact or is it the only fact in a world of questionable facts?

Love and Information is a play that mirrors the information overload of the information age through its shifting and indeterminate form. The liquidity of its dramaturgical structures encourages the production of many different permutations of the same play. Its structure takes the form of a dialectical network carrying a plethora of conflicting political messages about the effects of information overload. It does not draw a singular conclusion but instead asks the audience to read and reread its structure in different ways that lead to different conclusions. Its structure is like the Chinese characters in 'Chinese Poetry', whose component parts, 'mountain girl door', produce a multitude of different interpretations: 'The girl waits at the door of her house on the mountain'; 'To get the girl you have to go through a door into the mountain'; 'The mountain is a door only a girl can open' (Churchill 2012: 62). The play's disjointed, shifting, fluid form and its resistance to a single, unified interpretation, reflect the fragmentation, indeterminacy and intense distrust of all universal or 'totalizing' discourses that Harvey identifies as characteristic of works of art that are attempting to articulate the increasingly compressed and liquid nature of contemporary experience (Harvey 1990: 10).

The political character of serious drama, as explored in the first two chapters of this book, is a contradictory one. Its claim to a progressive socialist politics stands when it is considered on two of Jameson's three levels of analysis: content and form. The latter claim to a progressive socialist politics of form only holds, however, when serious drama is considered within the context of solid modernity. On Jameson's level of class origins and on the level of form, when considered within the context of the liquid modernity of contemporary British society, serious drama's politics can be read as reactionary.

Social reality can be thought of as constructed of a range of shifting social structures brought into being through collective intentionality. These social structures are political because they play a role in determining power relations. The social structures of social reality, however, are not fixed but need to be constantly renewed. Plays can be thought to articulate a reactionary politics when they reproduce, and so reaffirm, reactionary social structures through their dramaturgical structures. The structures of serious drama reproduce structures associated with solid modernity. Within a contemporary context, these structures can be thought of as reactionary because they are inadequate to capture the complex and ever-shifting social structures of liquid modernity. They misrepresent the complex mechanisms that underlie the processes of thinking, planning and taking action in a globalized world. This produces a gap between the representation of social reality (the ways in which it is understood to operate) and the lived experience of social reality (the ways in which it is experienced as operating). This gap makes it difficult for the social subject to have political agency, as their map for taking action no longer matches the actual landscape in which they are attempting to effect change. In order to take effective action in the world, it is necessary to understand how the world works. The next four chapters of this book will consider the specific ways in which a range of contemporary British plays can be read as attempting to address this gap in representation, by attempting to reflect, negotiate and critique the increasingly liquid social structures of contemporary social reality through their dramaturgical structures. Any rethinking of representations of social structures that better enables the social subject to understand how to have political agency within the complex mechanisms of a globalized society is a political act.

3

Time

[P]lays are neither in time nor about time, but are of time.

WILES 2014: 3

The first two chapters of this book investigated serious drama's claims to a progressive socialist politics. The first chapter concluded that this holds on the level of its content but is problematized in terms of its origins in a late-nineteenth-century class struggle over the dominance of the theatre between the middle and working classes. The second chapter concluded that the politics of serious drama at the level of its form are contradictory. Serious drama's claim to a progressive socialist politics holds when considered purely within the context of its historical origins, but is problematized when considered within a contemporary context as its dramaturgical structures reproduce representations of reactionary social structures.

The dramaturgical structures of serious drama reflect the values of the era of solid modernity in which it was born. There is, however, an increasing gap between the rational progressive representation of social reality presented through its dramaturgical structures and the liquid nature of contemporary lived experience. There is a need to find new dramaturgical structures that can reveal, negotiate and critique the increasingly liquid social structures of contemporary social reality. The next four chapters of this book explore some of the more liquid dramaturgical approaches currently in use in British theatre. The plays analysed in these chapters can be read as articulating a progressive politics as they attempt to reimagine social structures through their dramaturgical structures.

This exploration begins with plays that reimagine the structure of time. Bauman identifies time as the initiating 'factor of disruption' in the movement from solid to liquid modernity (Bauman 2012: 111). Time is also the backbone of dramatic structure. Shifts in temporal structures catalyse shifts in the representation of space, causation and character. In serious drama, time is thought to be successive and commensurate with lived time. Plots are predominantly organized along the temporal axis of succession. Liquid dramaturgical approaches are argued to reflect temporal shifts in the lived experience of contemporary social reality by moving the temporal emphasis from the axis of succession to the axis of simultaneity. The chapter concludes with analyses of four plays offering different dramaturgical strategies for the representation of temporal simultaneity. In *Time and the Conways* (1937), J. B. Priestley investigates the idea of simultaneous time. In *Constellations* (2012), Nick Payne explores the consequences of living in a multiverse. Caryl Churchill's *Heart's Desire* (1997) offers a dramaturgical strategy for representing simultaneous versions of the same moment. Finally, David Eldridge's *Incomplete and Random Acts of Kindness* (2005) attempts to capture the experience of time-space compression.

Dramatic time

Plays are woven from time. Their events are arranged in terms of their temporal relationship to each other. In serious drama, time is imagined as linear. One event follows the next, as the plot moves forward through time in a chain of cause and effect. Despite the fact that dramatic structure is essentially shaped by its temporal structures, the important role time plays in determining the shape of a play tends to be overlooked. As Waters notes, '[t]hat theatrical events take place in time is so self-evident it can often be forgotten' (Waters 2010: 71). This is because dramatic time is imagined to be so commensurate with lived experience of time that little attention is paid to its structures.

Dramatic time is imagined to have a high degree of physical unity with lived time, passing from the past into the future at a constant rate and divisible into the same consistent units of measurement.

Dramatic time is also imagined to have a high degree of moral unity with lived time. The temporal structures of a play mirror the temporal rhythms of everyday life and so seem as invisible as the temporal structures of the habitus that shapes 'normal' behaviour. Dramatic time, however, is as constructed as the social structures that shape social reality. It has a specific character that both reflects the social subject's lived experience of time and contradicts it in a number of important ways.

Dramatic time, like lived time, is imagined to be present tense. The difference between the narrative mode of the novel and the dramatic mode of the play is usually defined on this basis. A novel is past tense. It presents the reader with an account of 'what took place; no self-effacement on the part of the narrator can hide the fact that we hear his voice recounting, recalling events that are past and over, and which he has selected – from uncountable others – to lay before us'. In contrast, dramatic time is present tense: 'the personages are standing on that razor-edge, between the past and the future, which is the essential character of conscious being; the words are rising to their lips in immediate spontaneity'. As American playwright Thornton Wilder states: '[o]n the stage it is always now' (Wilder 1992: 71).

The present moment in performance is not a fixed point, but a succession of presents. As literary scholar Peter Szondi notes, although 'its internal time is always the present. That in no way means that the Drama is static [...] As the present passes away, it produces change, a new present springs from its antithesis' (Szondi 1987: 9). The audience is situated permanently in the present moment. From this position, they witness future events become present events and present events become past events. It is like walking up a down escalator. Future events come towards the audience, pass briefly beneath their feet and then move away into the past. The audience move forward towards the future at the same pace as events move backwards into the past. The present moment in drama is dynamic as opposed to static.

Plays generally contain both the narrative and the dramatic mode. In this respect, they are past tense as well as present tense. Characters recount events that happened before the play began and report offstage events. In performance, the narrative mode takes on a dramatic quality. The audience become aware of the process of narration. They hear events recounted in the past tense, but at the same time they witness the narrator compose their account in the present. The past events that are recounted and the present act of telling coexist. In this respect, the dramatic mode does not exclude the past tense.

Dramatic time is not commensurate with lived time. It passes at a different rate. As American writer Gertrude Stein notes, 'at the theatre there is a curtain and the curtain already makes one feel that one is not going to have the same tempo as the thing that is there behind the curtain' (Stein 2004: 59). The amount of dramatic time represented onstage in a single scene is almost always greater than the amount of lived time it takes to perform the scene. Dramatic time moves at a faster rate than lived time. The audience accept this accelerated rate as representative of the normal rate at which lived time passes, despite a physical disjuncture between the two. Literary theorist Manfred Pfister argues that dramatic time moves at a faster rate than lived time because it is compressed time. In the *Poetics*, Aristotle states that the plot of a play represents a 'single, unified action' (Aristotle 1996: 15). Plots usually only include events that drive this single line of action forward. Extraneous events and mundane, everyday actions, superfluous to the progression of the plot, are excised from the play. Dramatic time moves at a faster rate than lived time because it 'excludes or abbreviates certain sequences' (Pfister 1988: 285).

Dramatic time, like lived experience of time but unlike normative representations of time, is subjective. Clock time passes at a constant, measurable rate, whereas the rate at which both dramatic time and lived time pass varies from moment to moment. For example, in the final moments of English Renaissance playwright Christopher Marlowe's *Doctor Faustus* (Rose Theatre, London 1594), Faustus waits for the arrival of Lucifer to claim his soul. After line 142, the clock strikes eleven. After line 173, it strikes half past eleven. After line 192, it strikes midnight. The first half hour of dramatic time lasts thirty-one lines, while the second half hour lasts only nineteen lines. As Faustus approaches his fate, the rate at which dramatic time passes accelerates. Time is literally running out and the audience experience Faustus's sense of time speeding away from him. As Pfister points out, 'the introduction of a discrepancy between fictional and actual performance time is not designed simply as a way of economizing in dramatic terms, but actually reflects the discrepancy within the fiction itself between the empirical chronometry (the chiming of the bells) and Faustus's subjective perception of time' (Pfister 1988: 285). In this sense, dramatic time is like lived time, in that it is perceived subjectively.

Finally, dramatic time is organized on two axes: the axis of succession and the axis of simultaneity. Plots are fundamentally organized on the temporal axis of succession, and therefore this axis forms the main organizational structure of a play. Events happen one after another, tracing a line along this axis. In the *Physics*, Aristotle defines the movement of time as 'the number of precessions and successions in process'. Time, he argues, is dependent on events, an event being a change from one state to another. The passage of time is not noticeable unless something changes. Change is the means by which it is possible to differentiate this present 'now' from another previous or subsequent 'now', to establish what came before and what comes after. The process which connects these two 'nows' is time: '[w]hen we, accordingly, apprehend the extremes as distinct from what intervenes between them and when we mentally mark them as two "nows" (one coming earlier and the other coming later), it is then that we acknowledge and identify time' (Aristotle 1961: 80). Time is defined through the apprehension of change from an earlier state to a later one, in other words through a succession of events. Aristotle's definition of plot, the single-unified action, is also, like time, described as 'a series of events occurring sequentially' (Aristotle 1961: 14); or, as literary theorist Keir Elam defines it, 'complex successions of states'. Plot is the 'passage from an initial state (W_D at t_1) to a final state (W_D at t_x) through a series of intermediary states (W_D at t_n)' (Elam 2002: 105). Thus, the movement of the action of a play and the movement of time are based on the same principle.

The second temporal axis is the axis of simultaneity, of events that are happening at the same time: 'a number of different situations, actions or events coincide' (Pfister 1988: 276). It is most frequently invoked in plays, when characters onstage become aware of actions happening simultaneously offstage. The axis of simultaneity's role in the temporal organization of a play is considered so minor that few theorists examine its role in any depth. Szondi, for example, excludes it completely from his description of the temporal organization of drama. He states that 'the temporal structure of the Drama is one of absolute linear sequentiality'. He recognizes, however, that organizing the temporal structure of a play purely on the axis of succession restricts what a playwright is capable of representing: '[d]ramatists have regularly found themselves faced with material whose temporal dimension made it appear unsuitable for the Drama'. Szondi argues that Ibsen tends to dramatize the final chapter of his protagonists' lives because he is reaching for 'the possibility of expressing the essence of time, its duration, its passing and the changes it produces'. By starting towards the end of their stories, Ibsen can narrate other moments of time in his characters' conversations, presenting both past and present events simultaneously. The problem with this technique, Szondi notes, is that in these moments of narration, the action of the play is 'no longer "dramatic"' (Szondi 1987: 87). Representing the axis of succession appears to be an impossible task as it drives the playwright towards the narrative as opposed to the dramatic mode.

Dramatic time is not commensurate with lived time. The idea that they are identical is illusory. Dramatic time like lived time is predominantly present tense and experienced subjectively. Unlike lived time, dramatic time is abbreviated and so passes at a faster rate. Lived time is experienced as being both successive and simultaneous. Dramatic time in serious drama is thought of as organized along the temporal axis of succession. This is true of serious drama, even when it employs non-chronological plot structures.

Disrupted time

Edgar observes that some plays exhibit 'disrupted time' (Edgar 2009: 107). In this category, he includes plays which go backwards, plays with flashbacks or flash-forwards, plays that tell parallel stories happening at different historical moments in time and plays with circular plot structures. These temporal structures all offer different sequential organizations of events, but they do not necessarily disrupt chronological time. The audience can rearrange the events of most non-chronological plots to form a chronological story. Although these plays trace a range of different moves along the temporal axis of succession, the action of their dramatic narrative is still located firmly on it.

English playwright Harold Pinter's *Betrayal* (National Theatre, London 1978) tells a clear chronological story, even though its events are plotted moving backwards through time. The play depicts a love triangle between Emma, her husband, Robert, and his best friend, Jerry. It begins at the end of their relationship in 1977. Emma decides to leave Robert after discovering he has been unfaithful to her. She tells Jerry that when Robert confessed his betrayal, she told him about their affair. Jerry then visits Robert and discovers that Robert has actually known about the affair for years. Next, the audience are transported to 1975, to witness the end of Jerry and Emma's affair. Then to 1974, where a seemingly casual conversation between Jerry and Robert takes on aggressive undertones. Next to 1973, to witness Robert's realization that Emma and Jerry are having an affair. Emma then visits Jerry at their secret flat, but does not tell him that Robert now knows. Robert and Jerry have dinner together. Robert does not reveal that he knows. Then to 1971, to see Emma and Jerry moving into their secret flat together. Finally, to 1969, to see Jerry and Emma meet for the first time and realize they are attracted to each other. The backwards structure is essential to the question that the play raises: 'How did this situation arise?' If the play were plotted forwards, it would raise questions about how the situation would be resolved instead. *Betrayal* does not display a disrupted time structure because its plot can easily be rearranged into chronological order. There is no temporal disruption in its structuring of time.

In contrast, English playwright Laura Wade's *Breathing Corpses* (Royal Court, London 2005) utilizes a disrupted time structure. It tells the story of two murders and a suicide. The events of the play seem as if they could be neatly rearranged into a linear chronological structure but, unlike *Betrayal*, they cannot. The events of the story are set in motion when Ben murders his partner, Kate, and hides her body in a box in a storage unit. Jim, the owner of the storage units, discovers Kate's body and, haunted by this discovery, commits suicide in a hotel room. Jim's body is discovered by Amy, a chambermaid. He is the second dead body she has found. A few months later, Amy finds what she thinks is a third corpse.

Initially these events are plotted backwards. In the first scene Amy discovers Jim's body, in the second Jim discovers Kate's body and in the third scene Kate and Ben have an argument that provokes Kate's murder. It is also revealed that Kate discovered a girl's body in a park on an unusually hot September day. The fourth scene flashes forward to a point in time between Jim's discovery of Kate's body and his suicide, revealing how the discovery of her body leads to his suicide. The final scene flashes forward to a year after Kate's murder. Amy finds what she thinks is a third body in the same hotel room, but this time it is a living, breathing man called Charlie. He invites her out on a date, an early morning walk in a park on an unusually hot September day. The temporally impossible implication is that the corpse Kate discovered a year ago is Amy's.

Breathing Corpses traces a range of movements in time. The first three scenes move backwards. The fourth scene flashes forward. The final scene appears to move both forward in time, to a point after Jim's suicide, and backwards to a point before Kate finds Amy's body. In addition to this, the first and last scenes begin with an identical situation and identical dialogue, so creating an Escher-type loop of unending circularity. As Charlie observes, the town in which Amy lives seems to be the '[k]ind of place Dante'd draw circles round' (Wade 2005: 70). The characters of the play, like the inhabitants of Dante's circles of hell, are trapped in an eternal cycle of punishment; committing, being subjected to and witnessing the results of acts of violence. The play offers a model of time as a process of eternal recurrence, challenging the assumption that time is both linear and progressive in its movement.

Time and the Conways

English novelist and playwright J. B. Priestley's *Time and the Conways* (Duchess Theatre, London 1937) is an early example of a play that attempts to articulate a disrupted time structure. Like Charlotte Jones, whose *Humble Boy* was discussed in the previous chapter,[1] Priestley's ability to express his alternative understanding of time effectively is limited by the dramatic structures within which he is operating.

Time and the Conways traces the downfall of the wealthy Conway family during the interwar period. Acts one and three are set in 1919, during Kay Conway's twenty-first birthday party, when the family is at the height of their prosperity and full of hope for the future. Act two is set on Kay's fortieth birthday (Priestley

---

[1] See pp. 73–6.

states the act is set in 1937 but Kay's fortieth birthday would actually be in 1938). The family have now fallen into poverty and misery, despite all their efforts and ambitions.

Priestley attempts to express the notion of simultaneous time in *Time and the Conways*. The second act appears to be a flash forward, but it is not. At the end of act one, Kay is sitting on a window seat. At the beginning of act two, Kay is found sitting on the same window seat nineteen years later. Both no time and nineteen years have passed between these two moments of time. Kay is aware of all the events that have happened between these two points in time but, at the same time, it is as if she has leapt forward in time. Priestley indicates that Kay is somehow experiencing the future at the end of act one: she *'seems to stare not at but into something'* (Priestley 2000: 33). At the beginning of act three, when Kay is found sitting in the window seat again, back in 1919, Priestley indicates that she has gained an awareness of the family's future. He states that her surroundings are exactly the same as they were at the end of act one but, in the brief moment of time that has passed between the end of act one and the beginning of act three, 'KAY *herself has changed. Something – elusive, a brief vision, a score of shadowy presentiments – is haunting her. [...] She throws a look or two around the room, as if she had just seen it in some other guise'* (Priestley 2000: 62). Kay has experienced time as simultaneous rather than successive, gaining access to a future moment in time, alongside the present moment of time that she is most conscious of existing in.

Priestley is attempting to convey the idea that 'the single universal Time that is imagined to be hastening everything to decay and dissolution is an illusion; that our real selves are the whole stretches of our lives, and that at any given moment during those lives, we are merely taking a three-dimensional cross-section of a four or multi-dimensional reality' (Priestley 1937: ix). Priestley draws this concept of multidimensional reality from philosopher J. W. Dunne's *An Experiment with Time*. Dunne argues that reality is made up of at least five dimensions: three spatial dimensions (length, width and height), a fourth dimension of linear successive time and a fifth temporal dimension of the 'travelling "present moment"' (Dunne 1927: 143). The social subject sitting in this fifth dimension of time is able to perceive the four everyday dimensions of space-time. In order to become conscious of the fifth dimension,

the social subject would have to observe themselves from a sixth
dimension of time. In order to be conscious of the sixth dimension,
they would have to observe themselves from a seventh dimension,
and so on to infinity. At infinity, the social subject becomes a 'serial
observer' viewing a single, multidimensional time field, 'absolute'
time, which contains every point in time: '[t]he present moment
of this absolute Time must contain all the moments, "past,"
"present," and "future"' (Dunne 1927: 151). They can observe
all the moments of their life, past and future, in a single moment
of time. It is only the human mind, Dunne argues, that blinkers
this multidimensional view, narrowing time into an apparently
successive linear form.

Time and the Conways is informed by Dunne's conception of
time. In 1937, Kay laments the misery that time has inflicted on
her family – 'every tick of the clock – making everything worse'
(Priestley 2000: 59). Her brother Alan comforts her by explaining
that time is simultaneous rather than successive. He states that,
in that moment, they are only 'a cross-section of our real selves',
whereas '[w]hat we really are really is the whole stretch of ourselves,
all our time'. Life moves them on from 'one peephole to the next'
so time seems to be a linear succession of events. They are unaware
of the larger picture, that all points in time coexist simultaneously:
'we two, here now, are real and existing. We're seeing another bit
of the view – a bad bit, if you like – but the whole landscape's still
there' (Priestley 2000: 60).

Priestley illustrates this concept of time in the first act. The
action is set in the back room where the family are preparing for a
game of charades. The actual performance takes place in the next
room. As the family dress and prepare for their roles, the action in
the next room can be faintly heard. The action of the play takes
place in both rooms simultaneously. The audience, however, see
only one 'bit of the view' (Priestley 2000: 60). The wider landscape
is obscured.

When Kay returns to 1919, she remembers 1937/8. When,
in 1919, Carol enthuses about the future, Kay responds with 'a
terrible cry'. She is now painfully aware that Carol will die young.
She assumes Alan has also had the same experience as her and asks
him to comfort her, tell her '[s]omething you know – that would
make it different – not so hard to bear' (Priestley 2000: 81). But
Alan doesn't know yet. Priestley implies that Alan's understanding

of time in 1937/8 is drawn from Dunne's *An Experiment with Time*, first published in 1927. The Alan of 1919 has eight years to wait before he can rethink his notion of time. By locating the action of the first and third acts of the play prior to the publication of Dunne's book, Priestley implies that Dunne's ideas are based on a pre-existing phenomenon.

Priestley argues that thinking of time as simultaneous rather than successive frees us from pain, specifically from grief: 'the sense of bitter loss, the pain, the apparent dark tragedy of this life, are only like the shading in a picture of the grimmer features of a landscape' (Priestley 2000: ix–x). Kay feels the pain of Carol's impending death in 1919, but if time is simultaneous then she can comfort herself with the idea that, although Carol is dead in 1937/8, she will always be alive in 1919. This idea is illustrated by the game of hide and seek in act three. In order to be reunited with her, all Kay needs to do is discover where she is hiding by finding the right temporal peephole to look through. Alan adds a political dimension to the idea of simultaneous time. Successive time, he claims, promotes selfish and competitive behaviour, creating discord between human beings. If people feel they are 'creatures carried on that single-line track to the slaughter house' (Collins 1994: 212), then they 'snatch and grab and hurt each other' (Priestley 2000: 61).

Priestley attempts to communicate an experience of simultaneous time in *Time and the Conways*, but this often goes unnoticed. The play is read as purely about class. It is interpreted as an account of the decline of the selfish Edwardian bourgeoisie in the face of social progress: the second act 'flashes forward to show the same characters 20 years on, their hopes dashed, their promise unfulfilled', so painting a picture of the downfall of a 'self-regarding social class' who 'deserved everything it was about to get' (Fisher 2013). Although Priestley attempts to convey the concept of simultaneous time, the play's dramaturgical structures represent time as linear and successive. It is left to Priestley's characters to explain Kay's experience of simultaneous time through the dialogue. The play's exploration of time does not infuse and shift its dramaturgical structures. As Billington notes, Priestley's temporal theorizing remains 'an extra ingredient rather than something that grows organically from the text' (Billington 2009). The play's temporal ambitions are undermined by the nature of the dramaturgical structures on which it is built.

Constellations

Like Priestley, British playwright Nick Payne attempts to grapple with temporal theories that challenge everyday representations of time as linear and successive. While Priestley's experiments with time are limited by their presentation within the linear successive temporal structures of serious drama, Payne attempts to reimagine temporal structures through a reimagining of dramaturgical structures in order to convey alternative understandings of time. In *Constellations* (Royal Court, London 2012), Payne explores the same set of scientific ideas as Charlotte Jones in *Humble Boy*, drawing inspiration from the same book, Greene's *The Elegant Universe*, in which Greene explores the idea that our universe is only one of many universes in a multiverse.[2] The dramaturgical approach that Payne takes to representing these ideas, however, is very different.

At first glance, *Constellations* is a straightforward story of boy meets girl. Roland, an urban beekeeper, meets Marianne, a quantum cosmologist, at a barbecue. They go on a date, start a relationship and move in together. The relationship breaks down because one of them has an affair but then they bump into each other again and fall back in love. Roland proposes but Marianne is then diagnosed with a terminal brain tumour. Together they travel abroad so that Marianne can end her life by assisted suicide.

The play retains some of the conventions of serious drama. It features two characters who embody opposing sides of a dialectical debate. Roland wants to believe 'that ours is the only universe that exists', a singular universe in which every choice results in a definitive future; a rational universe in which everything has a clear and logical purpose (Payne 2012: 26). Roland's need to believe in a single universe is reflected metaphorically in the 'quiet elegance' of the lives that his honey bees lead. Female honey bees exist to collect pollen. Male honey bees exist to play a role in reproduction. Once male and female honey bees have fulfilled their purpose, they die. Roland wishes that human beings could attain this 'unfailing clarity of purpose' (Payne 2012: 53, 54, 57).

In contrast, Marianne believes that the universe is just one universe in a multiverse. She understands the universe through

---

[2]For an analysis of Charlotte Jones's *Humble Boy* see pp. 73–6.

string theory. This shift in understanding tiny subatomic particles, not as solid points but as microscopic vibrating loops of 'string', makes it possible that the conditions for the birth of a universe have occurred and continue to occur over and over again: 'the process continues, with new universes sprouting from far flung regions in the old, generating a never ending web of ballooning cosmic expanses'. Our universe could be one of many universes and the physics of these universes may be completely different from our own. Greene argues that life in these universes, if it exists at all, would not be 'anything remotely akin to life as we know it' (Greene 2000: 367).

Marianne's understanding of the multiverse takes into account the important role probability plays in quantum mechanics. Contrary to Einstein's assertion, quantum mechanics suggests that God does play dice with the universe. The future always involves an element of chance: '[a]ccording to quantum mechanics, the universe evolves according to rigorous and precise mathematical formalism, but this framework determines only the probability that any particular future will happen – not which future actually ensues' (Greene 2000: 107). The physicist Richard Feynman argues that, for any single future to occur, all possible futures must have been invoked. If an electron emitted from an electron source hits a piece of photographic paper, it has simultaneously travelled every possible path between the source and the photographic paper. Many parallel versions of the future occur simultaneously: 'every choice, every decision you've ever and never made exists in an unimaginably vast ensemble of parallel universes' (Payne 2012: 25).

Structurally, *Constellations* reflects Marianne's belief in a multiverse. The play consists of seven acts representing seven significant events in Roland and Marianne's relationship: the first meeting, a date, the confession of an affair, a chance reunion, a proposal, a cancer diagnosis and the moments before they go to an assisted suicide clinic. Each act consists of several scenes or 'universes', envisioning several different versions of the same basic event that 'co-exist simultaneously' (Payne 2012: 25). Between each version, Payne indicates that there is a 'change in the universe' (Payne 2012: 10). Roland and Marianne meet for the first time five times. In three universes, Roland is in a relationship. In one universe, he is uninterested. In the last universe, they are both attracted to each other. The play has a branching structure. Time is both successive and simultaneous. The audience explore a range of possible choices that could have been made in each situation before moving forward to the next event in time.

Sometimes, only a single version makes sense in terms of the forward action of the play, so it is clear which version of events is the 'right' universe. Only the final version of Roland and Marianne's first meeting suggests the possibility that they will embark on a relationship. At other times, any of the versions could move the action of the story forward. All the versions of the break-up scene lead to a future in which Roland and Marianne end their relationship and could make sense in terms of the forward action of the play. There is no single definitive version of Roland and Marianne's love story. Instead, the structure of *Constellations*, like the structure of Caryl Churchill's *Love and Information* (discussed in the previous chapter), offers a number of possible permutations.[3] The spectator is free to build their own personal version of the story within the parameters of the basic forward action of the play. Like Feynman's electron, the story 'splits off like a branching tributary to live out all possible futures in an ever-expanding arena of parallel universes' (Greene 2000: 108).

At times, different universes offer discrete and fundamentally different versions of a particular event. When Marianne breaks the news of her cancer diagnosis to Roland, the different universes offer parallel versions that are almost completely unique. In one, Marianne calmly breaks the news and Roland listens calmly. In another, Roland is angry with Marianne for going to the appointment without him. In a third, Marianne doesn't have cancer. In a fourth, Marianne is upset by the information on an online cancer forum. This version is iterated in a fifth universe in which the dialogue is replaced by sign language. The greater the differences between the parallel versions, the wider the possibilities for the characters' futures seem.

At other times, however, the possible futures offered in each of the parallel universes are not as different as they first appear. Scenes repeat the same sets of actions and the same snippets of dialogue. In the proposal act, Roland reads the exact same speech in three universes, while in a fourth he fails to say it because he

---

[3]See pp. 81–6

tries unsuccessfully to recite it from memory. At other times, small snippets are iterated rather than repeated. In the reunion act, Marianne suggests that Roland and she go for a drink in four universes in four slightly different ways. Although Marianne's offer is phrased slightly differently in each universe, the action of the scene is fundamentally the same. The more a particular section of dialogue or action is iterated, the more probable it feels that some permutation of this event occurred in some definitive version of the story, and the narrower the possibilities for the characters' futures seem.

Sometimes, entire scenes are repeated with no variation at all. In the final scene, before Roland and Marianne leave to go to the assisted suicide clinic, the first three universes offer identical versions. Roland tells Marianne the taxi is booked for nine. He asks if she is tired. She asks what the time is. He asks if she is cold. The fourth repeats the same action and dialogue and then continues with Roland questioning Marianne's decision to end her life. Marianne offers Roland two possible justifications in the fourth and fifth universes. This is followed by six brief one-line universes in which Marianne attempts to explain and Roland refuses to listen. In the final universe, Marianne offers another justification for her decision. When all twelve scenes are placed together, they form an almost singular version of events. The only variation is the justification Marianne gives. At the very moment Marianne repeatedly expresses a belief in the existence of multiple parallel universes in which their life together took a happier path – 'Knowing that another me and another you could be on holiday. Or at home. Or in our seventies. Or parents. Or with my mum. Or at work. Or healthy. Brings me solace'– the variations between the parallel universes are reduced to almost nothing (Payne 2012: 80). Marianne's future is becoming increasingly definitive and the possibility of an alternative future increasingly curtailed.

The play ends with a final version of Roland and Marianne's reunion, which combines different versions from different universes into a single scene. The final line creates a new version of events in which Roland asks Marianne out for a drink instead of Marianne asking Roland. The scene has two opposite effects. On one hand, the scene confirms Marianne's belief in a multiverse. She dies in one universe, but in another universe is reunited with Roland. On the other hand, the combination of sections from earlier scenes, the scene's standing alone without parallel versions and its position as the final scene of the play imply that it is a definitive version of events, confirming Roland's belief in a singular universe.

Roland's belief in a singular universe is also confirmed by the single repeated scene that forms the backbone of the play. In this scene, Marianne makes the decision to take her own life. The scene exists in six versions. There is a version of the scene between each of the seven basic acts that trace the progression of Marianne and Roland's relationship. This backbone scene exhibits no variation. Instead, each successive version adds more dialogue to the beginning of the scene, gradually revealing more and more of the conversation. The first version begins at the end of the conversation. Marianne explains that she cannot go back to work. The second reveals she is more frightened of being kept alive than of dying. The third reveals that Marianne's mother committed suicide when she became too sick to carry on. In the fourth, Roland asks to come with Marianne and she agrees. In the fifth, Marianne explains the process of committing assisted suicide. The sixth version reveals that Marianne is too sick to carry on. The scene's lack of variation suggests it is a definitive event in a singular universe.

Through its structure, *Constellations* holds Roland's singular universe and Marianne's multiverse in formal dialectical tension with each other. Payne, however, has stated a preference for Roland's point of view: 'I'd rather believe this is it, this is all that does exist' (Costa 2012). Payne presents Marianne's belief in a multiverse as problematic, as it raises questions about the nature of agency. If the possible consequences of every decision exist in separate universes, then where is the place of free will? If the choices that human beings make have no definitive effect on the course of the future, then what is the point in human existence: 'if everything I'm ever gonna do already exists, then what's the point in me' (Payne 2012: 26)? It also raises ethical questions. During his research, Payne met a cosmologist who pointed out that the existence of a multiverse 'could remove the idea of consequence' (Costa 2012). You could, for example, justify killing someone in one universe on the basis that the person would still be alive in other universes. If actions can be thought of as having no consequences, then the choices people make about their actions become both pointless and amoral.

The effect of a multiverse model of the universe on free will is addressed in the act in which Marianne and Roland go on a date.

In the sixth universe, Marianne argues that choices matter. Even if the consequences of every choice people make exist simultaneously in a maze of parallel universes, the decisions they make determine which of the possible futures they actually experience: 'if every possible future exists, then the decisions we do and don't make will determine which of these futures we actually end up experiencing'. In the seventh universe, Marianne argues the opposite. Our choices are meaningless because life is just a random sequence of events: '[w]e might think that the choices we make will have some say in the –' but ultimately '[w]e're just particles governed by a series of very particular laws being knocked the fuck around all over the place' (Payne 2012: 26–7). The equations of physics offer no evidence for the existence of free will: 'the wonders of life and the universe are mere reflections of microscopic particles engaged in a pointless dance fully choreographed by the laws of physics' (Greene 2000: 16). The forces of attraction that pull humans together and drive them apart are like the forces of attraction and repulsion between subatomic particles. Romance is like physics.

Structurally the play does identify one area in which the characters' decisions do matter and they do have a degree of control over their lives. In the final lines of the backbone scene, Marianne longs for a degree of control over her death:

Marianne I   I don't
We can't. I have to   have to   make a
I have to have a choice.
Control.

(Payne 2012: 18, 30, 42, 52, 61, 77)

This statement is repeated at the end of every version of the scene. The play's form suggests that Marianne is granted control over her death. The scene in which Marianne leaves to go to the assisted dying clinic has almost no variation in its parallel universes. The scene in which Marianne decides to take her own life has no variation and is positioned as the backbone of the play. The scene in which Marianne decides not to take her life does not exist.

In *Constellations*, Payne addresses the same ideas as Jones does in *Humble Boy*. While Jones's discussion of string theory is confined to the content of her play, Payne utilizes the dramaturgical structures of his play to convey a visceral sense of the

potential consequences of living in a multiverse.[4] While the dialectical tension in the play's structure between the idea of a single
rational universe and a more liquid understanding of the universe
as a multiverse remains unresolved, Payne's play highlights an
important relationship between agency and structure that has
political consequences. In order to know how to have agency, to
decide the direction and purpose of action, it is necessary to understand the nature of the universe you are acting within.

Heart's Desire

While *Constellations* presents a tension between a singular universe
in which events are ordered on the temporal axis of succession
and a multiverse where events are simultaneous, Caryl Churchill's
Heart's Desire (Out of Joint/Royal Court, London 1997) articulates a complete failure of the axis of succession, so revealing a
structural method for ordering dramatic time more predominantly
on the axis of simultaneity. The play consists of a single scene,
which repeatedly fails to complete itself. In the scene, a family
awaits the return of one of its members, Susy, from Australia. The
scene initially proceeds as if it were the first scene of a normal play.
Susy's mother, Alice, her father, Brian, and her aunt, Maisie, are in
the kitchen awaiting her arrival. The action of the scene, however,
soon comes to a grinding halt, stops, is rewound and starts again.
This happens twenty-six times. Each scene initially repeats the
action of the previous version of the scene, before offering what
is hopefully a more successful variation on it. If the variation is
successful, it is added to the existing text of the scene and repeated
the next time the scene is rewound. If the variation of the action
is unsuccessful, it is discarded and replaced. Once an addition has
been repeated, it is permanently incorporated into the cumulative
action of the scene.

The first version of the scene opens with Alice laying the table,
while Maisie fidgets. Brian enters in a red sweater. The scene
stops and resets to the beginning. It starts again with Alice laying
the table, while Maisie fidgets. This is now a permanent part of

---

[4]For an analysis of *Humble Boy* see pp. 73–6.

the action. Brian re-enters in a tweed jacket. The action stops and resets to the beginning. Alice lays the table. Maisie fidgets. Brian enters in an old cardigan and the dialogue commences with:

Brian She's taking her time.

Alice Not really.

Brian We should have met the plane.

Alice We should not.

(Churchill 2008: 65)

Then Maisie interjects with a long digression about Australian animals. This takes the action of the scene into a cul-de-sac. Maisie peters out and the action resets again to the top of the scene. Brian's entrance in the old cardigan and the first four lines of the dialogue are repeated. These are now a permanent part of the scene. Maisie's digression about Australian animals is not repeated. It is rejected. Instead Brian and Alice continue their conversation about whether they should have gone to the airport to meet Susy. This conversation develops into an argument that results in the breakdown of Alice and Brian's relationship. The scene reaches another dead-end. It resets again and repeats. The scenes continue to repeat in this pattern. There are twenty-six different versions of the scene before Susy arrives and Brian successfully delivers the final line, 'You are my heart's desire' (Churchill 2008: 92). Twenty-six different versions of a single event are compressed into one moment of time. The doorbell rings seven times. Susy appears at the door three times. Other callers include an unknown Australian woman, a ten-feet-tall bird, and a uniformed officer. Susy is simultaneously alive, killed in a tube accident and still in Australia.

The scene does not always reset to the beginning. The distance the scene is rewound varies, depending upon how far the unsuccessful elements added to the scene take the characters away from their goal of getting to the end of the scene. If the disruption is small, the scene resets back a short distance. When Alice garbles her words, the scene rewinds as far as her cue line:

Alice Are you pleased she's coming back?

Brian What's the matter with you now?

Alice You don't sleem peased – you pleem seased –

Reset to after 'coming back'.

Brian What's the matter with you now?

Alice You don't seem pleased, you seem cross.

(Churchill 2008: 74)

When the disruption is large – for example, when gunmen appear and shoot the family – the scene resets back to the beginning.

Maisie's digression on Australian animals articulates the idea that similar events happen simultaneously all over the world in many different variations:

Imagine going to feed the ducks and there is something that is not a duck and nor is it a waterrat or a mole, it's the paws make me think of a mole, but imagine this furry creature with its ducky face, it makes you think what else could have existed, tigers with trunks, anyway the platypus has always been my favourite animal.

(Churchill 2008: 65)

In Britain, the creature that emerges out of the water would be a water rat or a mole. In Australia it would be a platypus instead. Therefore, feeding the ducks in Britain and feeding the ducks in Australia are at once both the same action and different actions. The platypus, an animal that appears to be a random amalgamation of several different animals, becomes symbolic of this idea of variation. The existence of the platypus suggests that the events of evolution are random. Had evolution taken a different but equally likely path, then the creatures that now exist in the world would exist in different forms: 'tigers with trunks' (Churchill 2008: 65). Maisie's digression reflects the structure of the repeating scene. Both offer a picture of what else could have happened, if things had turned out differently.

The discarded fragments of action enlarge the audience's understanding of the characters and their relationships. Through Maisie's digressions, they learn not only of her fascination with Australian animals, but also of her fear of death, her expertise on the Hay diet and her physical fragility. The discarded fragments indicate that Maisie has some skeletons in her closet. Lewis hints that she may have a drinking problem. Her fear of being arrested suggests that she may have committed some terrible crime in the past.

The character of Lewis is another skeleton in the family's closet. He is Brian and Alice's son, but he is completely excluded from the final version of the scene and only exists within the discarded fragments. These discarded fragments, however, tell his story clearly. The first time he appears, he is presented as having a drinking problem. The second time, his drinking is linked to his father's rejection of him: 'Lewis, I wish you'd died at birth. If I'd known what you'd grow up like I'd have killed either you or myself the day you were born' (Churchill 2008: 75). The third time, Lewis expresses a desire to get all the family issues out on the table and resolve them. He is rejected again and goes off into oblivion with the words: 'No more. No more. No more' (Churchill 2008: 84). These three brief fragments give Lewis a narrative trajectory. The first fragment outlines his problem, the second presents its cause and the third offers the possibility of a resolution. The discarded fragments build to tell stories about characters that exist beyond the main action of the scene.

Finally, Susy arrives and the characters successfully reach the last line of the scene. The scene is then played through from beginning to end to cement it. When Brian reaches the final word of the scene, however, he cannot say it and the whole scene resets back to the beginning again. The action remains uncompleted. The play cannot move forward in time to the next scene. It fails to progress along the temporal axis of succession. By limiting this movement, Churchill offers a set of dramaturgical structures articulated not as a chain of successive events, but as a number of simultaneous possibilities. The focus is shifted away from the axis of succession towards the axis of simultaneity.

In her digression about Australian animals, Maisie articulates the idea of a set of simultaneous events occurring in many diverse locations as opposed to a set of successive events moving forward in time. Sociologist Roland Robertson notes that the forces of globalization have produced an 'intensification of consciousness of the world as a whole' in the social subject (Robertson 1992: 8). There has been a shift, Foucault argues, from a nineteenth-century conception of time as 'history' into an 'epoch of simultaneity' (Foucault 2011). The representation of this shift requires the representation of simultaneous events occurring in many different spaces at exactly the same time. The temporal axis of simultaneity demands an expression in spatial terms.

Incomplete and Random Acts of Kindness

Like *Heart's Desire*, English playwright David Eldridge's *Incomplete and Random Acts of Kindness* (Royal Court, London 2005) articulates a breakdown in the temporal axis of succession through its structure. Its protagonist, Joey, is in the middle of a nervous breakdown and suffering a form of temporal confusion that reflects the effects of time-space compression.[5] As in *Heart's Desire*, the failure of the temporal axis of succession draws attention to the axis of simultaneity. The play predominantly plots its events through spatial as opposed to temporal structures.

The play tells the story of Joey, a banker, forced to re-evaluate his life when his mother is diagnosed with terminal cancer. He takes his girlfriend, Kate, on holiday to the States and asks her to marry him. His mother dies and he discovers that his father, Ronnie, has started a relationship with his mother's nurse, Maureen. He has a breakdown. He leaves Kate and moves back in with his father, driving Maureen out of the house. He volunteers to tutor schoolchildren who are having difficulties with reading. He meets a young boy called Trevor but, just as he feels he is beginning to get through to him, Trevor is murdered. Joey becomes friends with Trevor's mother, Shanika, and begins to recover from his breakdown. He starts to help a new student with his reading. Maureen moves back in with his father and Joey moves out.

The play articulates Joey's subjective experience of time in his moment of crisis through its temporal structures. The events that happen to him are jumbled together rather than told chronologically,

---

[5]For an explanation of time-space compression, see pp. 79–81.

and mixed up with his memories and dreams. The play starts when Joey moves back in with his father and ends when he moves out. It is primarily organized around a set of father/son relationships: Joey's relationship with his father and his relationship with Trevor. Joey's relationship with Trevor forms a spine around which the events of the play are plotted. In the real world, Joey and his father struggle to rebuild their relationship. Meanwhile, Joey's relationships with the women in his life are explored through a jumble of memories. At the same time, Joey's imagination is haunted by the ghost of Trevor. Joey is present onstage throughout the play, indicating that the audience are always viewing the action from his subjective perspective.[6]

The action of the play reflects Joey's inability to shape his experiences into a coherent successive linear narrative. When Shanika tells Joey about Trevor's murder, Joey attempts to communicate his experiences in a stream of impressions, memories and thoughts:

Joey I went to Wales.

Shanika Did you?

Joey To Penally. There's a castle there. My mum and dad
   always took us as kids. I went with my best friend. Colin.
   He'll know what to do. I was going to write Trevor a letter.
   I – we saw the vicar. I went to a wedding once and a bishop
   conducted the service. Are you hungry? I've got a sandwich.
   Do you like cheese?

(Eldridge 2005: 43)

Joey's thoughts are not unconnected. He moves from thinking about his friend Colin, who knows what to do in a moment of crisis, to the thought that he did not know what to do to save Trevor. He connects the vicar he sees in a Welsh field to the bishop who married two of his friends. The events seem unconnected, however, because they are not arranged chronologically. Ronnie

---

[6]For a discussion of the shift from subjective to objective focalization in contemporary British drama, see p. 199–201.

attempts to guide Joey out of this confusion by offering a chronological account of what happened to him the day before:

> It's about getting up in the morning and doing things. To me it's
> about getting up, having a slice of bread and jam and getting in
> that cab and I'm happy in that cab. The people I've met. The
> wonderful things I've heard. The stories. Yesterday, I had a
> couple in there: they weren't talking. Young couple, looked like
> they wanted to die, both of them. I kept looking in the mirror. I
> saw him put his hand on her hand. And she put her hand on his
> hand. And he kissed her on her ear and she smiled and I came
> home full of it.
>
> (Eldridge 2005: 55)

Ronnie communicates the idea that life is not only about doing
things; it is about doing things that are connected in the right
order, a linear successive order. Ronnie gets up, has breakfast
and goes to work. The couple fall out with each other. The man
offers a sign of peace. The couple make up. Ronnie's life is made
meaningful both by the stories that he witnesses inside his cab and
the stories he hears. These coherent chronological narratives are
the 'wonderful things' that he feels are the secret to being happy
(Eldridge 2005: 51). If Joey cannot shape his experience in this
way then, in Ronnie's eyes, it is no wonder he is in a constant state
of distress.

The play abounds with images of Joey's struggle with linearity.
When Joey helps his father, Ronnie, build a fence, Ronnie constantly
questions Joey's ability to keep the line of the fence straight:

Joey holds a fence panel steady for Ronnie.

Ronnie Keep it straight.

Joey I am.

Ronnie Hold it.

Joey I am.

Ronnie Stroll on.

Joey I am holding it straight.

Ronnie It's not.

(Eldridge 2005: 26–7)

Even after the fence panel has gone, Joey's hands 'remain in mid-air', tracing the straight line that eludes him. There is an inability to follow straight lines inscribed in Joey's reading and writing. He writes a letter to Kate but his words are just 'ravings' (Eldridge 2005: 29). His words in their lines on the page fail to make sense. He is supposed to teach Trevor to read, to follow lines of words and make sense of them, but he fails to do this as well. Joey's failure to form straight lines reflects his inability to form a linear narrative.

The plotting of the play's events reflects Joey's failed attempts at structuring chronological narratives. Events become muddled and spatio-temporally compressed into the single present moment in which Joey is trying to synthesize his experiences into a coherent whole. About halfway through the play, Joey says to Kate that he feels as if they are 'floating, drifting' (Eldridge 2005: 40). As a spectator, I experienced a sensation of floating or drifting in time and space when watching the performance at the Royal Court. The set was a bare black stage. The characters flowed in and out of the action. There was no distinction in the staging between actual events, memories and dreams. There was no indication, beyond the text, as to the location of the play's action in time or space. Consequently, past, present and imagined events appear to occur within the same time frame, all at once. It is difficult to distinguish between events and to put the events in chronological order, so all the events of the play feel as if they have been collapsed into this single present moment. The play suggests, through its temporal structure, that the only moment of time that exists is the present, while articulating a relationship to space where several spaces seem to collapse into each other at once.

The play's dramaturgical structure reflects the structures of time-space compression. Temporal patterns within the play suggest that Joey is experiencing a perpetual present. Movements and interactions are repeated. This is particularly true of encounters between the two sons in the play. Joey and Trevor cross paths repeatedly as the action flows from scene to scene. They greet each other with a hello as they pass by. Joey physically mirrors Trevor. During their first encounter, Trevor *'takes a toothpick out of his hair and sucks it'* (Eldridge 2005: 6). Joey picks up this action: *'picks his teeth with a dental stick'* (Eldridge 2005: 9). Soon Joey has adopted Trevor's habit. While Trevor *'picks his teeth'*, Joey sports *'a toothpick in his mouth'* (Eldridge 2005: 20). The two sons of the play are equated with each other through mirrored repetitive movements. The scene in which Joey imagines Trevor's death begins with both characters facing each other, picking their teeth. Joey greets Trevor with the usual 'Hello', but Trevor refuses to mirror his greeting. Trevor has now changed his response to 'Hi' (Eldridge 2005: 29). The mirroring symbolizes Joey's deep need to connect with Trevor. The repetition of these encounters and Trevor's failure to respond adequately emphasizes how Joey's failure to form a functional relationship with the fatherless Trevor and, by extension, with his own father, lies at the centre of his distress. There is a disruption of the connection between father and son.

The figure of Trevor is frozen in time, like the images in the photographs he takes with his manual camera. In Joey's presence, he is presented as perpetually bleeding, marked by the violence of his death. When Joey and Trevor first meet, there is blood on Trevor's coat. Next time Joey sees him, his hand is bleeding. In a dreamed meeting, blood pours from Trevor's mouth. The blood becomes symbolic of Joey's failure to connect with Trevor. Trevor constantly floats at the edge of Joey's vision. When Joey tries to convince Kate to let him move back in with her, he is distracted by the presence of Trevor in the corner of his eye. The figure of Trevor, as constructed in Joey's mind, is always moving away from him. Every time they passed and greeted each other in the Royal Court production, Trevor was the one to move away. At times, Joey calls after Trevor's disappearing figure, 'Hello! Hello! Hello!' (Eldridge 2005: 26). Trevor is a figure perpetually present on the periphery of Joey's vision but always escaping his grasp.

In the creation of a perpetual present, Eldridge removes the temporal axis of succession from its position as the principal organizing structure of a play. While some critics found the play 'difficult to piece together' (Berkowitz 2005), others thought it 'beautifully structured' (Taylor 2005). But how is the play structured if not primarily on the temporal axis of succession?

Temporal movement is defined through space. The order of events is made clear by the movement of objects through space and references to particular spaces in the dialogue. Joey's mother's engagement ring first appears in scene nine, when Kate returns the ring to Joey. Later, Maureen gives the ring to Joey after his mother's death. In the same scene, Kate takes the ring from Joey and asks him to marry her. The next time the ring is seen, it is on Kate's finger indicating that she and Joey are engaged. The movement of the ring clearly indicates that, chronologically, the second scene comes first, then the third and finally the first. Maureen gives Joey the ring. Joey gives the ring to Kate. Kate returns the ring.

Spaces are used in a similar way. There are three distinct locations that indicate specific points in time. The first is Wales. There is only one scene set in Wales but references to it locate other scenes in a temporal relationship to it. In scene five, Joey mentions to Trevor that he is 'going to Wales' (Eldridge 2005: 6). In scene eight, Joey meets a priest in Wales who tells him about 'Odo de Barri' (Eldridge 2005: 13). In scene twelve, Joey mentions Odo de Barri to Trevor. This indicates that these three scenes are ordered chronologically. The hospital is another space that anchors events in time. There is a single scene set in the hospital, just after Joey's mother's death. Mentions of the hospital in other scenes locate them as happening before this point. In the penultimate scene of the play, Kate asks Joey how his mother got on at the hospital, locating this scene towards the beginning of the story, even though it comes towards the end of the play. America is the final space that orients the audience in time. In the penultimate scene, Kate talks about going to America. The scenes in America are located as happening after this scene, but before Joey's mother's death.

References to specific locations position events even more precisely in time. Joey and Kate's trip to America ends with 'the greatest bar on earth' where they 'have a cosmopolitan and watch all the helicopters flying around' (Eldridge 2005: 37). When they are engaged, Kate asks Joey if he remembers 'the lovely barman who served us the cosmopolitans' (Eldridge 2005: 65). Joey reminds her they cannot go back there now. The bar is the bar at the top of the World Trade Center. The first scene happens before 11 September 2001. The second scene happens after. Iraq is another location used as a temporal marker. The priest Joey meets in Wales mentions a big demonstration against the war in London that day. This identifies the date of the scene as 15 February 2003. There are references to the progress of the Iraq invasion. When Shanika tells

Joey about Trevor's death, he asks her if she has heard of 'Umm Qasr' (Eldridge 2005: 42). This positions this scene as happening around 21 March 2003, the day the Allies entered that particular town. Eldridge uses spatial references to define the temporal order of events and to locate some of these events at precise points in historical time.

In Joey's moment of temporal confusion, space becomes the principle by which he orientates himself. Space, however, starts to collapse in on itself, compressing many spaces into the same space. In his travels, memories and through the media, Joey flows quickly from space to space, annihilating the distance between them. Iraq is in his living room and America in his head. Amidst all this spatio-temporal chaos, Joey anchors himself through his personal relationships to space. He constantly repeats the facts he knows about Topanga Canyon:

> It begins in the San Fernando Valley.
> And runs to the Pacific Ocean.
> Some people think 'Roadhouse Blues' was written there.
> No one knows Marvin Gaye was there.
> There are racoons.
> Sometimes there are mudslides.
> Sometimes there are UFOs.
> I never saw any.
>
> (Eldridge 2005: 20)

He repeats them at moments of stress. In a dream, he tells them to Trevor to comfort him as he is dying. Topanga Canyon is a space in which Joey felt happy. He clings to this happy space in his confusion and distress.

Joey's spatio-temporal distress is a symptom of his mental breakdown. It can be argued, however, that the spatio-temporal structures that shape Joey's experience of his breakdown reflect the crisis in spatio-temporal structures that Harvey links to the experience of time-space compression under the pressures of global financial capitalism: 'the world sometimes seems to collapse inwards upon us' while 'time horizons shorten to the point where the present is all there is' (Harvey 1990: 240).[7] Thus, Eldridge's

---

[7]For an explanation of time-space compression see pp. 79–81.

play captures the experience not only of mental distress but, in a wider sense, of the postmodern condition.

Time in serious drama is predominantly present tense, abbreviated, subjective and organized on the axis of succession, even when it appears to be disrupted. Plays that exhibit liquid dramaturgies shift their temporal organization away from the axis of succession and towards the axis of simultaneity. Priestley's *Time and the Conways* offers an early but flawed attempt to represent simultaneous time through the temporal structures of drama. The play articulates ideas about simultaneous time in its content, but its representation of simultaneous time is hampered by the successive linear temporal structures, which form the basis of its dramaturgical form. Payne explores the simultaneous time frames of the multiverse through *Constellations'* liquid dramaturgical structures and raises questions about the meaning of agency in an indeterminate universe. In *Heart's Desire*, Churchill points towards the idea that the representation of simultaneous moments in time involves an understanding of the increasingly simultaneous nature of space in a globalized world. Finally, Eldridge's *Incomplete and Random Acts of Kindness* conveys the experience of time-space compression, revealing that the representation of simultaneous time demands a dramaturgy predominantly organized through space.

The next chapter will examine the effects of this temporal shift from the axis of succession towards the axis of simultaneity on the representation of space. Shifts in the representation of time necessarily cause shifts in the representation of space as spatio-temporal structures exist in 'wedlock' (Bauman 2012: 111). It will investigate the ways in which a range of contemporary plays have attempted to structure their meaning predominantly through spatial as opposed to temporal structures. As time shifts from the axis of succession towards the axis of simultaneity, it argues that representations of space become less concrete and more virtual, reflecting a corresponding shift in lived experience.

4

Space

[T]he theatrical text is defined and perceived above all in spatial terms.

ELAM 2002: 56

The previous chapter explored how the nature of temporal drama-turgical structures is shifting in a range of contemporary British plays. It concluded that the representation of time is moving from an understanding of time as successive towards an understanding of time as simultaneous. This chapter explores the effect of this temporal shift on spatial dramaturgical structures, arguing that while serious drama predominantly thinks of space in terms of solid concrete settings, liquid dramaturgies present space as virtual, fluid and multi-layered. This reflects Bauman's observation that, in liquid modernity, the social subject lives simultaneously both in 'real' spaces and in the virtual spaces generated by new technologies: at once 'physically close' and 'infinitely remote' (Bauman 2012: 154).

This chapter begins by examining the nature of dramatic space and the spatial codes that can be used to define it. Through an analysis of English playwright and theatre maker Tim Crouch's *The Author* (2009), it interrogates the differences between dramatic space and lived space. The previous chapter explored the idea that the representation of simultaneous time demands an organization through space. Following Stein, this chapter explores the idea of virtual space and its potential as an organizational structure. Harold Pinter's *Party Time* (1991) and Sarah Kane's *Blasted* (1995) are argued to organize meaning spatially through a layering of seemingly irreconcilable virtual spaces. Finally, the shifting virtual spatial structures of Scottish playwright David Greig's *San Diego* (2003) are examined in terms of the ways in which they are productive of new spaces with new sets of social structures.

Dramatic space

Plays are fundamentally structured in space as well as time. Their spatial structures describe tangible worlds that are brought into three-dimensional life in front of an audience. Plays articulate what Waters terms a 'micro-geography' (Waters 2010: 54). The spatial structures of serious drama, however, like its temporal structures, are undertheorized. Like dramatic time, dramatic space is imagined to be so commensurate with lived space that little attention is paid to it. As English playwright Noel Greig observes, dramatic space is commonly reduced to setting, the concrete 'location(s) that the story takes place in' (Greig 2005: 119). Dramatic space is often thought of as an unmediated representation of real space. Just as Diderot hoped it would be, a living room onstage is imagined to be identical with a living room in an actual house.[1] The choice of setting usually frames the action taking place in it appropriately. Characters adhere to the normative spatio-temporal rhythms of everyday life, doing the right thing in the right place, and so the spatial structures of serious drama can be read as articulating a reactionary spatial politics.

Elam argues that dramatic space is defined through four different spatial codes: architectural, interpersonal, scenic and virtual. The first code, the architectural, is related to the physical organization of the performance space. Some elements of this space, such as the material fabric of a theatre building, are set in 'fixed-feature' spatial relations. The spatial relationship between these elements cannot be altered. Other elements are 'semi-fixed-features' (Elam 2002: 62). The spatial relationship between them can be altered. For example, in flexible theatre spaces, the relationship between the stage and the audience can often be shifted between 'end on', 'thrust' and 'in the round' arrangements.

---

[1] See pp. 31–3.

The second spatial code is the interpersonal, which is related to the position of actors' bodies in space: 'the distance between the characters' and 'the position of the characters within the stage space' (Elam 2002: 56). Following anthropologist Edward T. Hall's work on *proxemics* (Hall 1966), Elam identifies four different types of interpersonal relationships defined by the physical distance between people: intimate (physical contact and near touching), personal (1.5–4 feet), social (4–12 feet) and public (12–25 feet) (Elam 2002: 65). Onstage, interpersonal distances define the degree of intimacy or formality between characters. A dissonance between a character's definition of their relationship to another character and the interpersonal distances enacted between them creates subtext.

Stages can be divided into zones. These zones are encoded with spatial significance. For example, a figure occupying a downstage position on a proscenium arch stage appears more dominant than a figure occupying an upstage position (Elam 2002: 59). Different movements across a stage also have different resonances. Diagonal movements from upstage right to downstage centre, for example, are conventionally read as confident, conveying an increase in power.

The third spatial code, the scenic, visually defines the world the characters are imagined to inhabit. This is predominantly achieved through the use of set, costume and props. The scenic code helps to locate the play's action in a specific time and place. The location of the action also has a shaping effect on character behaviour. As Noel Greig observes, '[l]ocation and setting spell out certain "rules", or conventions of behaviour' (Greig 2005: 121). The scenic code can therefore be used to reveal the ways in which a character's behaviour is determined by their environment. This is particularly true of realist dramaturgies, as Pfister notes, with their focus on the way in which 'figures are conditioned by external circumstances' (Pfister 1988: 265). In this case, as Noel Greig observes, the scenic code becomes 'an active driving force, not just a background' (Greig 2005: 125).

The scenic code can be used symbolically to reflect the state of an individual or of society as a whole. The apparently naturalistic setting of Ibsen's *Hedda Gabler* (Königliches Residenz Theater, Munich 1891) provides the audience with a symbolic representation of Hedda's character. The French windows express her desire for freedom, the picture of her father symbolizes the influence he has over her life and the stove is a physical representation of her fiery passion. The spatial relationship between Hedda and these objects indicates her inner emotional state. For example, when her husband, Tesman, mentions that her former admirer, Loveborg, has returned to town, Ibsen indicates that Hedda '[s]*its in the armchair by the stove*', so suggesting her passionate feelings for Loveborg (Ibsen 2002: 30). The scenic code can also define a character's relationship to the world they inhabit. A harmony between the visual appearance of a character and the scenic code suggests they are well integrated into their world. Conversely, dissonance suggests they are at odds with their world. The scenic spaces that characters inhabit shape, drive and express their actions and feelings.

The final spatial code is the virtual. The virtual code depicts 'a domain which does not coincide with its actual physical limits, a mental construct on the part of the spectator from the visual clues that he receives' (Elam 2002: 67); for example, the pictorial representation of a space larger than the stage on a backdrop. Arguably, the virtual code also includes spaces described through words and produced as images in the mind of the spectator. Pfister describes these virtual spaces as 'word-scenery' (Pfister 1988: 269). They are what Lefebvre terms representational or imagined spaces[2] because they exist purely in the imagination. Lefebvre argues that such imagined spaces offer the possibility of political change through a reimagining of everyday spatial structures.

As Elam observes, dramatic space, like dramatic time, is highly structured. It can be described in terms of the performance space, the positioning of actors within that space, scenic setting and the virtual spaces invoked. At the heart of Elam's spatial codes is an understanding of lived space and dramatic space, not as commensurate, but as standing in a dialectical relationship to each other.

The Author

Tim Crouch's *The Author* (Royal Court, London 2009) is a play that attempts to annihilate the difference between lived and

---

[2]For Lefebvre's definition of representational or imagined spaces, see pp. 71–2.

dramatic space through the use of physical unity.[3] As discussed in chapter 2, physical unity demands that the spatio-temporal structures of a performance reflect the audience's lived experience of time and space during the performance. Szondi argues that physical unity produces immersion because it is the basis of what he terms 'absolute' form (Szondi 1987: 8). Absolute form describes drama's attempt to position itself as presentational rather than representational; 'not a (secondary) representation of something else (primary); it presents itself, is itself'. The actor is the character; the 'actor-role relationship should not be visible' (Szondi 1987: 9). The presence of both the author and the spectator is denied. The dialogue is not written, nor is it addressed to any listeners beyond the dramatic world of the play. The drama is 'conscious of nothing outside itself'. The spectator is encouraged towards a position of 'complete identity' with the dramatic action and is 'pulled into the dramatic event' as if nothing else existed outside it (Szondi 1987: 8). Absolute form immerses the spectator in the world of the play.

Some recent attempts at absolute form rely not on immersing the spectator in a dramatic world, but instead situating the performance in the world of the spectator. The performers play themselves, acknowledge the presence of the audience and share the same space and the same time frame as them. If the performance space is a theatre, then the performance is set in a theatre. If the performance starts at 7.45 p.m., then the time is 7.45 p.m.. If the performance has a performance time of seventy-five minutes, then the time period represented in the performance is also seventy-five minutes. As the performers in German playwright Peter Handke's *Offending the Audience* (Theater am Turm, Frankfurt 1966) inform the spectators: 'You don't see a room that pretends to be another room. Here you are not experiencing a time that pretends to be another time. The time on stage is no different from the time off stage. We have the same local time. We are in the same location' (Handke 1997: 9).

Crouch's *The Author* tells the story of a violently shocking play, through the eyes of the writer who writes it, the actor and actress who are in it and an audience member who watches it. The violence represented in the play slowly seeps into the lives of

---

[3]For an explanation of physical unity, see pp. 69–70.

its makers. The actor violently attacks the audience member. The author is accused of abusing the actress's baby and commits suicide in a floatation tank.

Crouch states that his plays 'subscribe to the Aristotelian unities' (Crouch quoted in Bottoms 2009: 67). In *The Author*, he uses the unities of time and place to create absolute form by locating the action of the play in the venue the play is being performed in. Dramatic space appears to be commensurate with the audience's lived experience of space. The play is set 'within the heart of the audience' (Gardner 2009). There is 'no "stage"' (Crouch 2009: 16). Instead, two seating banks are positioned opposite each other with no performance space in-between. The audience sit looking at each other. The actors sit among the audience and are part of them. During the performance, dramatic time appears to pass at the same rate as lived time. Audience member Adrian refers to flashing lights fifteen minutes before the end of the performance, and fifteen minutes before the end of the actual show the audience of *The Author* are treated to a '*brilliant light show*' (Crouch 2009: 46). Actor is blended with character. Actors share the same names as their characters. Tim Crouch is the writer Tim. Vic Llewellyn and Esther Smith are the actors Vic and Esther. Adrian Howells is the audience member Adrian. The actors tell a story about past events, but in the telling of it they appear to share the same present moment as the audience. The play appears to produce absolute form.

In actuality, Crouch's use of physical unity in *The Author* emphasizes rather than erases the differences between dramatic and lived space. I saw the play at both the Royal Court and the Northwall Arts Centre in Oxford. Crouch states that: '*The Author* is set in the Jerwood Theatre Upstairs at the Royal Court Theatre – even when it's performed elsewhere' (Crouch 2009: 16). In Oxford, the dramatic nature of the space of the play is obvious. Sitting in the Northwall Arts Centre, the audience are told they are in the Jerwood Theatre Upstairs at the Royal Court. There is a dual awareness of space; of dramatic versus lived space. The illusion of physical unity is broken.

Even when the play is performed in the Jerwood Theatre Upstairs at the Royal Court, a tension between dramatic and lived space persists. The Royal Court in Crouch's play is a fictionalized representation of the Royal Court. Most of what is said about the Royal Court in the play is true. The rehearsal room is '[j]ust to the side of this building' (Crouch 2009: 51). Friends do get 'five pound off the top ticket prices' (Crouch 2009: 32). One very important fact, however, is not true. The play that Tim describes having written for the Royal Court was never performed there. The play has echoes of plays that have been staged there. The audience are told, for example, that the stage crew find it difficult to clear up all the blood after the show: 'The stage was a mess at the end of the show. Poor old stage management spent hours clearing it up at the end' (Crouch 2009: 45). This echoes the real difficulties of clearing up stage blood recorded in the show reports of an actual production at the Royal Court, Simon Stephens's *Motortown* (2006): '[t]here was too much blood tonight so we had trouble cleaning the blood' (Sierz 2011: 131). During a performance of *The Author* at the Jerwood Theatre Upstairs, the audience inhabit two spaces at once, the fictional Royal Court and the actual Royal Court. The tension between dramatic and lived space persists.

A similarly dual relationship exists between dramatic and lived time. The play appears to run in continuous time but the action is actually split into scenes separated by musical interludes and silent darkness. Crouch identifies the moments of music as allowing the audience some relief from the pressure of the performance: '[m]usic is present in the play as a release valve. It brings us into the here and now and helps the audience to feel good about being together' (Crouch 2009: 16). This note reveals that the audience actually experience more than one time frame while watching the play. Part of the function of the interludes is to bring them back into the present moment. The audience of *The Author* experience the same three distinct time frames they would while watching a conventional play. They experience a sense of actual lived time. Alongside this they experience two time frames within the dramatic world of the play. They see what is happening in the present moment and they imagine what has happened in the past as the characters narrate their story to them. What is unusual about *The Author*, however, is the balance between these two time frames. The action within the present time frame of the play is minimal. The actors tell their story to the audience or wait with them during the interludes. The action that happened on the stage of the theatre in which the audience is now supposedly sitting happened in the past. The narrow gap between the seating banks where the stage should be remains empty, but the characters' retelling of the action that was once played on and around that empty stage builds images in the virtual space of the audience's minds.

The interludes allow the audience a break from the pressure of the action created in the virtual space of their own imaginations; a moment to return to the present and be together with those around them. Crouch states that the relief these moments provide should be a 'treat' and yet these interludes feel uncomfortable (Crouch 2009: 16). These interludes create discomfort by manipulating the audience's sense of the rate at which time is passing. Dramatic time appears to run at the same rate as lived time during the performance, but in the interludes time feels suspended. Nothing is happening. The audience and the actors wait. When music is played it does provide relief, as Crouch suggests. Its rhythm measures out the time that passes, making its passing more comfortable. Something is happening. In moments when the audience are plunged into silent darkness, however, the pause seems interminable. The audience experience an uncomfortable suspension of time. Dramatic and lived time are not commensurate during performance. Dramatic time is repeatedly suspended, while lived time continues to pass at a steady rate.

Crouch indicates pauses in the text of *The Author*, not with the usual notation of 'pause', but with the word '*[s]pace*' (Crouch 2009: 17). These moments are a creation of space, rather than a duration of time. The audience are given space to review what they have just been told. They are free to survey the virtual landscape the play builds in their imaginations and to consider the relation of its elements to each other. There is space for them to reflect on their emotional responses to the acts of violence the play describes.

At first glance, physical unity appears to be produced between the representation of dramatic time and space in *The Author* and the audience's experience of lived time and space during the performance. The dramaturgical structures of the performance, however, work to make the audience more conscious, rather than less conscious, of the dialectical tension between lived space and time and dramatic space and time. The performance plays with the idea that it happens in the space of the audience, in a shared space of lived space and time. In reality, *The Author* is a play whose action predominantly takes place not in the shared space of the theatre auditorium, but in the virtual space of each individual audience member's imagination.

Lang-scapes

The Author is a play that predominantly takes place in the virtual space of the audience's imagination. Stein offers a way of thinking about how language creates such virtual spaces within the audience's imagination. Through her consideration of such virtual spaces, she offers a model of how the dramaturgical structure of a play could be predominantly organized through a system of spatial as opposed to temporal relationships.

Stein's thinking about dramatic structure originates in a realization that the tempo of a play and the tempo of an audience's emotional response to it are out of sync. The audience's emotion is always either 'behind or ahead of the play': 'the scene as depicted on the stage is more often than not one might say it is almost always in syncopated time in relation to the emotion of anybody in the audience' (Stein 2004: 58). The answer to this problem, Stein suggests, is to organize the structure of a play on a spatial rather than temporal model: 'if a play was exactly like a landscape then there would be no difficulty about the emotion of the person looking on at the play being behind or ahead' (Stein 2004: 75). By halting the forward temporal drive of the action, the audience are able to bring their emotional responses to the play back into sync with it. As scholar Jane Palatini Bowers explains, '[b]ecause the text does not impel us forward in time, we can suspend our normal anticipatory response to theater and engage the event in a meditative way, suspended in the experience of the thing in and of itself' (Bowers 2002: 140).

Stein argues that when time is halted, our awareness expands into space. This space or landscape, as Stein terms it, is a static one: 'nothing really moves in a landscape but things are there'. The magpies she sees in skies over the landscape in Ain are frozen in space: 'they hold themselves up and down and look flat against the sky' (Stein 2004: 80). This halting of time allows the audience to survey the elements of the play as they would a landscape whose elements are positioned in spatial relationships to each other. As these elements are frozen in space, the audience can consider them in any order they wish to; they can return their attention to one element many times or consider the relationship between any element and any other element as they choose: 'any detail to any other detail' (Stein 2004: 77). This produces an audience who are free to critically reread and reconnect the play's events.

Stein's theory of landscape is commonly thought of in terms that seem more at home in visual as opposed to textual dramaturgy. Stein's landscapes 'frame and freeze visual moments' (Carlson 2002: 147), but, as theatre scholar Marvin Carlson points out, Stein's landscape is actually a 'lang-scape' (Carlson 2002: 149). They 'exist only in the language and the audience's imagination'. They are virtual spaces: 'spatial configurations of language itself that, like landscapes, frame and freeze visual moments and alter perception' (Carlson 2002: 147). Sometimes, these lang-scapes are created through the description of a visual landscape: 'Saint Therese very nearly half inside and half outside outside the house and not surrounded' (Stein 1949: 446). At other times, they are more conceptual landscapes built purely upon language: 'With wed led said with led dead said with dead led said with said dead led wed said wed dead led dead led said wed' (Stein 1949: 476). Here, the same five words are positioned in different relationships to each other as if trying to map the entire constellation of ways in which they could be connected to each other.

In her plays, Stein reaches for a way of spatially ordering a narrative to define not the passage of time, but rather several simultaneous moments in time. Stein's play *Four Saints* (1934) is inspired by sets of photographs she saw in a photographer's shop window in Paris. These sets of photographs show a single person moving through the different stages of their life (a girl slowly transformed into a nun) or performing different actions (a soldier taking off his armour). These photographs describe character in spatial as opposed to narrative terms: '[a]ll these things might have been a story but as a landscape they were just there' (Stein 2004: 81). The text of *Four Saints* includes lang-scapes that reflect the movement Stein observed in the photographs:

Saint Ignatius well bound.
Saint Ignatius might be very well adapted to plans and a distance.
Barcelona in the distance. Was Saint Ignatius able to tell the
     difference between palms and Eucalyptus trees.
Saint Ignatius finally.
Saint Ignatius well bound.
Saint Ignatius with it just.

Saint Ignatius might be read.
Saint Ignatius with it Tuesday.
Saint Therese has very well added it.

(Stein 1949: 455)

As the lang-scapes succeed one another, their elements are reorganized. Stein guides the audience's imagination around a set of continually altering images. First, we see Saint Ignatius 'well bound', then the image alters to present him 'adapted to plans and a distance' and so on, until Saint Ignatius is finally transformed into Saint Therese. Stein leads the audience's eyes and ears from state to state without any regard for chronology. She returns to particular lang-scapes and encourages rereading through this repetition. For example, Saint Ignatius is 'well bound' twice. By organizing her text in space as opposed to time, Stein can describe sets of simultaneous states and suggest non-chronological relationships between them.

The previous chapter concluded that, when dramatic time is predominantly organized on the axis of simultaneity, dramatic space takes on an organizational role. The mechanics of such spatial organization are hard to envisage within the context of Elam's first three codes of dramatic space. Within the fourth, virtual, code, however, the expression of simultaneous moments in time and the organization of meaning on a primarily spatial basis seem more possible. Stein's lang-scapes offer a dramaturgical method for achieving this.

Party Time

The spatial dramaturgy of Pinter's *Party Time* (Almeida Theatre, London 1991) uses lang-scapes to generate a dialectical tension between two seemingly irreconcilable spaces, a space of privilege and a space of brutality. The play is set in a space of privilege. Gavin is throwing a party in 'a very elegant and wealthy apartment' (Pinter quoted in Smith 2006: 91). Outside, however, a brutal round-up of undesirables is taking place.

The world outside the party is obscured from view. Within the scenic code, there is no visual indication of the nature of the space beyond the door through which the party guests enter the room.

At three points in the play, the audience's attention is drawn to a half-open dimly lit second door, through which no one enters or exits. The action pauses and the lights on the party dim, while the 'light beyond the door gradually intensifies' until '[i]t burns into the room' indicating the presence of a concealed space beyond (Pinter 2005: 298, 309, 313).

The party guests offer a succession of lang-scapes to describe the unseen world beyond the room. These lang-scapes predominantly depict spaces of privilege: an exclusive tennis and swimming club, a place of 'pure comfort' and 'real class' (Pinter 2005: 283) with 'first class' food (Pinter 2005: 286); boats on which Gavin's guests like 'cooking' (Pinter 2005: 295) and 'fucking' (Pinter 2005: 296); and a rejuvenating 'paradise' island (Pinter 2005: 300). Pinter's description of the party in the scenic code is indeterminate: 'A large room. Sofas, armchairs, etc. People sitting, standing'. The party's position as a space of privilege is only indicated by the presence of '[a] WAITER with a drinks tray' (Pinter 2005: 281). The guests picture the party as a privileged space. It is an event of 'elegance, style, grace, taste'. All the guests are 'beautifully dressed' (Pinter 2005: 299). Pinter leaves a potentially productive gap between the guests' characterization of the party and its description in the scenic code. The party guests' vision of their world is open to question.

The party guests' lang-scapes emphasize the importance of cleanliness. Gavin fondly reminisces about West Country barber shops where barbers used 'hot towels' that 'burnt all the black-heads out of your skin'. Douglas proudly remembers how, when Liz and he were starting out, they were still able to live cleanly despite their hardships. Liz kept the flat looking 'immaculate' with '[n]o maid, no help, nothing' (Pinter 2005: 309). The party guests are repeatedly praised for maintaining a pristine appearance. Melissa is praised for her 'wonderful figure' (Pinter 2005: 293). Fred is admired for being 'so trim, so fit' (Pinter 2005: 307).

Within these clean, idealized spaces, however, there are under-lying currents of brutality. Love, sex and violence are enfolded into each other. Liz reveals she has fallen in love with a man she saw being lugged away to be raped by another woman. She remembers the man as being like prey, 'a wounded deer' (Pinter 2005: 289). The woman was a sexual predator, 'her legs all over him' like 'she was going to crush him to death' (Pinter 2005: 288). The woman's actions provoke both violent feelings in Liz – 'I could have cut her throat' – and romantic desire. As Charlotte observes: 'for you it was love, it was falling in love' (Pinter 2005: 290).

The image of the man being lugged away like a deer positions violence as inherent in nature itself. The birds Melissa remembers seeing as a girl are all birds of prey: 'I loved hawks too. And eagles. But certainly hawks. The kestrel' (Pinter 2005: 298). These birds hover over her looking for prey. Wild tropical storms rage on Douglas's paradise island and provoke wildness in him. He feels as if he could fight any man, woman or child or even 'take a wild animal on' (Pinter 2005: 300).

Outside, violence has invaded the spaces of the town, moving ever closer to Gavin's flat. When Melissa arrives, she reports that: 'The town's dead. There's nobody on the streets, there's not a soul in sight, apart from some ... soldiers. My driver had to stop at a ... you know ... what do you call it? ... a roadblock' (Pinter 2005: 286). The character of the town's space appears to have changed. It is an unfamiliar space full of unfamiliar objects. Melissa struggles to find the correct words to describe the people and things in it.

The instigators of the violence outside are present within the space of the party. Douglas identifies the violence as part of a programme to bring peace. This peace, however, is a 'cast-iron peace' imposed by violent means (Pinter 2005: 293). Gavin apologizes for the 'traffic problems' guests encountered on their way to the party (Pinter 2005: 312). The disruption outside, he reveals, is the result of a 'bit of a round up', invoking the Nazi practice of randomly rounding up civilians in the street for summary execution or transportation to labour camps during the Second World War (Pinter 2005: 313).

For Pinter, the action of *Party Time* exemplifies how political power operates:

> there *are* extremely powerful people in apartments in capital cities in all countries who are actually controlling events that are happening on the street in a number of very subtle and sometimes not so subtle ways. But they don't really bother to talk about it, because they know it's happening and they know that they have the power.
>
> (Pinter quoted in Smith 2006: 92, emphasis in original)

Pinter's description of the operation of political power operates on a spatial basis. Those who occupy the space of privilege exercise control over the spaces of those whom they brutally repress. These spaces of brutality exist on the periphery, concealed from view. Lefebvre argues that capitalist space creates centres of accumulation that, like the space of the party, 'concentrate wealth, means of action, knowledge, information and "culture"', and act as points of political power. These centres 'expel all peripheral elements with a violence that is inherent in the space itself' (Lefebvre 1991: 332).

The party is literally a party. A political party expanded out into space. Gavin, the host, is a pivotal figure in the party. He defines the nature of what is happening outside the party for everyone inside the party. He even defines the nature of '[n]ormal service', that is, normal everyday behaviour: the 'secure and legitimate paths' along which the 'ordinary citizen be allowed to pursue his labours and his leisure in peace' (Pinter 2005: 313). Gavin's position within the power structures of the party is undefined. Like Dusty, the audience 'don't know what his position is' (Pinter 2005: 310). He wields power but the operation and nature of that power remain invisible.

The party's values are equally invisible. They are represented by the idea of the tennis and swimming club. Everyone at the party belongs to the club or has been invited to join. The club offers protection. Melissa observes that her membership 'saved my life' (Pinter 2005: 294). The party guests cleanse themselves of brutality at the club, performing a 'regime' that enables them to live a 'clean life' (Pinter 2005: 307). The cleanliness of the people within the party, however, is only an outer appearance. They lack an inner sense of morality. When Melissa tries to define 'a moral sense, a moral awareness' (Pinter 2005: 311) that they all share, she can only define it as 'unshakeable, rigorous, fundamental, constant' (Pinter 2005: 310). She cannot specify what their shared values are.

The enemies of the party are defined in the same non-specific terms. They are that 'lot' (Pinter 2005: 302). They are the opposite of the guests at the party. They are the dirty, while the party guests are the clean. Their presence spoils the pristine appearance of the privileged. They do 'vulgar and sordid and offensive things' (Pinter 2005: 310). They are the blackheads that need to be 'burnt' out of the clean skin of the privileged by barbers with hot towels (Pinter 2005: 283).

While the privileged space of the party is visible onstage, the repressed are violently thrown offstage into concealed spaces. They are present only in their absence. They are the missing and the dead. They are 'not on anyone's agenda' (Pinter 2005: 296). In the final moments of the play, however, these concealed spaces of brutality burst onto the stage. The party guests freeze, their figures silhouetted by the intense burning light emitted from the half-open door, which opens to reveal one of the missing, Jimmy. Jimmy is located in a space of 'terrible noises' (Smith 2006: 314). His existence has been erased. His identity is past tense: 'I had a name'. His own heartbeat recedes from him: 'not my heartbeat' but 'someone else's heartbeat'. His body recedes from him, becoming a negative space. He '[d]on't hear don't breathe am blind' (Pinter 2005: 314). As theatre scholar Charles Grimes observes, Jimmy 'speaks, paradoxically, only to tell us that he has no words and no existence' (Grimes 2006: 125). Theatre scholar Richard Allen Cave extends this idea beyond language to the visual. Jimmy's 'silhouette against the burning whiteness of that "beyond"' is 'a body reduced to a point where it is recognizable only by its outline' (Cave 2009: 139). Jimmy represents, as Luckhurst notes, a state of complete 'depersonalization' (Luckhurst 2009: 116).

The space of brutality Jimmy inhabits is no space. It is a space in which everything 'stops', 'closes', 'shuts' (Pinter 2005: 314). Jimmy describes the space purely in terms of sound: 'doors bang'; there are 'voices'. The blinding light that illuminates Jimmy obliterates any visual sense of space. Despite its brightness, the lang-scape he conjures is a soundscape suffused with blackness that consumes even time itself: 'I see nothing at any time any more'. The blackness consumes him and he consumes the blackness: 'I sit sucking the dark' (Pinter 2005: 314). He disappears into the negative space he inhabits and the negative space disappears into him.

In *Party Time*, Pinter uses a succession of lang-scapes to explore the relationship between power and space, creating a dialectical tension between a privileged space of power and a concealed space of brutality. Theatre critic and scholar Martin Esslin finds Pinter's use of space unconvincing, deeming the play 'an unhappy hybrid'. Judging the play in terms of the realist dramaturgy of serious drama, Esslin expresses discomfort with Pinter's use of British cultural references within an imagined world that bears no resemblance to the reality of British society:

If the play was meant to be set in an English or British milieu, it would be politically unconvincing. No such round-ups, disappearances or tortures and quick deaths are likely in this milieu and to suggest anything like it would amount to a case of paranoia. Are the British conditions and linguistic quirks thus meant to suggest another country? In that case location is left too vague, and the English idioms and party manners become very much out of place.

(Esslin 2000: 213)

Esslin finds it difficult to reconcile the democratic space of British society, with its soft forms of social control, with the authoritarian space of the society depicted in *Party Time*, with its hard methods of social control. He argues that these two spaces cannot exist simultaneously because they are contradictory spaces, and searches for a unity that will fold them into a single concrete space. These two spaces, however, produce meaning through their contradictory relationship. By using lang-scapes to layer a democratic space on top of an authoritarian space, Pinter produces a productive spatial dialectic that highlights how soft forms of social control, while appearing to be non-violent, have brutality concealed within their very core.

Blasted

Like *Party Time*, English playwright Sarah Kane's *Blasted* (Royal Court, London 1995) juxtaposes a space of privilege with a space of brutality and, through layering them, attempts to articulate a relationship between the two. The play begins in a hotel room in Leeds. Ian, a middle-aged journalist, has invited a young girl, Cate, to spend the night with him. The hotel room is a space of privilege: '*a very expensive hotel room*' (Kane 2001: 3). Once in the room, Ian proceeds to insult and sexually abuse Cate. The following morning Cate escapes through the bathroom window. A soldier suddenly enters and a mortar bomb explodes through the building. A violent civil war has broken out. The soldier's girlfriend has been raped and killed. The soldier avenges her by raping Ian. He then sucks Ian's eyes out and shoots himself. Cate returns to the hotel room with a baby. Ian begs her to shoot him. Cate secretly removes the bullets from the gun. Ian attempts to shoot himself and fails. The baby dies. Cate buries it under the floorboards. Cate leaves to find food. Ian masturbates, attempts to strangle himself, shits, laughs, has a nightmare, cries and hugs the soldier's body for comfort. He eats the baby's body, climbs into the baby's grave and dies. It rains. Ian is resurrected. Cate returns with food and feeds him. Ian thanks her.

The spatial dramaturgy of *Blasted* echoes the spatial dramaturgy of *Party Time* in its juxtaposition of two seemingly irreconcilable spaces: a British space of privilege and a space of brutality modelled on the 1990s Balkan conflict. Esslin's criticism of Pinter's spatial dramaturgy is echoed by the initial critical response to *Blasted*. Billington argues that: '[t]he difficulty with the play was always structural – that it yoked together two apparently irreconcilable worlds' (Billington 2001a). Like Esslin, he complains that these two spaces cannot be logically unified into a single concrete space. He finds their pairing absurd: 'I was intrigued to notice, however, that public disorder had not interfered with room service or with soccer matches at Elland Road' (Billington 1995).

Indeed, Kane's own description of how these two spaces came to be paired together emphasizes their irreconcilable nature:

> I switched on the news one night while I was having a break from writing, and there was a very old woman's face in Srebrenica just weeping and looking into the camera and saying – 'please, please, somebody help us, because we need the UN to come here and help us'. I thought this is absolutely terrible and I'm writing this ridiculous play about two people in a room.
>
> (Kane quoted in Saunders 2002: 38–9)

Kane's description of the moment of inspiration, however, indicates the simultaneity of the two spaces. In a globalized world, spaces of privilege and brutality are experienced simultaneously. Images of extreme human suffering are beamed direct into privileged homes, while images of privilege reach the eyes of the less privileged through television, advertising and the internet. Kane argues that these two spaces do not simply coexist. The space of privilege plays a role in producing the space of brutality: 'it's obvious, one is the seed and the other is the tree' (Kane quoted in Saunders 2002: 39).

As in *Party Time*, the space of brutality is initially unseen. It approaches slowly. The space outside the hotel room is positioned as threatening from the beginning of the play. Ian tells Cate that it is 'too dangerous' to go outside (Kane 2001: 28). Whenever the phone rings or there is a knock on the door, he '*starts*' (Kane 2001: 6, 12, 16, 28). This undefined threat slowly solidifies itself into the reality of an approaching civil war. A car backfiring outside sounds like gunfire (Kane 2001: 28). Later, Cate looks outside and casually observes that it '[l]ooks like there's a war on' (Kane 2001: 34). The next time there is a knock on the door, the soldier enters bringing the edges of the space of brutality with him. He claims the space by urinating on the bed. Seconds later, the space of brutality rips through the privileged space of the hotel room.

There is a blinding light, then a huge explosion.

[...]

The hotel has been blasted by a mortar bomb.
(Kane 2001: 39)

The force with which the space of brutality explodes through the space of the hotel room reflects the inward-looking nature of the space of privilege. The world beyond the hotel room is hidden from view. Cate and Ian only take brief glimpses outside. As theatre scholar Graham Saunders observes, Kane presents British society as insular. Even as a journalist, Ian has no interest in the wider world. When he reports on a serial killer in New Zealand, his article focuses exclusively on the single British victim. As Ian explains to the soldier: 'I'm a home journalist, for Yorkshire. I don't cover foreign affairs' (Kane 2001: 48). Ian is blind to the suffering of those outside the space of privilege. His blinding offers a physical image of his blindness to the misery of others.

Blasted attempts to challenge the idea of British society as civilized, free from the seeds of brutality: the 'widespread attitude' that 'what was happening in central Europe could never happen here' (Sierz 2000: 98). As Radosavljević notes, the play achieves this through 'a twofold use of place: a juxtaposition between a culturally specific and that which would have been considered positively "universal"' (Radosavljević 2012: 504). The space of brutality is usually positioned as the culturally specific space of the 1990s Balkan conflict. The space of privilege is read as a generic globalized space, in line with Kane's characterization of the hotel as the kind that *'could be anywhere in the world'* (Kane 2001: 3).

The spatial dramaturgy of the play, however, can be read as offering a reversal of this reading. The privileged space of the hotel room is culturally specific. Kane locates the hotel *'in Leeds'* (Kane 2001: 3). The play is littered with references to British culture: 'A-levels' (Kane 2001: 13), 'United beat Liverpool 2–0' (Kane 2001: 19), 'English breakfasts' etc. (Kane 2001: 34). In contrast, the space of brutality is generic. There are no geographical or cultural references to link it to a specific location. The descriptions of violent acts within the space of brutality are non-specific:

Went to a house just outside town. All gone. Apart from a small boy hiding in the corner. One of the others took him outside. Lay him on the ground and shot him through the legs. Heard crying in the basement. Went down. Three men and four women. Called the others. They held the men while I fucked the women.

(Kane 2001: 43)

As Saunders notes, the space of brutality was specifically characterized as the space of the 1990s Balkan conflict in early drafts of the play but, in the final draft, these specifics were removed. For example, the soldier loses his Slavic name, 'Vladek', becoming simply 'Soldier' (Saunders 2002: 53). Kane herself states that the spatial dialectic is between a specifically British space and a generic space of civil war: 'the safety and civilization of peacetime Britain and the chaotic violence of civil war' (Kane quoted in Saunders 2002: 45).

The space of privilege and the space of brutality, however, share common features. Both are spaces of tribalism. The soldier takes time to establish which tribe Ian is from: 'Welsh as in Wales' (Kane 2001: 41). Ian characterizes football grounds as spaces of tribal warfare by suggesting sending 'a bomber over Elland Road' to finish off the 'queers' and the 'wogs' (Kane 2001: 19). Ian and the soldier are flipsides of the same character. Ian is also a soldier. He claims to have been a '[k]iller' in the service of the British government (Kane 2001: 30). Ian imagines the soldier in scene one, symbolically bringing him into being within the space of privilege. He foresees the very situation he later finds himself in with the soldier:

Cate Who'd have a gun?

[...]

Ian Someone like me.

[...]

Cate Why would they shoot at you?

Ian Revenge.

(Kane 2001: 29)

Ian commits acts of sexual violence against Cate, just as the soldier commits acts of sexual violence against Ian. He does this because she is the enemy: 'I love this country. I won't see it destroyed by a slag' (Kane 2001: 32). The soldier is positioned as an extreme version of Ian. Ian has raped Cate but the soldier has raped many women: 'You did four in one go, I've only ever done one' (Kane 2001: 44). Ian recognizes that the soldier is like him but '[w]orse' (Kane 2001: 40). Both the soldier and Ian commit acts of sexual violence at gunpoint. The soldier holds the gun to Ian's head and rapes him. Ian holds the gun to Cate's head and simulates sex with her. The same images are repeated in both the space of privilege and the space of brutality. One space is not simply the product of the other. They are simultaneously one and the same space. The space of privilege is a space of brutality. Spatial unity is observed: 'the time and action are disrupted while the unity of place is retained' (Kane quoted in Saunders 2002: 41).

Instead of offering a juxtaposition between the two seemingly irreconcilable spaces of privilege and brutality, *Blasted*'s spatial dramaturgy offers a succession of spaces of brutality. The space of privilege becomes a space of war. At the beginning of scene five, Cate buries the dead baby under the floor, transforming the space of war into a graveyard, a space of death. Kane states that, with

Ian's death, the graveyard is transformed into a space of hell: 'he's in hell – and it's exactly the same space he was in before, except that now it's raining' (Kane quoted in Saunders 2002: 59). Spaces shift and consume each other but, at the same time, space remains the same. Each successive space retains scenic features linked to previous spaces. The hotel room is blasted but traces of its elements remain visible but transformed in the debris. The flowers in the hotel room in scene one become the petals on the baby's grave in scene five.

Cate experiences a similar liquidity and layering of space during her fits:

The world don't exist, not like this.
Looks the same but –

(Kane 2001: 22)

This layering of space is accompanied by a layering of time: 'Feels like I'm away for minutes or months sometimes, then I come back just where I was' (Kane 2001: 10). The liquid spatio-temporal structures that Cate experiences during her fits are reflective of the liquid spatio-temporal structures of the play's dramaturgy. *Blasted*'s spatial structures layer a series of seemingly irreconcilable simultaneous spaces into a single space. Its temporal structures move in minutes and months at the same time. The events of the play happen close together in time. Scene two takes place the morning after scene one. Scene three takes place on the same day as scene two. The passing of time, however, is also measured by the sound of the rain between scenes, suggesting the passage of months not minutes. Between scenes one and two, there is '[t]he sound of spring rain' (Kane 2001: 25). Between scenes two and three, there is '[t]he sound of summer rain' (Kane 2001: 39). This duality of time matches the duality of space. Layered temporal and spatial schema run side by side.

Blasted presents its audience with a dramatic world that is liquid and layered, reflecting an uncertainty about the nature of space. Lived spaces are no longer concrete and discrete. In a globalized world, they simultaneously layer concrete, mediated and virtual spaces. The only thing that is certain about space, Kane suggests, is that it is infused with an inherent brutality.

San Diego

While *Blasted* layers space, collapsing seemingly irreconcilable spaces into one another, David Greig's *San Diego* (Tron, Glasgow/ Edinburgh International Festival 2003) is generative of new spaces. In the play, a playwright called David Greig is on his way to San Diego to visit the La Jolla Playhouse. Once in San Diego, he gets lost and is stabbed by an illegal immigrant called Daniel. The Pilot who flew David Greig's plane to San Diego and a prostitute called Amy try to save him, but he dies. Another David finds himself as a patient in a mental hospital. He falls in love with a patient called Laura, the Pilot's daughter. Together they escape to a beach in Scotland, where Laura attempts to commit suicide and David saves her. The subplots of the play tell the stories of: a woman, Marie, who is having a spiritual crisis; an actor, Andrew, who is playing a fictional pilot in a film; an illegal immigrant, Daniel, who is searching for his mother with the help of two tramps, Pious and Innocent; and a group of Davids working in a conceptual advertising agency.

The play is organized on a predominantly spatial as opposed to temporal basis. The characters travel through capitalist spaces, inscribed with the pressures of consumption and globalization, and pre-capitalist spaces, inscribed with images of agro-pastoral villages and nomadic communities. The capitalist 'space of accumulation' (Lefebvre 1991: 263), with the marketplace at its centre, is placed in negotiation with pre-capitalist 'absolute space', with the sacred at its centre instead (Lefebvre 1991: 234).

As in *Blasted*, space in *San Diego* is shifting and uncertain. All the characters are lost. The San Diego that the characters are lost in is not the 'real' San Diego but an imagined San Diego, dreamt up by the playwright David Greig during a twenty-minute drunken nap, as his plane comes in to land. In the original production, the face of the actor playing David Greig surveyed the play's action from a video screen, reminding the audience they were watching a 'strange surreal dream play' (Greig 2003). The space of the plane in which David Greig has his dream is a site of time-space compression. The plane crosses time zones as it flies, compressing many moments in time into the same moment. It is both '3.17pm San Diego Time, 11.17pm London time' (Greig 2010: 8). It is a space that simultaneously compresses many spaces into a single space. In Toronto airport, a Scottish playwright flying to the American city of San Diego drinks Canadian 'Molson' beer while watching a 'Filipino woman refuelling a 747' (Greig 2010: 7) and reading an article in a 'British newspaper about a Quebecois biologist' who led a flock of orphaned geese back to 'their summer breeding grounds in the Arctic' (Greig 2010: 8).

At the same time, the space inside the plane is positioned as offering spatio-temporal security amid the spatio-temporal confusion outside. As a David who works in the conceptual ad agency observes, a 'person needs to know where they are, where they're going and what time it is'. In a plane, they do. The only time that exists is universal coordinated time, which is unaffected by shifts from time zone to time zone. The space inside the plane stays the same as the plane moves through space. Tickets state each passenger's destination so they can be sure 'where they're going'. The moving map on the back of the seat enables the passenger to locate themselves in space and each passenger is given an allocated seat, so they know exactly 'where they are'. The plane is a space in which the social subject can feel safe and insulated against spatio-temporal confusion. It 'is the only space where we can be certain we belong'. It is 'home' (Greig 2010: 82).

The plane is represented as both a capitalist and a pre-capitalist space. The plane is a symbol of global financial capitalism, of the networks and flows that connect its spaces. The consultants at the conceptual ad agency, however, rethink the plane as a pre-capitalist village. The plane is a community in itself. The Boeing 777 is designed to carry 256 passengers, which one of the Davids states is the size of the ideal human community: 'The human mind evolved to cope with a community of two hundred and fifty-six people' (Greig 2010: 83). The inhabitants of this flying pre-capitalist village have a sense of 'belonging'. It is their 'place of birth' (Greig 2010: 72). They enact the spatio-temporal rhythms of everyday pre-capitalist society:

Men chew betel nut
They spit juice on the ground
In a lazy arc
It's slow. It's a rhythm.

(Greig 2010: 74)

The village has a 'symbolic centre', a 'transformative space'. It is neither 'a pub' nor a 'village square' nor a 'Banyan tree' (Greig 2010: 74). It is a 'place of praying' filled with '[s]moke' and '[d]arkness', a 'secret chamber', the domain of the 'shaman' or the 'magician' (Greig 2010: 76). The village's sacred centre identifies it as an absolute space.

Absolute space is a 'fragment of agro-pastoral space' inhabited by 'peasants, or by nomadic or semi-nomadic pastoralists' (Lefebvre 1991: 234). It is a space that is lived and embodied rather than represented and known: 'meaning addressed not to the intellect but to the body' (Lefebvre 1991: 235). The sacred space at its centre is endowed with religious or magical power. It is a holistic space, 'at once and indistinguishably mental and social, which *comprehends* the entire existence of the group concerned' (Lefebvre 1991: 240, emphasis in original). This agro-pastoral absolute space is relocated by the consultants to the plane. The 'cockpit' becomes the space's magical centre and the pilot its 'chief' (Greig 2010: 77). The plane's spatial characterization is a contradictory one. It enfolds within it spaces of dislocation and belonging, spaces of global financial capitalism and absolute space.

The space of San Diego also enfolds the seemingly contradictory spaces of global financial capitalism and absolute space. The first half of the play is dominated by spaces of global financial capitalism: spaces of work (a film set, a brothel and a call centre) and spaces of transit (a plane, a motel and the freeway). Things are produced and consumed. The Pilot, Andrew and the Stewardess drink beer and whisky, Pious and Innocent shape meat into patties and David the patient and the Pilot look at pornography. Space itself is consumed. The desert is literally eating San Diego: 'the desert is hungry for the city' (Greig 2010: 45). The body, too, becomes subject to this hunger. Laura consumes her own flesh, describing this process in food preparation terms, invoking the processes of the meat industry. She tells the counsellor that she is not cutting herself but 'butchering' herself. She wants to be 'cured' (Greig 2010: 48). Laura grounds her relationship to David in a series of puns equating love with consumption: 'Do you want me tender?' (Greig 2010: 84). Laura's blurring of love, sex and consumption does physical harm to her body: '*Laura comes in, limping badly*' (Greig 2010: 89). She screams when she cuts herself (Greig 2010: 36, 86). The processes of global financial capitalism are positioned as harmful to the social subject.

In the second half of the play, absolute spaces appear within San Diego, eventually dominating the space of the city. The characters who were lost find a sense of belonging within these spaces. Daniel and Pious visit Paul McCartney to find out the truth about Daniel's mother. Paul McCartney's office corresponds to the sacred space of the chief in the village. It's a 'place you're not allowed into' (Greig 2010: 76): 'It's dark. It's behind a door. And it contains ... everything' (Greig 2010: 77). The office is positioned as a 'transformative place' (Greig 2010: 74). It is where Daniel realizes his true reason for coming to San Diego. The fictional pilot Andrew is playing in the film is found by a fictional Bedouin in the desert on *'the point of death'* (Greig 2010: 89). The Bedouin is not a real Bedouin, but his *'white disdash'* imbues him with the same authority (Greig 2010: 94). The Bedouin offers Andrew's wife, Marie, sanctuary in his fictional encampment, which echoes the consultant's concept of the plane as a village. Both are villages with a 'well' (Greig 2010: 75, 95) and spaces where men and women have different social lives (Greig 2010: 74–5, 94–5).

As the play progresses, its spaces become dominated by nature, becoming increasingly sandy. The action moves between a beach in San Diego, the Nevada Desert and a beach in Scotland. In these sandy environments, characters find a sense of belonging. They are all in need of 'more desert' (Greig 2010: 101). Laura reconnects with a strong, innate sense of direction on a beach in Scotland:

I know where I'm going
It's in my brain
I know – I can see a direction

(Greig 2010: 114)

She becomes focused and purposeful, like the geese that fly past on their way to Greenland. As the play ends, David Greig returns his characters to the elements. Sea enters the space. In San Diego, Amy the prostitute and the Pilot meet on a beach and *'walk into the sea holding hands'* (Greig 2010: 120). Daniel's mother promises him that '[w]e'll go swimming in the ocean' (Greig 2010: 112). In the end, Daniel returns not to the sea but to the air. He takes flight on the plane 'high up in the Jetstream' (Greig 2010: 119). There is a spatial progression in the play from the networks and flows of financial capitalism through spaces of pre-capitalist societies back to the natural 'simplicity' of the desert, the beach, the sea and the air (Greig 2010: 100).

The character of these absolute and natural spaces, however, is not clear-cut, as they remain enfolded within spaces of global financial capitalism. The Bedouin encampment, where Marie finds sanctuary, is part of a film set. It has 'total coverage' for her mobile phone (Greig 2010: 76). It is both ancient and modern simultaneously. The plane is rethought as an agro-pastoral village as part of a rebranding of air travel in order to allay the anxiety that 'acts as a disincentive to air travel' (Greig 2010: 82). A utopian reading of the play is disturbed by the fact that its absolute spaces are the product of capitalism. Despite this, the play can still be read as resisting capitalism as, within its seemingly capitalist spaces, earlier spaces from different modes of production continue to persist. As Lefebvre argues: '[n]othing disappears completely […] what came earlier continues to underpin what follows' (Lefebvre 1991: 229).

As *San Diego* folds the spaces of global financial capitalism and absolute space into each other, it generates layers of lived space, representations of space and imagined spaces.[4] San Diego is simultaneously a physical space, a representation of space defined by a guidebook and an imagined space existing only in David Greig's dream. At the beginning of the play, a disjuncture between lived space and representations of space is enacted. The characters are lost in the city. The transport and communication networks that connect its spaces are disrupted. Laura tries to call her father but the phone is never answered. David Greig's 'automatic' car fails to take him to the correct destination (Greig 2010: 15). Representations of space, such as maps, that should help the characters locate themselves, are useless. All the geographical points of reference by which the characters could orientate themselves have vanished. The Pilot cannot find the street names that would help Amy locate him. He cannot see the ocean from his apartment, despite its name, 'Pacific View' (Greig 2010: 18). Maps of space no longer reflect the physical infrastructure of the city.

Representations of San Diego's space fail to match the lived experience of its space because the San Diego the characters inhabit is not the real San Diego. David Greig has been reading the

---

[4]For Lefebvre's definition of lived space, representations of space and imagined spaces, see pp. 71–2.

Blue Guide to San Diego on the plane: 'I always like to know the facts about a place'. The San Diego in which the play is set is an expansion of the San Diego described in the guidebook. The facts about the city become expanded out into the dramatic space of the play. David Greig informs the audience that San Diego serves as the 'backdrop for several episodes of *America's Missing Children*' (Greig 2010: 7). San Diego is indeed a space where people disappear from view. The illegal immigrants Pious, Innocent and Daniel do not officially exist. Daniel's mother is missing. Laura can never reach her father, the Pilot, on the phone. Andrew and Marie's baby is never seen, but only heard breathing through a baby monitor.

San Diego is a space that is both 'anonymous' and 'familiar' (Greig 2010: 38). The guidebook states that: 'San Diego has featured in almost no fictions, films, novels or plays' (Greig 2010: 7). It is, instead, the generic American city, used in films as 'a substitute for other American cities' (Greig 2010: 35). It is a city of reproduced spaces. Its theatre is 'an exact reproduction of Shakespeare's Globe' (Greig 2010: 34). Its inhabitants stay in houses that are not homes, global hotel chains, motels and anonymous apartment blocks, connected by a system of nameless highways. The inhabitants themselves are anonymous. It is a city where 'everybody is called Amy' (Greig 2010: 56).

San Diego is positioned as the embodiment of the American dream. The guidebook claims that it 'has the highest quality of life of any city in the United States' (Greig 2010: 7). This idea is embodied in Patience/Amy, Daniel's Nigerian mother, who came to San Diego with nothing and worked her way out of a 'massage parlour' (Greig 2010: 111) and 'into real estate' (Greig 2010: 112). The privileged space of those who attain their American dream is contrasted with the space of those who are excluded from that dream. The poor are violently pushed away from the centre. Pious and Innocent are left to scrape a life together on the peripheries, inhabiting a space '[u] nder the freeway, beside a small muddy gutter' (Greig 2010: 24). The violence innate within this space is hinted at in the guidebook's observation that the Pacific's water is 'the same temperature as blood' (Greig 2010: 38). Blood runs through the peripheral spaces in the play. David Greig bleeds to death in the dust at the side of a highway. Innocent is shot under a freeway bridge.

David Greig's San Diego is what Lefebvre terms an abstract space. Abstract space is generated by representations of space, such as maps or plans, and generates a 'false consciousness' (Lefebvre 1991: 310) of space because it contains 'representations derived from the established order: statuses and norms, localized hierarchies and hierarchically arranged places, and roles and values bound to particular places' (Lefebvre 1991: 311). Abstract space is 'repressive in essence' (Lefebvre 1991: 318). David Greig's San Diego is an abstract space because it is generated from a representation of space in a guidebook rather than from lived experience. Such abstract spaces are positioned as a source of both disorientation and distress for the social subject. David has 'attention deficit disorder' (Greig 2010: 54). Laura is suicidal and self-harms. Marie is suffering from severe anxiety: 'After every breath, I'm scared the next breath isn't coming' (Greig 2010: 12). Marie's baby is suffering from a rash caused by the heat or the water or the 'terrible world' they inhabit, '[s]o terrible even his skin reacts to it' (Greig 2010: 60).

The lived space of San Diego is enfolded in the representations of its space in a guidebook and in turn these representations of space are enfolded in virtual spaces. David Greig's San Diego is ultimately the imagined space of his dreams. San Diego is a space in which other spaces are imagined. The film set imagines the Nevada Desert to be a desert in the Middle East. It imagines a Bedouin and a Bedouin camp. Andrew the actor plays the imaginary pilot of an imaginary plane, which crashes into this imaginary desert. San Diego acts as an 'unnamed backdrop' and so is open to constant reimaginings (Greig 2010: 7). It is a dynamic and shifting space, which 'disorders representations of space and transforms them into representational space' (Lefebvre 1991: 232). As such, it is productive of new spaces, articulating new sets of social structures and the power relations that go hand in hand with them. It is a politically productive space that produces spaces within the space of global financial capitalism that are or have the potential to be free from its governance. Through its spatial dramaturgy, David Greig's *San Diego* imagines a space that has agency.

In serious drama, dramatic space is often thought of as setting. Elam's spatial codes suggest, however, that dramatic space is more than a simple representation of lived space. Crouch, in attempting to annihilate the difference between lived and dramatic space in *The Author*, emphasizes the irreconcilable nature of the two, shifting the action of the play from the concrete space of the theatre into the virtual space of his audience's imaginations. Stein explores the potential of such virtual spaces (or lang-scapes) and raises the possibility of ordering meaning on a spatial as opposed to a temporal basis through them. In *Party Time*, Pinter employs lang-scapes to explore the political relationship between the seemingly contradictory spaces of privilege and brutality. By layering these spaces, he suggests a symbiotic relationship between them. Both Kane and David Greig present the audience with a series of liquid spaces that consume each other. In *Blasted*, these shifting, simultaneous spaces are united by the presence of brutality at their core. In *San Diego*, they become productive of new spaces with new sets of social structures, suggesting that space is capable of changing its political character.

Dramatic narratives are plotted through time and in space. Shifts in spatio-temporal structures inevitably cause shifts in the nature of the dramatic narrative. The next chapter will examine the proposition that as the spatio-temporal structures of drama become increasingly liquid, simultaneous and virtual, the causal structures that shape dramatic narratives become more networked and more indeterminate.

5

Plot

The new school of play-writing must systematically see to it that its form includes 'experiment'. It must be free to use connections on every side

BRECHT 1964: 46

The previous two chapters explored shifts in the spatio-temporal structures of drama in contemporary British plays in response to shifts in the social structures that shape lived experience under the pressures of global financial capitalism. They argued that as modernity becomes more liquid in character, temporal structures become more simultaneous, while spatial structures become more virtual.

As dramatic narratives are plotted through time and space, a shift in the spatio-temporal structures of drama inevitably causes shifts in the structure of the dramatic narrative. This chapter will explore the ways in which the structure of the dramatic narrative has responded to these shifts, arguing that as spatio-temporal structures become more simultaneous and virtual, dramatic narratives become more networked and indeterminate, presenting the world as 'an infinite collection of possibilities' (Bauman 2012: 61). The first half of the chapter examines the causal structures that underlie plot structure. It argues that the plot structures of serious drama are connected through linear mechanical causation and driven by desire. Consequently serious drama's political character can be thought of as determinist, capitalist and reflective of solid modernity's belief in progress as 'a road with an *a priori*, pre-ordained finishing line' (Bauman 2012: xi). English playwright

Mike Bartlett's *Contractions* (2008) is analysed as a play that exposes the capitalist political character of serious drama's plot structures through its dramaturgical structures. Plot structures based on alternative causal models are explored through analyses of English playwright debbie tucker green's *Generations* (2007) and English director Rupert Goold and English dramaturg Ben Power's adaptation of Italian playwright Luigi Pirandello's *Six Characters in Search of an Author* (2008). These alternative plot structures are argued to encourage processes of reading and rereading. The second half of the chapter investigates a shift in the traditional relationship between plot and story through an exploration of English playwright Martin Crimp's *The City* (2008) and English playwright Mark Ravenhill's *The Experiment* (2009). It argues that this shift has an ethical dimension through its questioning of the politics of socio-psychological causation.

Plot and story

Dramatic narratives are composed of two distinct elements: plot and story. Edgar defines story as 'the bare, chronological succession of events' and plot as 'the events as they are ordered and connected' (Edgar 2009: 19). The relationship between plot and story can be viewed from two different perspectives. In the first, story is the raw material from which writers construct plots. In the second, plot is the raw material from which audiences generate stories.

The division of dramatic narrative into plot and story dates back to Aristotle. Aristotle views story as a stable referent and plot as a variant of it. Tragedies are based on pre-existing stories. Playwrights adapt these into tragic form through the process of plotting. Not all the events of the original story are included in the plot: 'one should not compose a tragedy out of a body of material which would serve for an epic' (Aristotle 1996: 30). Instead, the playwright selects a set of unified events from the story. Plotting also involves the 'organisation of events' (Aristotle 1996: 11). Unlike the random events of everyday life, Aristotle argues that the events of a plot have a recognizable structure: 'action in real life becomes muthos [plot], that is, an ordered sequence of events' (Aristotle 1999: 10).

Similarly, Russian formalist Viktor Shklovsky defines story as the basic storyline and plot as the structure through which that storyline is told: 'the plot of Eugene Onegin is not the love between Eugene and Tatiana but the appropriation of the story line in the form of digressions that interrupt the text'. Like Aristotle, Shklovsky views story as 'nothing more than material for plot' (Shklovsky 1990: 170). Shklovsky sees plot structure as the product of 'the artist's conscious choice' (Shklovsky 1990: 44). The writer's decisions about which story events to include and their organization carry meaning. Therefore, the structure of a plot reveals the author's intention, the 'force of will driving an artist to create his artefact piece by piece as an integral whole' (Shklovsky 1990: 41).

From this perspective, story is thought of as the stable entity. Plotting is the act of interpretation. As literary theorist Jonathan Culler observes, there are 'various contrasting ways of viewing and telling a given story, and this makes "story" an invariant core, and a constant against which the variables of narrative presentation can be measured' (Culler 1981: 170). Meaning is located in the different ways the same story is plotted by different writers.

The relationship between plot and story can easily be turned upside down. Plot can be seen as the raw material from which audiences construct stories. Elam argues that, while watching a play, the spectator works 'at piecing together into a coherent structure the partial and scattered bits of dramatic information that he receives from different sources. The effective construction of the dramatic world and its events is the result of the spectator's ability to impose order upon a dramatic content whose expression is in fact discontinuous and incomplete' (Elam 2002: 88–9). This approach assumes that audiences, like playwrights, are experts in dramatic structure. The playwright constructs a play with reference to a set of rules. The audience then use the same rules to decode it, building their own story by making sense of the incomplete information given in the plot. Each spectator 'anticipates events, attempts to "bridge" incidents whose connection is not immediately clear and generally endeavours to infer the overall frame of action from the bits of information he is fed. In trying to project the possible world of the drama, the spectator is principally concerned with piecing together the underlying logic of the action' (Elam 2002: 108). Story is no longer the stable entity; it is a shifting construct within the mind of the spectator: 'an abstraction from the *sjuzet*/plot [...] a *paraphrase* of a pseudo-narrative kind, made, for example, by a spectator or a critic in recounting the "story" of the drama' (Elam 2002: 108, emphasis in original). Plot is now seen as the stable entity instead. The audience's construction of story from plot becomes the interpretative act.

These two different perspectives locate the production of meaning in different places: 'In the first the plot is seen as an interpretation of the story. In the second the plot generates the story [...] through the need for the characters and the audience to find a cohesive story behind the plot' (Culler 1981: 175–6). The first locates meaning in the writer's construction of the plot. As Edgar puts it, 'the play's meaning is demonstrated by the way it's put together' (Edgar 2009: 28). The second locates meaning in the act of reading. As Barthes observes, 'a text's unity lies not in its origin but its destination' (Barthes 1977: 148).

Causation

According to Aristotle, plotting involves the linking of events through what Althusser terms mechanical causality to produce unity of action.[1] The causal structures that link the plot's events are important because they determine the plot's structural shape and its degree of complexity. The degree of its complexity, in turn, determines its magnitude or size.

Aristotle claims that beauty consists of two elements: magnitude and order. The appropriate magnitude for a tragedy is 'such as can readily be taken in at one view'. In the case of plots, they 'should be such as can readily be held in memory' (Aristotle 1996: 14). To achieve this, Aristotle recommends reducing the story down to its essential components by disposing of irrelevant events: '[i]f the presence or absence of something has no discernible effect, it is not part of the whole' (Aristotle 1996: 15). The ideal tragic plot can be summed up in a brief outline. For example:

A man has been away from home for many years; he is kept under close observation by Poseidon, and is alone; at home

---

[1]For an explanation of mechanical causality, see pp. 64–5.

affairs are in such a state that his property is being squandered by the suitors, and plots are being laid against his son. Despite being shipwrecked he reaches home, reveals his identity to a number of people and attacks. He survives and destroys his enemies.

(Aristotle 1996: 28–9)

A single action is not synonymous with a single protagonist. The actions of a single person are not necessarily linked to each other: 'a single individual performs many actions, and they do not make up a single action' (Aristotle 1996: 15). A single unified action describes a set of events linked by mechanical causality. Each event must occur 'because' of another event, not just 'after' it (Aristotle 1996: 18). English novelist E. M. Forster elaborates this idea in his definition of the difference between story and plot: '[t]he king died and the queen died' is story but '[t]he king died and then the queen died of grief' is plot (Forster 2005: 86). A unified plot is a chain of cause and effect. It is 'a complete, i.e. whole, action' as it has 'a beginning, a middle and an end' (Aristotle 1996: 13). A beginning is an event which is not caused by something that precedes it, but results in another event that occurs because of it. A middle is both caused by an event that precedes it and results in another event that occurs because of it. An end is caused by an event that precedes it but does not necessarily cause anything. This chain of causation must arise in line with probability: 'a series of events occurring sequentially in accordance with probability or necessity' (Aristotle 1996: 14).

For an event to be probable or necessary, it must be an event that 'would happen' (Aristotle 1996: 16). The event must seem possible within the bounds of society's conception of how the world works and what it perceives as probable human behaviour. Probability has a political character. The shifting nature of understandings of what is probable is illustrated by Aristotle's own examples of the limits of probable human behaviour. As the social reality of ancient Greece was different from contemporary social reality, some of Aristotle's statements about probable human behaviour seem at odds with modern conceptions of it. Aristotle deems it improbable, for example, that a woman would display courage or cleverness in the same way men do (Aristotle 1996: 24).

Aristotle identifies two types of unified plot. The simple plot is one 'in which the change of fortune comes about without reversal or recognition'. The complex plot is one in which the change involves reversal or recognition. Aristotle considers the complex plot superior to the simple plot. A reversal is a change in the direction of the play's action: 'a change to the opposite in the actions being performed'. A recognition is 'a change from ignorance to knowledge' (Aristotle 1996: 18) that is most effective 'when it occurs simultaneously with a reversal' (Aristotle 1996: 19). The most effective kinds of reversal or recognition arise out of a chain of logical causation, occurring 'as a result of what has happened before, out of necessity or in accordance with probability' (Aristotle 1996: 18). The reversal must be plausible and seem, in retrospect, inevitable. Chance events may astonish an audience, but events are more astonishing if 'they appear to have happened as if for a purpose' (Aristotle 1996: 17).

For the complex plot, Aristotle transforms his original trio of beginning, middle and end into complication, reversal and resolution. Complication is a chain of events leading to a reversal of fortune. The reversal instigates a change in fortune, producing a change in the direction of the play's action and in how the hero's previous actions are read. The resolution is the chain of events set into motion by the reversal. For example, in ancient Greek playwright Sophocles' *Oedipus Rex*, Oedipus needs to solve the murder of King Laius to save the people of Thebes from the plague. During the complication, it is revealed that he ran away from the parents who raised him in Corinth to escape a prophecy that he would murder his father and sleep with his mother. It is also revealed that Oedipus killed an old man on his way to Thebes, where he is now king and married to Laius's widow, Jocasta. At the point of reversal, Oedipus realizes that his real parents are Laius and Jocasta and that Laius was the man he murdered on the road. The play's reversal reveals that by trying to avoid his fate, Oedipus has actually fulfilled it. It establishes the 'correct' reading of events.

Desire

Contemporary serious drama looks to Aristotle as an authority but repurposes his theories to fit its own dramaturgy. For example, a contemporary translation of Aristotle observes that 'the goal of life is an activity not a quality' (Aristotle 1996: 11). Aristotle cannot mean the idea translated as 'the goal of life' in the psychological sense these words now imply. Psychology only appeared as a concept in the late-seventeenth century and our modern sense of it is shaped by its rise as a discipline in the nineteenth century. It is more likely that Aristotle is referring to his own concept of final causes. To explain an action by invoking its final cause is to explain it in terms of its innate purpose. For example, the final cause of rain is to provide water. Rain has no desire to provide water. Rain's final cause is innate within its form. It rains because raining is rain's role in the world. The twentieth-century translation psychologizes Aristotle, revealing an important lens through which the *Poetics* is now viewed, that of desire.

In serious drama, plot is driven by desire. As Edgar notes, this idea rises to prominence with the rise of naturalism and 'was codified by the Russian director Konstantin Stanislavski into a theory of acting which implies a theory of writing' (Edgar 2009: 48). Stanislavski's system of actor training shifts actors away from the performance of feeling towards the doing of actions. It is rooted in the belief that human action is motivated by desire. In *An Actor Prepares*, Stanislavski outlines a system of objectives, actions and obstacles as an analytical tool for actors to use in the creation of a role. The same system is now frequently employed as a playwriting tool. A character is thought of as having an 'objective'. They want something. In order to get it, they have to overcome 'obstacles' that stand in their way. In order to do this, they perform 'actions', specific activities aimed at bringing them closer to their objective. An action can be a physical activity or a perlocutionary speech act (something that is said to encourage the listener to do something). British director Max Stafford-Clark defines an action by using 'a transitive verb' that describes 'the character's intention or tactic' – for example 'to seduce' or 'to threaten' (Stafford-Clark 1997: 66). In a play, each line of dialogue or stage direction constitutes an action through which a character hopes to achieve their objective. For example:

Objectives for the scene: Kite wants to seduce Wilful [Silvia], Silvia wants to fend off Kite

Kite: **Befriends** – Sir, he in the plain coat is Captain Plume; I'm his sergeant and will take my oath on't.

Silvia: **Warns** – What! You are Sergeant Kite!

Kite: **Pleases** – At your service.

Silvia: **Snubs** – Then I would not take your oath for a farthing.
(Stafford-Clark 1997: 67)

The action of one character causes a reaction from another character, producing a chain of causation with every interaction.

The progression of a play as a whole is understood in terms of its super-objective. This is the main line of action that runs through the whole play, drawing all the smaller lines of action within its scope. Stanislavski defines the super-objective as the 'basic purpose of the play'. Everything in a play must point towards the super-objective: 'even the most insignificant detail, if it is not related to the *super-objective*, will stand out as superfluous'. Each scene, composed of its chain of action and reaction, draws towards this over-arching line, producing a linear mechanical plot, not dissimilar to Aristotle's single unified action. Stanislavski defines a play's quality in terms of the quality of its super-objective: 'the greater the literary work, the greater the pull of its super-objective' (Stanislavski 1988: 271, emphasis in original). A play without a strong through line of action has a 'kind of deformed, broken backbone [and] cannot live' (Stanislavski 1988: 277).

Brecht

German playwright and director Bertolt Brecht positions his epic theatre in direct opposition to Stanislavskian dramatic theatre, which he claims 'follows Aristotle's recipe' (Brecht 1964: 87). He argues that Aristotelian plot structure, with its linear mechanical causation, encourages the audience towards a purely emotional engagement with the action of a play. Emotional engagement, he argues, can only occur when the action of a play progresses between two points in a predictable manner: 'emotions will only venture on to completely secure ground'. Dramatic plots with their 'single inevitable chain of events' have a supply and demand structure that provides secure ground for emotional engagement. They engage the audience by creating desire, 'a growing demand', in each spectator for the 'supply' of an event, mirroring capitalist consumption (Brecht 1964: 45). This is problematic because emotional engagement is undesirable in political theatre. It clouds critical thinking and breeds a state of passivity in the audience: 'entire rows of human beings transported into a peculiar doped state [...] Their tense, congealed gaze shows that these people are the helpless and involuntary victims of the unchecked lurching of their emotions' (Brecht 1964: 89).

Linear mechanical plots reduce the spectator's ability to take political action because they present an unalterable vision of the world: 'bundling together the events portrayed and presenting them as an inexorable fate, to which the human being is handed over helpless' (Brecht 1964: 87). Aristotle argues that plots deal with what '*would* happen' under a given set of circumstances: 'the kind of speech or action which is consonant with a person of a given kind in accordance with probability or necessity'. The action should be 'universal' (Aristotle 1996: 16). This produces, Brecht argues, the sense that event A always leads to event B, which always leads to event C under a given set of circumstances, falsely suggesting that this chain of events constitutes a universal pattern. There is little sense of what else '*could* have' happened if the characters had made different choices or taken different courses of action. Dramatic theatre's determinacy 'wears down' the spectator's 'capacity for action' (Brecht 1964: 37).

Brecht is searching for a dramatic form that suggests what '*could* happen' instead of what '*would* happen'. Character actions are presented as specific to a particular character acting under a particular set of social conditions: 'the conduct of the persons [...] is not fixed and "universally human"' (Brecht 1964: 140). Social conditions are historicized as 'the social relationships prevailing between people of a given period' (Brecht 1964: 139). This creates a theatre in which characters are capable of altering, not only their own individual path, but the nature of the social conditions under which they live. Brecht's theatre aims to arouse the spectator's 'capacity for action' (Brecht 1964: 37).

Linear mechanical plots not only wear down the spectator's capacity for action; they also narrow their structures of thinking. They do not allow divergences or digressions. They keep the action of the play on the straight and narrow. As the spectator moves forward with the action, their perception is blinkered. They can only think 'within the confines of the subject'. Their structures of thinking are restricted. Brecht states that 'this passion for propelling the spectator along a single track where he can look neither right nor left, up nor down, is something that the new school of play-writing must reject' (Brecht 1964: 44).

Instead, Brecht urges playwrights to find plot structures that ask the spectator to reread what they see, encouraging them to think critically beyond the parameters of what is presented to them: 'it is perhaps more important to be able to think above the stream than to think in the stream'. He calls this 'complex seeing' (Brecht 1964: 44). Complex seeing encourages the audience to reread and critically examine the attitudes behind different readings. Through complex seeing, the act of reading itself is estranged.

Brecht suggests that plot structures that produce complex seeing move 'in curves'; employ 'montage' instead of 'growth'; progress by 'jumps' instead of 'evolutionary determinism' (Brecht 1964: 37); and have 'no objective but only a finishing point' (Brecht 1964: 45). They employ the use of 'diversions' to disrupt the supply and demand system of dramatic theatre and disable the production of emotional engagement by producing broken-backed plot struc-tures. Stanislavski may dismiss broken-backed structures as dead, but Brecht argues that, as well as discouraging empathy, such structures break the illusion that events are inevitable, revealing them instead as 'human contriving' (Brecht 1964: 87). Brecht encourages playwrights to use as many different forms of causal connection as possible in their search for new plot structures: 'use connections on every side' (Brecht 1964: 46).

Brecht's thoughts on scene structure usefully clarify the kind of plot structure he has in mind. Rather than thinking of a chain where 'one scene makes another', the playwright should think of 'each scene for itself' (Brecht 1964: 37). A Brechtian scene is contained within itself: 'the individual scenes contain their own meaning'. It does not set up the next scene or raise expectations about how the action will develop. It is not necessary to see the previous scene in order to understand the current scene. Each scene is both complete in itself and part of a plot structure in which the scenes are not merely 'subordinate, purely functional component parts to an ending in which everything is resolved' (Brecht 1964: 279).

Brecht favours the use of irregular rhythms and patterns in plot structures, as they draw the audience's attention to the structured-ness of plot. Brecht explains this concept most clearly when he discusses the effect of irregular verse structures in poetry. Regular verse structures identify the words being heard as a poem, but not the particularities of the actual poem being read. The words of the poem 'glide past the ear' without the listener attending to their content. The poem does not 'cut deep enough' into the listener's consciousness (Brecht 1964: 120). Irregular rhythms help the listener to listen, drawing their attention to the poem by disrupting their expectations. The listener questions the poem. Is it a poem? How is it a poem? The particularity of the poem, in terms of its structure, its content and its attitude to that content, is actively registered. The same notion can be applied to dramatic structure. Familiar dramatic structures glide past the spectator like the regular rhythms of verse. The spectator recognizes that they are watching a play, but not the actual content, form and attitude of the play. Disrupted dramatic structure draws the spectator's attention to the particularity of the play by confounding their expectations; the spectator questions whether what they are seeing is a play and if so how it relates to their normal conception of a play. The spectator is activated, because rather than being fed causal links by the playwright, they have to build the connections between dramatic elements themselves. The spectator is asked to actively make sense of what they are seeing, rather than trusting the playwright to make sense of it for them by guiding them towards a 'correct' reading of events.

Brecht outlines two dramaturgical tools for encouraging complex seeing in the spectator. The first is the 'not ... but ...'. This is a gestic construction defining a dialectical attitude, which implies that 'every sentence or gesture in a performance conveys a decision' – 'not that, but this' – containing both the negation of one possibility and the affirmation of another. For every choice a character makes, the writer must allow 'the other possibilities to be inferred' so that the character's actual choice 'only represents one out of the possible variants'. All the things a character 'doesn't do' must be 'contained in what he does' (Brecht 1964: 137). As well as conveying what did happen, a playwright must convey all the possible events that could have happened but did not. The idea of contradiction rather than unity becomes central, producing a plot structure that does not 'rule out all the individual's deviations from the straight course', but instead uses 'such deviations as a motive force of the play's dynamics' (Brecht 1964: 46). The represented always gestures towards the unrepresented.

Theatre scholar Sean Carney links Brecht's 'not ... but ...' to the Freudian concept of *Verneinung* or de-negation. The negation contained in the 'not ... but ...' both negates and at the same time affirms the possibility that is denied. As psychoanalyst Jacques Lacan observes: 'what is simultaneously actualized and denied comes to be avowed' (Lacan 1992: 64). In order to negate a possibility, it is necessary to first of all acknowledge that possibility, and by doing so affirm its existence. The concept of the 'not ... but ...' suggests the possibility of a dramatic structure that presents the audience with an ever-branching web of represented and non-represented possibilities.

Brecht's second tool is the footnote: '[f]ootnotes and the habit of turning back in order to check a point need to be introduced into play-writing' (Brecht 1964: 44). The footnote represents a failure of the linear to contain or represent thought. Thought has overspilled the representational structures available to articulate it, exposing their insufficiency. As Jameson puts it, the footnote 'designates a moment in which systematic philosophizing and the empirical study of concrete phenomena are both false in themselves; in which living thought, squeezed out from between them, pursues its fitful existence in the small print at the bottom of the page' (Jameson 1971: 9). Carney argues that the footnote transforms the passive spectator into 'a reading spectator' (Carney 2005: 34). The play becomes an object that must be read and reread. Complex seeing is induced. Each rereading produces a different reading, so that the text can never be enclosed within one definitive reading.

Both the footnote and the 'not ... but ...' challenge Aristotle's law of magnitude. A plot structure that aims to generate a plethora of possible readings cannot be taken in 'at one view' (Aristotle 1999: 14). Second, they shift the relationship between plot and story away from an Aristotelian perspective, in which plot is seen as an interpretation of the story, towards a viewpoint from which plot is seen as the raw material from which the audience generate a variety of stories, depending on how they choose to interpret the events of the plot.

Contractions

Brecht calls for playwrights to abandon linear mechanical causation. Mike Bartlett's *Contractions* (Royal Court, London 2008), however, demonstrates how a rigid adherence to the logic of linear mechanical causation can act as an effective critique of linear mechanical causality.

The craft of playwriting is haunted by the spectre of the 'so-called' rules of playwriting, which are frequently invoked but rarely explicitly stated. These 'rules' are commonly presented as 'universal' (Hilliard 2014: 385) and ahistorical: 'laws inherent in the nature of the art itself' (Matthews 1906: 19). Playwrights are usually encouraged to challenge this view by breaking these 'so-called' rules. Noel Greig instructs playwrights that 'rules are there to be broken' (Greig 2005: 99). There is, however, a problem with the concept of such rule-breaking in political terms. To break a rule, it is necessary to invoke the rule in question. Rule-breaking breaks rules, while at the same time reaffirming them.

Philosopher Slavoj Žižek argues that breaking the rules actually helps maintain the status quo. He suggests that on the underside of the law there is a shadowy, unwritten code that permits but does not acknowledge certain kinds of transgression. These approved transgressions are vital to ensuring public order as they cement social bonds within a community through a sense of common guilt: 'What most deeply "holds together" a community is not so much identification with the Law that regulates the community's "normal" everyday rhythms, but rather *identification with a specific form of transgression of the Law*'. For example, in the military, transgressions of official regulations, such as the hazing of new recruits, are thought to increase the cohesion of the unit. These approved transgressions also allow potential agitators, 'who, although they violate no public rules, maintain a kind of inner distance and do not truly identify with *l'esprit du corps*', to break some rules without threatening the stability of the community (Žižek 2006: 64, emphasis in original).

Žižek positions breaking the rules as a politically normative act and argues instead that a strict adherence to the rules is more politically productive. An '*over-identification*' with the rules '*frustrates*' the system and exposes its underlying nature (Žižek

2006: 65, emphasis in original). For an example of successful overidentification, Žižek looks to the work of Neues Slowenisches Kunst. In 1987, a group of artists related to the movement, Novi Kolektivizem, won a competition to produce a poster to commemorate the Day of the Communist Yugoslav Youth. Their winning poster was a reproduction of a 1937 Nazi propaganda poster in which the insignia had been altered to Yugoslavian equivalents. The poster identified so completely with the values of the communist system in Yugoslavia that it was chosen to represent those values, but the revelation of the poster's origin effectively exposed the regime's underlying authoritarian nature.

Contractions is a play about a rule and the breaking of a rule. It exposes the political character of linear mechanical causation through an overidentification with it in its plot. The play is about Emma, who falls in love with her colleague, Darren. Unfortunately, she forgets, chooses to ignore or has not read a clause in her employment contract prohibiting her from having romantic relationships with her colleagues: 'No employee, officer or director of the company shall engage with any other employee, officer or director of the company in any relationship, activity or act which is wholly, predominantly or partly of a nature which could be characterised as sexual or romantic, without notifying the company of said relationship, activity or act' (Bartlett 2008: 7).

In the first section of the play, Emma assumes, as Žižek suggests, that there is a level of transgression permitted by any system of rules. She ignores the rule, assuming it is one of those rules that can be broken. When the Manager reminds her of the rule, Emma decides not to inform her about her relationship with Darren, despite the fact that her contract compels her to do so. For Emma, the freedom to bend rules is part of what it means to be human. She encourages her manager to break the rules on this basis:

> You're a person.
> You could just let me go.
> If you wanted to.

> (Bartlett 2008: 48)

On the surface, the play deals with an interpersonal struggle between Emma and her manager. It charts Emma's relentless pursuit of her personal desires despite the obstacles in her way, and in doing so adheres firmly to a Stanislavskian plot structure based on linear mechanical causation. Every action Emma takes towards being with Darren produces a reaction from the Manager towards breaking them up in accordance with the rule. In the first section of the play, Emma deliberately flouts the rule by going out for dinner with Darren. When questioned about this by the Manager, she replies that the dinner was not romantic. The Manager tells Darren the dinner was not romantic. Darren then breaks up with Emma. In the second section of the play, Emma follows the terms of her contract to the letter. She tells the Manager about her relationship with Darren. The Manager asks her to sign a new contract setting out an end date for the relationship. Emma gets pregnant, thinking this will extend the end date. The Manager threatens her with breach of contract, forcing her to end the relationship. Emma has the baby. The Manager relocates Darren to Kiev, because the baby constitutes a continuing sexual relationship. The baby mysteriously dies. Emma argues that Darren can now return from Kiev. The Manager informs her that Darren does not think there is anything for him to come back for now that the baby is dead. Darren and Emma's relationship is ended again. Emma's actions are all successfully reversed by the Manager, bringing her back into line with the rule.

Emma employs emotional means to achieve her objective and becomes increasingly emotional as the play progresses. In scene eight, she attempts to win the Manager over by encouraging her to empathize with the painful situation the couple are in:

> he said that we would have to leave. That he couldn't bear the thought of not being with me. He held my hand and told me that no one could pull us apart. He said that he would protect me, and that we could live as a family. That we would make it work somehow. But I said with a baby, we can't afford to be out of work, we just can't, the way things are these days. That we had to think of the baby first. Then he started to cry and I took my hand away, and we sat for about five minutes not saying anything.
>
> (Bartlett 2008: 32)

By scene twelve, Emma's emotional agitation reaches such a height that she can only express herself by vomiting.

The Manager operates on a purely rational plane. She is the embodiment of global financial capitalism. She has no name and is purely identified with her job title. She views the world in terms of economic relations and the contracts that are used to define and protect them. She is without compassion in her quest to secure maximum efficiency from her employees. Emma repeatedly appeals to the Manager's humanity, asking her to acknowledge a human need for: 'Mess. Play. Failure' (Bartlett 2008: 49). The Manager, however, cannot be humanized. All Emma's emotional attempts to do this fail. The Manager understands nothing about human emotions. She responds to Emma's description of the couple's pain by pointing out Emma's inability to measure time correctly: 'I've got that you sat together without saying anything for ten minutes' (Bartlett 2008: 32). She defines romance in legal terms, according to the company's contractual definition of it: 'Any gesture, indication, communication (verbal or otherwise), appearance, message, understanding or organised meeting or event which is perpetrated with a view to advancing the relationship towards love' (Bartlett 2008: 12).

The Manager is concerned with the accumulation of capital, not the well-being of her employees. She only remembers her 'duty of care' (Bartlett 2008: 46) and sends Emma to 'see someone' (Bartlett 2008: 47) when her 'sales figures are down' (Bartlett 2008: 46). The Manager understands personal relationships purely in economic terms as a threat to productivity. By the final scene, Emma, too, has learnt to define herself in economic terms. She measures her own health through the health of her sales figures: 'My sales figures are back to normal after the meeting with the doctor [...] I think it's all going very well' (Bartlett 2008: 51). She has been moulded into a model employee, but the process has dehumanized her.

There are moments in the play where Emma appears to be able to escape this dehumanizing system. Each time, however, her escape is foiled by her need for money. It is the need to cover the financial cost of the baby that forces Darren and Emma to split up. They cannot afford to risk redundancy. When Emma attempts to leave the company herself, the threat of being sued for breach of contract forces her to stay. She is trapped by what Randy Martin terms the financialization[2] of everyday life. Her financial obligations trap her

---

[2]Randy Martin argues that as people take on larger levels of debt, they begin to behave more like businesses. Risk-taking replaces labour as the basis for the generation of personal capital. Debts grow and the social subject becomes locked into working to pay them off (Martin 2002).

into the system: 'without money you can't live any life, can you?' (Bartlett 2008: 32).

Contractions presents an image of a financialized society, in which the social subject assumes they are free and able to bend the rules, but in which indebtedness and the need to accumulate capital controls their every move. Bartlett's strict adherence to linear mechanical causation viscerally conveys the inescapable situation Emma contractually ties herself into by 'propelling the spectator along a single track where he can look neither right nor left, up nor down' (Brecht 1964: 44). Bartlett employs the very structure Brecht dismisses as inscribed with the logic of capitalism to critique the socio-economic relations of capitalism itself.

Generations

While Bartlett uses a strict adherence to linear mechanical causation to reveal the dehumanizing effect of the logic of capitalism, debbie tucker green's *Generations* (Young Vic, London 2007) offers an alternative model of plot construction, one that invokes Althusser's concept of expressive causality.[3] The play tells the story of the devastation of a black South African family at the hands of a mystery disease. The plot consists of a single scene repeated in five variations. In each variation, each character speaks almost exactly the same lines of dialogue, but at the end of each variation a character exits the stage and their contribution to the scene is lost. The scenes are underscored at points by the singing of an African choir, whose dirge invokes the names of those who have died from the mystery disease. The singing describes an emotional journey from 'jubilation to hushed lamentation' during the progress of the play (Bassett 2007).

The structure of the play is iterative. Iteration, according to philosopher Jacques Derrida, is repetition with variation. Derrida observes that communication through language is commonly thought of as a process of passing an 'original' utterance full of meaning from one person directly to another. Derrida argues instead that communication is a process of iteration, involving

---

[3]For an explanation of expressive causality, see pp. 64–5.

the repetition of recognizable written and spoken marks, which do not contain meaning in themselves but are part of a shared code: 'a network [*une grille*] that is communicable, transmittable, decipherable, iterable for a third, and hence for every possible user' (Derrida 1988: 8). People understand each other because communication involves the citation of recognizable utterances from a shared code or of new utterances which can be deciphered within the context of that shared code. For example, the phrase 'raining cats and dogs' communicates the idea of heavy rain because it is a recognizable formula within the shared code of the English language.

Iteration, however, 'does not signify simply [...] repeatability of the same, but rather alterability' (Derrida 1988: 119). Part of what is iterated is always different. Only part of the iterated utterance remains the same. For example, in communicating Derrida's concept of iterability, I inevitably alter it, even if I succeed in explaining the concept clearly: '[i]terability alters, contaminating parasitically what it identifies and enables to repeat "itself"; it leaves us no choice but to mean (to say) something that is (already, always, also) other than what we mean (to say)' (Derrida 1988: 62).

Iteration plays a role in everyday rituals. It would be difficult to understand the significance of a ritual 'if its formulation did not repeat a "coded" or iterable utterance, or in other words, if the formula I pronounce in order to open a meeting, launch a ship or a marriage were not identifiable as *conforming* with an iterable model' (Derrida 1988: 18, emphasis in original). For every ritual, there are constitutive rules that generate a basic script. Each individual instance of the ritual, however, contains variations on that script. For example, weddings have basic constitutive rules but can take many different forms.

The iterated scene in *Generations* presents an everyday ritual: cooking the family meal. The family's conversations while cooking concern cooking and courtship. These two ritual activities constitute rites of passage passed down from generation to generation. The conversation ostensibly revolves around the passing down of cooking skills: 'I was the cooker – you was the cookless – I was the cooker who coached the cookless' (tucker green 2005: 72). The family members all understand, however, that cooking has sexual connotations:

Grandma He looked like he needed a meal.
     You looked like you needed a meal.

Dad I needed a meal.

Grandad He looked like I did.

Grandma You needed more than a meal.

(tucker green 2005: 73)

These rites of passage are shared experiences. When describing their individual experience of these rituals, the characters reproduce the same phrases. Mothers remind their daughters: 'I coached you to / cook' (tucker green 2005: 72). Courtship is also described through the reproduction of shared formulae:

Mum This is how they start –

Grandma oh.

Jnr Sister Sis, 'this is how they start'

Dad have to start somewhere –

Mum oh.

Grandad laughs.

     This is how your Father started with me.

Grandma This is how your Father started with me.

(tucker green 2005: 72–3)

Grandma, Mum and Jnr Sister reproduce each other's words and reactions exactly. The use of quotation marks around the younger family members' dialogue implies this process of direct citation. They are learning to reproduce the community's rituals.

The rest of the play enacts the breakdown of the reproduction of these shared rituals. At the end of each iterated scene a member of the family's death is lamented by the choir and they leave the stage.

The youngest generation of the family disappears first: Jnr Sister after scene one; Boyfriend and Girlfriend after scene two. The middle generation follow: Dad after scene three; Mum after scene four. In the final scene, only the grandparents are left. Whereas the first iteration enacts the passing on of shared rituals, the last iteration becomes a lament for this broken chain of inheritance as the older generation are left to iterate what remains of the scene alone. The lines that once celebrated shared experience become a mournful dirge for the younger generations that have been lost.

With each death, the scene decays as that character's words and actions are lost. Despite this, each iteration continues to make sense within its own context. The omitted lines alter the meaning of the scene so that, with every iteration, its sense shifts. In the first iteration, an exchange between the Jnr Sister, the Girlfriend and the Boyfriend implies that the Boyfriend is attracted to the Jnr Sister:

Boyfriend 'You look like – '

Jnr Sister 'Does she look like someone who can't?'

Boyfriend 'You look like someone who could – '

Girlfriend 'Do I look like someone who couldn't?'

Jnr Sister 'She doesn't look like someone who / couldn't.'

Boyfriend 'You look like someone who should.'

(tucker green 2005: 74)

In the second iteration, the surviving lines imply that the Boyfriend is attracted to the Girlfriend instead:

Boyfriend 'You look like – you look like someone who could – '

Girlfriend 'Do I look like someone who couldn't?'

Boyfriend 'You look like someone who should.'

(tucker green 2005: 79)

Though the words remain the same, their meaning and tone is significantly altered.

Each iteration invokes previous iterations. The omitted lines and the missing actors' physical presence remain as a palpable absence. As the content of the scene decreases, the weight of the loss increases. As the *Guardian* theatre critic Lyn Gardner notes, 'the stage suddenly becomes crowded with an appalling absence' (Gardner 2007). Subtle changes in tense and subject in the dialogue accentuate this absence by shifting characters out of the present moment and into the past. Dad's comment about his daughter, '[s]he doesn't cook' (tucker green 2005: 71), shifts to '[s]he didn't / cook' after she dies (tucker green 2005: 82). In the first two iterations, Mum's line 'This is how your Father started with me' is directly addressed to her daughters (tucker green 2005: 79). After both daughters die, the subject of the line alters so that it is addressed to Dad: 'This is how you started with me' (tucker green 2005: 83). After Dad is gone, the line is addressed to Grandma and changes its subject again: 'This is how he started with me' (tucker green 2005: 86). With each death, family members lose their roles within the family. Grandad shifts from 'don't pay your Grandfather no mind' (tucker green 2005: 83) to '[d]on't pay your Father no mind' (tucker green 2005: 86) to '[d]on't pay it no mind' (tucker green 2005: 88). After his granddaughters die, he is no longer a grandfather. After his daughter dies, he is no longer a father. Theatre critic Gerald Berkowitz, writing in the UK's leading theatre industry newspaper *The Stage*, observes that in performance these 'small horrors' such as 'the discovery that Grandfather can no longer be called by that name' produce 'the play's most powerful moments' (Berkowitz 2007).

The main movement in *Generations* is towards decay, but, as Derrida states, the variation inherent in iteration, despite being a corruption of original meaning, generates new meaning. Though the 'moment of its production is irrevocably lost', an iterated utterance gains meaning through its transposition into new situations: '[o]ne can perhaps come to recognize other possibilities in it by inscribing it or *grafting* it onto other chains' (Derrida 1988: 9, emphasis in original). This generative process happens with the lines of dialogue in *Generations*, as they are iterated, gathering new meanings and altering their perlocutionary nature as the context of the situation shifts. The scene itself not only loses content, but gains it. The cause of the deaths is gradually revealed. In the first and second iteration, the Boyfriend articulates the presence of something as an unfinished: 'The –' (tucker green 2005: 75, 80, 81). He is unable to complete the utterance, identifying the nature of this presence: 'The what is there to say?' (tucker green 2005: 75, 81). In the third iteration, the Dad expands the Boyfriend's incomplete utterance to: 'This thing' (tucker green 2005: 84). In the fourth iteration, the Grandma expands it, specifying the nature of the thing: 'This big dying thing' (tucker green 2005: 87). Finally, in the fifth iteration, Grandad expands it again, identifying the presence of the disease: 'This thing. This dying thing … This unease. This dis-ease' (tucker green 2005: 89). Through the process of the iteration, the presence of the disease slowly comes to light.

tucker green's use of an iterative structure can be read as a model of expressive causality. The decay of the family, and by implication a community and its culture, is caused by the presence of a mysterious disease that pervades every element of the community's experience. Rather than telling a story that progresses through linear mechanical causation, tucker green presents us with a worsening situation and slowly brings its cause into focus.

Six Characters in Search of an Author

In *Generations*, tucker green uses iteration to encourage the spectator to read and reread a single basic scene and draw different meanings from it. In contrast, Rupert Goold and Ben Power's radical reworking of Pirandello's *Six Characters in Search of an Author* (Headlong/Chichester Festival Theatre 2008) can be read as encouraging rereading by utilizing the Brechtian strategies of the 'not … but …' and the footnote to create a networked plot structure, evoking Althusser's idea of structural causality.[4]

The first three acts follow the basic plot of Pirandello's original, but Goold and Power relocate the action from a theatre to a television studio. The Producer, Joanna, is editing a drama-documentary about assisted suicide when six mysterious characters appear, demanding she tell their story instead. The six characters view

---

[4]For an explanation of structural causality, see pp. 64–5.

their story as an Aristotelian tragedy based on linear mechanical causality. They are victims of inexorable fate. The events and their individual roles in them are unalterable: 'no matter how many times our story is told, we are always the same' (Pirandello 2008: 62). Once the action of the story has been set in motion, it cannot be stopped. There is a greater force at work behind it, an author or 'creator', driving it ever forward towards its preordained conclusion, selecting and ordering its events. Goold and Power compare the characters' conception of their author to the idea of a God who 'controls aspects of our existence. Including when we begin and when we end' (Pirandello 2008: 36–7). At the same time, they challenge the idea that human destiny is determined by a divine force by introducing the notion of assisted suicide through the drama-documentary. Assisted suicide offers people a degree of control over their fate.

For Joanna, translating experience into a linear mechanical plot is a way of accessing the objective truth about the world. A fictitious documentary about the 1990s Balkan conflict is presented as the ideal example of this process: 'when the Serbian soldier just cracked [...] we just *knew*, that he'd been there at the massacre. And the whole story, the entire thing, hinged on that one moment' (Pirandello 2008: 15–16, emphasis in original). The documentary's plot structure is recognizably Aristotelian. It relies on a moment of reversal that produces a 'correct' reading of events. The ideal drama-documentary is described as sharing some of the dramaturgical features of serious drama. It offers a range of 'intellectual positions, pro-life versus pro-choice, etc.' embodied in the journeys of individual characters (Pirandello 2008: 12). Events are framed within a dramaturgy that produces political impact by creating the illusion of authentic reality: 'keep it real. Mirror up to nature' (Pirandello 2008: 16).

Joanna should be a good author for the characters' story but she struggles to articulate it coherently through a linear mechanical plot structure. Despite the supposedly fixed nature of their story, the characters cannot agree on a singular version of events. They each offer their own subjective retelling of the story and their squabbling over the truth produces a type of Brechtian 'not ... but ...'. For example, the Father and the Stepdaughter disagree over the details of their incestuous liaison. To the Stepdaughter's statement that she was wearing a black dress because she was in mourning, the Father remembers responding: 'I understand, I understand'. In contrast, the Stepdaughter remembers the Father's response as being: 'Well, then, why don't we just take off your dress?' Each character articulates a version of events that supports their own sense of their socio-psychological impact on them: 'all the reasons why I am what I am'. The Father wants 'to piece together a sentimental scene' to protect himself (Pirandello 2008: 55). The Stepdaughter demands that the events be played out in their full horror. Joanna is simultaneously presented with multiple, competing and radically different versions of the story.

The inability of a linear mechanical plot to authentically capture the complexity of reality is highlighted at the beginning of the play. The editing of the drama-documentary distorts the content of the raw footage, shifting the nature of reality. In the opening sequence, the doctor, Lully, is *dabbing at her eye*, unable to hold back her tears at the thought of a child taking their own life. In the unedited footage, however, the action is different: '*[s]he stops mid-sentence, blinks and then giggles. She dabs at her eye*' (Pirandello 2008: 11). Her tears are caused by a loose contact lens. Lully's detached, routine attitude to the child's suicide is edited into a less authentic but more socially acceptable one.

Joanna's adherence to a linear mechanical plot structure forces her to exclude important elements of the reality she is trying to capture, excising any seemingly superfluous connections the drama-documentary makes with the world outside. When Lully's husband links assisted suicide and the character of Hamlet, this connection is discounted as a 'red herring' (Pirandello 2008: 13). The editing process narrows the view, obscuring the full complexity of reality. As the Father explains: 'You look at the world through your viewfinder and you see only shadows. Behind you is the fire' (Pirandello 2008: 61). Joanna's view of the world through the camera's lens becomes the modern equivalent of Plato's cave. Her drama-documentary is full of images that are *at a distance and in shadow* (Pirandello 2008: 9). The fictitious Balkans documentary is entitled *Shadows*, suggesting that even this model example fails to capture an authentic reality (Pirandello 2008: 15).

Goold and Power radically rework Pirandello's original play by adding an entirely new fourth act. The scenes of this act, which Bassett aptly titled 'A Dozen Endings in Search of an Editor', take the form of a series of expanding footnotes (Bassett 2008b). Instead of moving the plot forward, these footnotes add extra layers of meaning to the previous action, encouraging a process of rereading. Goold and Power justify this radical addition to Pirandello's play by referring to the idea that Pirandello was constantly rewriting *Six Characters in Search of an Author*. As a result, the text of Pirandello's original is unstable: 'Pirandello did about six different versions, I mean, he never left the thing alone' (Pirandello 2008: 84). This idea is reinforced in a footnoted scene in which Pirandello struggles and fails to produce a definitive version.

The fourth act begins by replaying the first, repeating its action exactly: '*every move replicated*'. This time, however, the act is played with a directors' commentary over the top. Before the action begins, a projection shows a cursor passing over a DVD menu for 'SIX CHARACTERS REMIX' and selecting the directors' commentary (Pirandello 2008: 73). The directors' commentary footnotes the scene, flagging up the importance of details that might have seemed incidental in the first viewing, such as the film's Danish location. The directors, by implication Goold and Power, stress the importance of authenticity in creating the initial scene of the play. Like the fictitious Producer, they work to capture the reality of the world they are representing: to make 'the world of Joanna and her crew [...] feel as realistic as possible'. By focusing on this, however, they reveal layers and layers of inauthenticity. For example, Lully, supposedly one of the founders of the assisted suicide clinic, is actually just a character played by an actress, Anna-Maria. They praise the authenticity of her performance, while at the same time emphasizing its constructed nature: 'even though everything she does is totally naturalistic, you're always aware that she's acting' (Pirandello 2008: 75). The commentary reveals the creative team's influences – 'Jonze/Kaufman films', 'Lars von Trier' (Pirandello 2008: 78) and 'Haneke' (Pirandello 2008: 79). The editing process is reversed. Instead of narrowing the range of possible connections that can be made, the commentary adds lateral links, creating a web-like structure that widens the scope for interpretation, increasing the number of possible readings of events.

At the end of the first scene, there is a knock on the door on the soundtrack. The onstage action is paused as the Father is heard greeting the Writer and Director. The audience are invited to imagine that the Writer and Director will now be subject to a visit by the six characters and that the whole process of retelling their story will begin with a different set of storytellers. A Russian doll structure is suggested, where the first version of the play's basic plot is framed by another variation, which in turn is framed by yet another variation and so on to infinity. Temporal dramaturgy is dislocated. The footnoted scenes start to take the audience further and further into the past, while Joanna, who observes these scenes alongside them, stays firmly in the present.

Just as the audience are led to believe that another retelling of the six characters' story is about to begin, the action cuts to a new scene in which two theatre-makers (who in the original production visually resembled Goold and Power) try to persuade an Executive to fund a radical reworking of Pirandello's *Six Characters in Search of an Author*. Whereas the directors' commentary commented on the finished production of the play, this footnote comments on the play before it even exists. The theatre-makers describe the idea of the directors' commentary scene that opens the fourth act, creating a footnote to the previous footnote. They reveal the inspirations behind their proposed radical reworking and these inspirations are all around them. The play's setting is inspired by an office they have seen down the hall from the Executive's office. The audience view this scene through the windows of that office, which is also the editing suite where the action of the first three acts took place. The Executive in the fourth act is played by the same actor who played the Executive in the first act, so it becomes clear that the character in the first act is based on the Executive the theatre-makers are now talking to. The action of this footnote is again ended by the entrance of the six characters, who hack the two theatre-makers to death.

The final conversation of the scene is a discussion of Pirandello's difficult relationship with *Six Characters in Search of an Author*. This conversation is footnoted in the following scene. The action of the play moves to Pirandello's study in 1925. In Italian, Pirandello discusses his inability to perfect the play with his maid, the figure in whom he embodies the idea of artistic inspiration (Pirandello 1925). He is 'getting nowhere' (Pirandello 2008: 85) and 'can't seem to find an ending'. The characters then enter and finish the play for him: '[t]he FATHER *writes quickly and certainly in the book and then folds it shut*' (Pirandello 2008: 86). The act finishes with a final footnote in which Hamlet, who was deemed irrelevant in the first act, makes an appearance, asserting his relevance and linking the end of the play back to the documentary at the beginning, with its Danish location and its theme of suicide. The six characters then assist Joanna to commit suicide. The final stage direction, 'An End', avoids narrative closure, emphasizing both the unstable nature of Pirandello's original and the multiple possible other endings suggested by the footnotes (Pirandello 2008: 87).

The final image of Joanna taking her own life at the clinic returns the audience to the drama-documentary footage at the start of the play. The back office of the set is now clearly 'an exact replica of the Dignitas clinic' (Pirandello 2008: 87). The process of rereading starts again. Elements that seemed insignificant in the first viewing of the drama-documentary footage are highlighted in the process of rereading. In the clinic's waiting room, the six characters, another 'family, dressed in black, also waiting', come into view. The nondescript house in the opening shots of the documentary is recognizable as the characters' house. Yet more new connections are made and spread like a 'virus' (Pirandello 2008: 82). The promise of a rational explanation is continually held out to the audience in the fourth act only to be 'hijacked', as the six characters enter and take over each scene (Pirandello 2008: 82). The play's structure reflects Lully's observations on death: 'We all seek the elegant closure of a great novel or a magisterial symphony – the dying fall – but life is often more random [...] a meandering series of commas and hesitating, unfinished sentences' (Pirandello 2008: 13). The audience are left to pull together the connections, searching in vain for a singular version of events, just as the characters do.

Through its dramaturgical structure, Goold and Power's adaptation of Six Characters in Search of an Author suggests that the complexity of social reality exceeds the degree of complexity that can be expressed through a linear mechanical plot structure. It demonstrates that Brecht's alternative dramaturgical tools, the 'not ... but ...' and the footnote, can be successfully utilized in practice to create plays that break with Aristotle's stricture that the magnitude of a work of art 'should be such as can readily be taken in at one view', encouraging instead a process of reading and rereading (Aristotle 1996: 14). The resulting networked structure not only offers an ever-increasing number of alternative readings, but can be read as an attempt to produce a plot structure that exhibits structural causality, repeatedly revealing in footnote after footnote the mechanisms of its own construction.

The City

Goold and Power's adaptation of *Six Characters in Search of an Author* actively encourages its audience to generate a variety of different stories from the vast network of connections made within its plot structure. It views story not as the raw material for plot formation, but as an abstraction created from the plot in the mind of each individual spectator. In recent years, plays such as Martin Crimp's *The City* and Mark Ravenhill's *The Experiment* have exploited this view of plot and story to create dramatic narratives that disrupt the story-making process. These plays contain recognizable plot elements, but their dramaturgical structures make it impossible for the spectator to organize all of these elements into a coherent story.

Martin Crimp's *The City* (Royal Court, London 2008) presents its audience with what literary theorist Brian Richardson terms an 'irretrievable, contradictory, potential and self-negating *fabula*' (Richardson 2007: 66, emphasis in original). Its plot structures disrupt the story-making process to the point where there appears to be no access to a story at all. *The City* appears to be about a middle-class couple, Clair and Chris, who live in a city. The facts of Clair and Chris's story, however, are difficult to establish. Clair works as a translator and wants to be a writer. She creates a city in her imagination that she hopes to people with her stories. Chris works in the city. They supposedly have two children. One of their neighbours, Jenny, is a nurse whose husband is working as a doctor in a war-torn city. Clair meets a writer, Mohamed, and a sexual liaison is hinted at. Chris loses his city job and ends up working behind a meat counter in a supermarket instead.

British theatre critics offered radically different interpretations of the play. As Billington notes, the play's lack of narrative coherence 'allows the audience to create its own story' (Billington 2008d). Robert Hewison, writing in the major UK newspaper *The Times*, argues that the play is a critique of capitalism. He reads the play's title as referring to London's financial district and contextualizes

Clair's internal city, which by the end of the play is destroyed and deserted, as representative of the destructive effects of capitalism: 'the City is a city of the mind, a place of the imagination that is as broken and bereft as Fallujah, itself an emblem of the commercial warfare that is business life' (Hewison 2008). In contrast, Paul Taylor, writing in the *Independent*, argues that the play is about a failing of imagination: 'a play where stories fall apart and where the characters are gradually revealed to be, at least partly, the deformed figments of an imagination that's resentful at its lack of true creativity' (Taylor 2008). Paul Taylor's thesis fits neatly with the words of Fernando Pessoa that Crimp quotes on the title page of the script: '[e]verything we do, in art and life, is the imperfect copy of what we intended' (Crimp 2008: 5).

If, as Paul Taylor suggests, Clair is the author of the play, then what the play lacks is not imagination but story. Clair has plenty of imagination. She imagines fully realized socio-psychological characters. Jenny, the nurse, is haunted by images of the war her husband is involved in. Mohamed, the writer, is separated from his daughter and then must deal with her sudden death. Clair also imagines a fully realized world for her characters to inhabit, where some live in a pristine city 'full of green squares, shops and churches' (Crimp 2008: 61), while others 'cling on to life' in a war-torn city (Crimp 2008: 22). The problem is not Clair's lack of imagination, but an absence of story. She fails to make the clear casual connections between the elements of her plot that would make sense of it.

The play gives the impression of having a conventional plot structure. It contains a series of events and hints at connections between them through coincidence, repetition and imagery. The first scene offers many of the conventional features of opening scenes. It starts with an inciting incident. Clair and Chris's ordinary routine is disrupted by an unusual incident that should kick the action of the play into gear:

Chris How was your day?

Clair My day was fine. Only –

(Crimp 2008: 7)

Clair reveals that she has met a writer, Mohamed, who has given her a diary. Chris reveals that he is in danger of losing his city job.

Heavy exposition is used to establish Clair and Chris as characters. They tell each other things they would both already know, drawing attention to the unnaturalness of conventional exposition. For example, Chris establishes that they have children by reminding Clair that '[t]here are, as you are well aware, two small children sleeping in this house' (Crimp 2008: 13).

The play draws attention to the process of establishing causal links between plot elements. There is a sense of the play being constructed as it is spoken. For example, when Clair describes her meeting with Mohamed to Chris, she appears to be actively building relationships between characters and finding motivations for their actions as she speaks:

> The girl – because they'd just got off the train – the girl had been brought here to stay with the sister-in-law. But the man – the father – had decided at the last moment to buy his little girl a diary [...] his sister-in-law despised him. Which is why [...] the moment he was out of sight she'd deliberately dragged the little girl off.
> (Crimp 2008: 7–8)

Characters outline the socio-psychological causes driving both their own actions and the actions of others, rationalizing them: 'I'm saying I love you because I feel good about myself. I have some very good news' (Crimp 2008: 30). Despite the sense that causal connections are actively being built between plot elements, the causal connections the play offers fail to yield a coherent story. There is an abyss at the heart of the play. The audience become increasingly aware of their role in the process of constructing story because their efforts to do so are frustrated.

In the second scene, things have altered. The characters introduced in the first scene have shifted positions. The nurse who took the child from the railway station is now Jenny, the nurse who lives next door. It is as if the nurse character has been recast in a more suitable role. Jenny's function within scene two is to introduce the world outside the city, which she fulfils with a long, expositional speech about her husband's experiences far away in a war-torn city.

Scene two acts as a key to the rest of the play. The scenes that succeed it are connected to it and to each other through echoes of it. For example, the image of Jenny's war-torn city is echoed by Clair's image of a destroyed city in the final scene:

they're attacking a city – pulverising it, in fact – yes – turning this city – the squares, the shops, the parks, the leisure centres and the schools – turning the whole thing into a fine grey dust [...] people in all sorts of unexpected places, clinging on to life [...] deep under the city – in the drain.

(Crimp 2008: 22–3)

The houses had been destroyed, and so had the shops [...] I looked for the people still clinging on to life [...] in the drains [...] there was nothing – nobody – just dust.

(Crimp 2008: 62)

Crimp's use of language invites the audience to make such connections. His descriptions lack specificity. There is an absence of adjectives. When Crimp does use adjectives, they tend to be simple and childlike, for example: 'your house is much bigger than my tiny flat' (Crimp 2008: 20). This universalizes the objects referred to. The tiny flat could be any tiny flat. There is little to distinguish one object from another. The audience are encouraged to connect objects to each other as if they were one and the same object. For example, the 'small knife with a stainless serrated blade being used to cut the soldier's heart out' (Crimp 2008: 24) ominously becomes the *'small serrated kitchen knife'* that Jenny gives Clair for Christmas (Crimp 2008: 55).

Objects are also linked to each other through visual repetition. Jenny and the girl are strongly linked in this way. The nurse's outfit the woman is wearing in scene one is worn by Jenny in scene two and by the girl in scene four. The pink jeans Mohamed's daughter is wearing in scene one are worn by both Jenny and the girl in scene five. In scene two, Jenny reveals that she plays the piano. In scene four, Chris and the girl are sitting by a piano. In scene five, Jenny *'runs her fingers over the keyboard without making any sound'* (Crimp 2008: 54). Later, the girl attempts to play the piano but keeps getting stuck. A strong connection is implied between Jenny and the girl through these images, but never defined. There is connection but no story.

The play also draws links through coincidence. Everyone knows each other. A local supermarket is a vortex of coincidence for Chris. He first bumped into Jenny there: 'I've seen you somewhere [...] looking in a freezer cabinet in the supermarket' (Crimp 2008:

19). The man behind the meat counter turns out to be an old school friend. There is a sense that, as Aristotle dictates, nothing is random in the play's action. Everyone is somehow part of the story. These coincidences, however, cannot be reconciled. They cannot be pulled together into a single, neat, overarching storyline.

The play contains as much contradiction as coincidence. Characters contradict what they say by what they do. In scene two, Jenny delivers a two-page monologue despite her initial insistence that she does not have any time to talk. Characters describe what they are doing in the moment of doing it – 'you and I are sitting in front of the fire' – but their actual actions contradict what they claim to be doing: '*There is no fire. They are not sitting*' (Crimp 2008: 56). The play's mimetic impulse is challenged. There is a disjunction between the actions outlined in the dialogue and the actions performed onstage.

The play's failure to yield a coherent story is reflected in the unfinished stories that the characters tell. Chris tries to tell Clair the story of being locked out of his building twice. Both times he is interrupted and, in both cases, it is implied that Clair was not listening anyway:

Chris But I've already told you this.

Clair Told me what? Have you?

(Crimp 2008: 15)

The ability to communicate through story has been lost. The structures of storytelling lie empty and broken like the crumbling buildings in Clair's city: 'I looked for the people still clinging onto life – what stories they could tell! – but even there – in the drains, the basements [...] there was nothing – nobody – just dust'. The structures persist but they no longer function to support 'the stories and characters of life' they once did. As Clair states, 'the stories fell apart even as I was telling them' (Crimp 2008: 62).

By presenting recognizable plot structures but preventing them from being linked into a coherent story, Crimp demonstrates that it may be possible for plot to exist without story. This is represented, however, as a nihilistic move. In the play's final moments, the girl attempts to play the piano but finds she can go no further than the fourth bar of the music. She is stuck and, like all the play's unfinished stories, cannot progress. A world without stories is a dead world. Clair's city is deserted. Jenny's piano-playing is full of technique but lacks soul: 'there's no life to my playing' (Crimp 2008: 21). For all its structural bravado, Crimp's play betrays a degree of anxiety about the absence of story at its heart.

The City articulates anxiety about the separation of plot and story that it enacts. The decoupling of this relationship, however, creates space for a radical rethinking of the dramaturgical structures of the dramatic narrative. As Richardson notes, useful as conventional concepts of plot and story remain, through reimagining them it may be possible to 'articulate new, more expansive concepts of story, plot, progression and temporality' (Richardson 2007: 66), which may in turn enable playwrights to write plays which are able to capture more effectively the '[f]iction, fragmentation, collage and eclecticism' of contemporary lived experience under the pressures of global financial capitalism (Harvey 1990: 98).

The ethics of the disrupted story

Despite The City's anxieties about the absence of story, the disrupted story can be read as having an ethical dimension. Philosopher Jean-François Lyotard argues that narratives play a role in defining the legitimacy of actions. Narratives 'define what has a right to be said and done' with a particular society (Lyotard 1984: 23). Lyotard positions narrative as a form of knowledge. Knowledge, Lyotard argues, is not purely a set of denotative statements of what is considered true or false, but also includes the notion of competence, of 'knowing how' – for example, 'knowing how to live' (Lyotard 1984: 18). Narrative is a form of knowledge because narratives define a set of criteria of competence, playing an important role in communicating the knowledge of 'how to live'. In a narrative, characters' actions offer positive and negative models of behaviour: 'narratives allow the society in which they are told, on one hand to define its criteria of competence and, on the other, to evaluate according to those criteria what is performed or can be performed within it' (Lyotard 1984: 20). Narratives legitimate and delegitimate certain actions, defining which actions are acceptable within a particular society and which are not.

Serious drama is positioned as having social value because it enables an understanding of the actions of others, actions that might otherwise appear unacceptable. It explains these 'unacceptable' actions in terms of socio-psychological causation. A character's actions are seen as determined either by their psychology or the social and economic conditions under which they live. For example, the actions of Ibsen's Hedda Gabler can be read as the result of either her unconventionally masculine upbringing or her position as a woman in a society that offers women an unacceptably narrow range of social roles or a combination of both. Serious drama can be argued to have social value because it enables society to understand the socio-psychological causes of 'unacceptable' actions. These can then be addressed to prevent such 'unacceptable' actions being repeated in the future.

In the field of social psychology, the relationship between narrative and the acceptability of the actions it narrates is presented as problematic. Social pyschologists Arthur G. Miller, Anne K. Gordon and Amy M. Buddie note that a large number of books, offering accounts of real incidents of harm doing, begin with a preface in which the writer expresses a concern that to narrate these harmful actions is to condone them. For example, the historian Christopher Browning introduces his account of how a battalion of German policemen were transformed into mass murderers with the following disclaimer:

> I must recognise that in the same situation, I could have either been a killer or an evader – both were human – if I want to understand and explain the behaviour of both as best I can. This recognition does indeed mean an attempt to empathize. What I do not accept, however, are the old clichés that to explain is to excuse, to understand is to forgive. Explaining is not excusing; understanding is not forgiving.
>
> (Browning 2001: 18)

Miller et al. conducted a series of experiments to determine the validity of Browning's concern that to explain is to condone. In one experiment, participants were asked to read a description of a harmful act. Half the participants were asked to write a narrative explanation of the situation. The other half were not. The participants who had written the narrative explanation were significantly more likely to see the harmful act as justified or caused by the external situation. They were less likely to label the perpetrator as evil. Therefore, Miller et al. concluded that the act of narrativization produces a more condoning attitude.

Miller et al. argue that the act of narrativization focuses the participant on the socio-psychological conditions under which the perpetrator committed the harmful act, creating an understanding that 'perpetrators are, to an important degree, not personally responsible for their actions' and that the participant 'were he or she in the same situation, might be highly susceptible to the same actions'. The more complex and extended the act of narrativization, the more likely it was to produce a condoning attitude. When the harmful act was presented without the opportunity for narrativization, participants tended to view the act from a dispositional causal perspective, 'attributing harm doing to the perpetrator's personal character' (Miller et al. 1999: 226).

Both of these causal perspectives are problematic. The dispositional causal perspective distances the subject from acknowledging their own proclivity towards negative social behaviours. The socio-psychological perspective is equally unacceptable because it appears to encourage the condoning of any action, no matter how harmful. From the perspective of this experiment, serious drama's use of socio-psychological causation is problematic because it is likely to condone any harmful act it represents, even if the playwright's intention is otherwise.

The Experiment

Mark Ravenhill's monodrama *The Experiment* (Southwark Playhouse, London 2009) can be read as an attempt to delegitimate rather than condone a harmful action. This short monologue[5] tells the story of someone or some people involved with some scientific experiments on a child or some children, which are being conducted in the hope of finding a cure for some incurable disease. The speaker's account of these events is, however, extremely disrupted.

---

[5]The play, as performed at Southwark Playhouse in 2009, consisted of parts one and three of the published text only.

The Experiment, like *The City*, presents a series of plot elements, which suggest the possibility of a coherent story, while at the same time making it impossible for the audience to construct one. The plot elements feel connected because they belong to the same dramatic world. Objects described within the narrative act as concrete referents. The presence of a 'bed' (Ravenhill 2013: 430), a 'house' (Ravenhill 2013: 429), a 'garden' and a 'fence' indicates a naturalistic frame to this story (Ravenhill 2013: 431). Like Crimp, Ravenhill offers generalized descriptions of these objects. The house in which the characters live is 'big' and 'old' (Ravenhill 2013: 429). The child's room is 'lovely' (Ravenhill 2013: 430). This lack of specificity enables the audience to imagine the objects as they choose. The object becomes a template onto which the audience can project images from their own experience. The house, for instance, could be a cottage in a Welsh village or a terrace in south London. The word house, which is mentioned repeatedly, could refer to one specific house or many different houses. It is both one house and every house. The spectator is able to connect these unspecified everyday objects together into a concrete, individualized image of the world in which the action is taking place.

Like *The City*, *The Experiment* both encourages connections and contains irresolvable contradictions. Individual sentences contain contradictory compound phrases. The neighbour's response to the experiments is 'sarcastic mocking teasing furious understanding' (Ravenhill 2013: 433). The time span is 'two three six months years' (Ravenhill 2013: 431). Where an object is described in specific terms, its description is protean. The size of the house expands and contracts, altering every time it is referred to. At first, it is 'modest' (Ravenhill 2013: 429), then it is a 'great big manor', next it is 'cramped' (Ravenhill 2013: 430), then 'big' again and so on (Ravenhill 2013: 431). It becomes difficult to maintain a consistent picture of the house and, by implication, the social status of the speaker. The exact socio-economic conditions under which the speaker is making his decisions are unclear.

It is impossible to explain the speaker's actions in terms of their situational causality or to even identify the exact nature of their actions. The speaker's account repeatedly contradicts itself. At times, three possible actions are offered in response to one event, as if several possible responses exist simultaneously at the same moment. For example, when asked if they will agree to the experiments, the speaker states:

Was totally opposed
I understood immediately
I was dumbstruck, didn't know what to do

(Ravenhill 2013: 430)

All three actions exist as possibilities in the audience's mind, but there is no indication of which action represents the speaker's actual response.

In order to create a coherent story, the spectator is forced to make a tiny selection from a large set of possible events. Many different stories can be constructed from the play's plot elements. There is no definitive version of events. Therefore, it is impossible to judge the speaker in socio-psychological terms as there is no concrete sense of the exact circumstances surrounding the situation and how he responded to it. This failure of the speaker to explain the experiments on the basis of socio-psychological causation means that the audience are also denied the possibility of understanding them from this perspective, suggesting that this particular harmful act lies beyond the bounds of acceptability. Ravenhill's *The Experiment* uses a disrupted story to challenge the ethics of using socio-psychological causation in serious drama to enable an understanding of and, by implication, condone harmful actions.

The dramatic narrative of serious drama presents human action as driven by personal desire and moving forward through linear mechanical causation. Its plot structures carry the hallmarks of solid modernity's belief in rational positive progress: 'a movement towards the splendid vision on the horizon' (Bauman 2012: xi). Brecht argues that these structures can be thought of as articulating a capitalist politics of form and calls for playwrights to explore new, less determinate forms of plot structure. Sometimes, however, as Žižek argues, it is more politically productive to adhere strictly to a rule than to break one. In *Contractions*, Bartlett adheres strictly to the logic of linear mechanical causation to reveal a correspondence between the logic of financialization and the plot structures of serious drama. tucker green and Goold and Power employ alternative systems of causation to suggest alternative models for plot structure. tucker green's use of expressive causality in *Generations* encourages the audience to read and reread a single scene in order to discover the cause of a terrible situation. Goold and Power produce a Brechtian plot structure that articulates a structural causality and encourages its audience to enter into a cycle of reading and rereading. Goold and Power's plot, in particular, reflects the indeterminate nature of liquid modernity in its 'network-like' (Bauman 2012: 25) structure: 'a matrix of random connections and disconnections and of an essentially infinite volume of possible permutations' (Bauman 2007: 3).

Crimp and Ravenhill challenge serious drama's understanding of plot and story as interdependent structures by presenting their audiences with recognizable plot structures, but preventing them from linking these structures into a single coherent story. Ravenhill adds an ethical dimension to this approach by using it to disrupt the audience's ability to locate socio-psychological causes behind character behaviour, and in doing so suggests that some actions are unacceptable regardless of the circumstances under which they are committed.

The plays explored in this chapter articulate plot structures that are more networked and less determinate, reflecting the liquid nature of contemporary social reality in their form. At the same time, they question the validity and ethics of socio-psychological causation. If socio-psychological causation is under question, then this has an effect on how character is understood to function. If characters are no longer understood as shaped by their circumstances and their experiences, then how are they defined? The next chapter will explore this question, arguing that dramatic character is currently undergoing a shift from an objective to a subjective focalization.

6

Character

*Without believing that art progresses, we can still say
that it is continuously in motion, among all civilisations,
and that this motion reflects different phases of the
human mind.*

ZOLA 1968A: 354

The previous chapter explored shifts in the plot structures of
contemporary British plays in response to shifts in the social
structures that shape lived experience. As temporal structures
become more simultaneous and spatial structures more virtual,
plot structures become more networked and more indeterminate.
These shifts in plot structure have resulted in a questioning of
socio-psychological causation. If socio-psychological causation is
in question, then this automatically has an effect on how character
is constructed.

This chapter begins by examining the structural role character
plays in drama. It puts forward the idea that character is a lens
through which the social subject imagines themselves and their role
within society and explores some of the different ways in which the
social subject has been imagined through dramatic character over
the course of history. It argues that, in contemporary liquid dramaturgies, the focalization of character shifts from an objective to a
subjective viewpoint, presenting the social subject's understanding
of both their world and of themselves as a uniquely individualized
perspective. Neilson's *Realism* (2006) presents its protagonist's view
of the world through a dramatization of the inside of his head. In

Pornography (2007), English playwright Simon Stephens presents his characters through the use of a predominantly narrative as opposed to dramatic mode. The chapter argues that this shift in focalization reflects a shift in the social subject's understanding of identity under the pressures of global financial capitalism from a solid concern with 'social standing' to the endless fluidity of 'self-determination' (Bauman 2012: 32). Bauman claims that this obligatory and perpetual project of self-determination generates existential uncertainty. The social subject of liquid modernity finds themselves condemned to a 'state of unfinishedness, incompleteness and underdetermination [...] full of risk and anxiety' (Bauman 2012: 62).

This shift in focalization to the subjective mode presents the social subject as increasingly isolated, reflecting Bauman's argument that liquid modernity is 'a powerful *individualizing* force' (Bauman 2012: 148, emphasis in original) that raises questions about the nature of community in a globalized world by creating a disjuncture between 'individually conducted life policies on the one hand and political actions of human collectives on the other' (Bauman 2012: 6). The final section of this chapter argues that the exploration of increasing individuation in contemporary British drama is paralleled by an exploration of new forms of the collective. Both Stephens's *Pornography* and Ravenhill's *Shoot/Get Treasure/Repeat* (2007) are argued to offer new understandings of community in the face of increasing individuation.

Dramatic character

Character is the most frequently mystified element of dramatic structure. There is a tendency, within the context of serious drama, to think of characters as living, breathing beings instead of as elements of dramatic structure. Serious drama's socio-psychological characters are imagined to behave independently and unpredictably, with a high degree of free will, driving the action of their own stories. As American playwright Janet Neipris notes of one of her characters: 'I hadn't anticipated he would do that. He had taken on his own life. His words were rushing out at such a speed I could hardly keep up with them on the typewriter' (Neipris

2005: 33). The playwright is positioned as powerless in the face of their characters' surprising choices. As English playwright Alan Ayckbourn observes: 'I have started plays in my time fairly sure of where a character was going, and have been quite amazed at what they've blurted out' (Ayckbourn 2002: 46).

Characters, however, are not real people. They do not possess volition or free will. Characters are imaginings of the social subject. They are representations of how people understand themselves to be, both as human beings and as members of a particular society at a particular moment in time. Neipris, despite feeling in thrall to her characters' impulses, acknowledges a fundamental difference between a human being and the representation of a human being in the form of a character. Human behaviour has a tendency to be chaotic, mysterious and complex. In contrast, the actions of dramatic characters can usually be logically explained. In creating a character, the playwright takes on board 'the responsibility of making order of a life' (Neipris 2005: 36).

The structure of character is as constructed as the structure of plot. Character actions are determined by sets of character rules that limit the range of actions certain characters can perform under particular sets of given circumstances. Some of these rules are aesthetic, in that they relate to the ways in which specific character types are understood to behave within the context of specific dramatic genres. Other rules reflect the social structures that define normal everyday behaviour within the society for which the play is written.

The rules that define character play an important role in shaping the overall structure of a play because they place limitations on the direction of the play's action. British playwright Steve Gooch compares the structure of a play to a game of chess. Characters, he argues, are like chess pieces. Each chess piece obeys a set of rules that restrict the ways in which it can move. For example, a knight can only move in an L-shape. Each move that a piece makes contributes to the overall shape of the game. Like chess pieces, different characters obey different sets of rules that limit the actions they can perform. The overall action of a play is determined by the sum of all the individual actions of its characters, just as the overall shape of a chess game is determined by the sum of all the moves of the individual chess pieces. Therefore, character actions can be seen as the building bricks that determine the overall shape of a play's action (Gooch 2004: 25).

During the twentieth century, structuralist thinkers proposed systems of narrative analysis that attempted to define the specific relationship between individual character actions and overall narrative structure. Russian formalist Vladimir Propp argues that the narratives of Russian folktales are drawn from a set of thirty-one possible events. Each event describes a character action, such as 'THE HERO LEAVES HOME' (Propp 1968: 39, capitals in original) or 'THE FALSE HERO OR VILLAIN IS EXPOSED' (Propp 1968: 62, capitals in original). Each folktale is composed of a selection of these events. The thirty-one events have a fixed order. Events can be omitted from the sequence but the order in which they happen always remains the same.

The character actions that each of these events describes are attributed to one of seven specific character roles: the villain, the donor, the helper, the princess and her father, the dispatcher, the hero and the false-hero. For example, event six is a character action that can only be performed by the villain: '[t]he villain attempts to deceive his victim in order to take possession of him or of his belongings' (Propp 1968: 29). Each character role is associated with a limited range of character actions, a 'sphere of action'. For example, the villain can only perform actions that fit within the categories of 'villainy', 'a fight or other forms of struggle with the hero' and 'pursuit' (Propp 1968: 79). Propp's sphere of action defines a set of what Lyotard terms criteria of competence[1] for each character. Certain types of character, and, by implication, certain types of people within society, are associated with the capability to perform certain types of actions.

Each character role and its related character actions can, however, be performed by different named characters: '[t]he names of the dramatis personae change [...] but neither their actions nor functions change' (Propp 1968: 20). Thus, Bába Jagá, Morózko and the forest spirit are different named characters but they all play the role of the donor when they test and reward the stepdaughter. Conversely, one named character may play many different character roles with different spheres of action. For example, the same named character can perform character actions attributed to the role of the villain and the role of the helper at different points in the same narrative.

---

[1]For an explanation of criteria of competence, see p. 181.

Though Propp's system of named characters, character roles and character actions is frequently applied to drama, it is specific to the genre of the Russian folktale. Philosopher Étienne Souriau attempts to articulate a comparative system specifically for drama in *Les Deux cent mille situations dramatiques*. Souriau's system, like Propp's, is based on named characters taking on character roles with different spheres of action. Souriau, however, articulates the difference between narratives as differences in the combination of six character roles (the lion, the sun, the earth, the opponent, the scale and the moon) as opposed to differences in a sequence of character actions (Souriau 1950: 83–104). Semiotician Algirdas Julien Greimas attempts to draw both Propp's and Souriau's methods together into a single, universal method of narrative analysis. Greimas's system consists of six actants or forces (object, subject, sender, receiver, helper and opponent) that can be used to define the basic structure of any narrative (Greimas 1983: 197–221).

In structuralist terms, narratives consist of individual named characters, who take on a range of different character roles, which are defined in terms of a sphere of character actions that act as criteria of competence, defining which actions each character type is capable of performing. Certain types of behaviour are seen as being appropriate for certain types of character. This raises the question of why particular behaviours are imagined to be appropriate for particular character types but not others. In order to understand this, it is necessary to consider that the idea that certain types of people are capable of certain types of actions and incapable of others is a product of the social structures that define the ways in which people understand both themselves as social subjects and their role within a particular society at a particular moment in time. Narratives play a role in both supporting dominant understandings of the social subject and reimagining the social subject in ways that alter how people see both themselves and the society in which they live.

Characterization and the social subject

The history of dramatic character is often presented as the logical progression from two-dimensional character types to fully realized three-dimensional characters that authentically reflect human experience. The socio-psychological character of serious drama is commonly seen as the successful culmination of this endeavour. This chapter challenges this teleological narrative, arguing instead that shifts in principles of dramatic characterization over time reflect shifts in society's understanding of the social subject. There is change but there is not necessarily progression. As Fuchs suggests:

> each epoch of character representation – that is, each substantial change in the way character is represented on the stage and major shift in the relationship of character to other elements of dramatic construction or theatrical presentation – constitutes at the same time the manifestation of a change in the larger culture concerning the perception of the self and the relations of self and world.
>
> (Fuchs 1996: 8)

An individual's sense of themselves as a social subject at any point in time is the product of the social structures that shape their understanding of everyday social reality and of normal human behaviour.[2] As social structures shift, the individual's sense of themselves as a social subject shifts.

From this perspective, shifts in the representation of the social subject in the aesthetic realm have a political dimension. Jameson argues that 'the cultural monuments and masterworks that have survived tend necessarily to perpetuate only a single voice in this class dialogue, that of the hegemonic class' (Jameson 1983: 71). The accepted principles of characterization at any point in time produce representations of the social subject in line with dominant understandings of normal everyday human behaviour and of social relations, reinforcing the status quo. In contrast, challenges to accepted principles of characterization can be seen as an attempt to reimagine the social subject and are indicative of shifts within the social structures of a society towards new understandings of the self and social relations.

For example, the principles of characterization articulated by the theorists of ancient Greek and Roman theatre position the social subject as playing a fixed role within society, for which they

---

[2]For an explanation of how social structures shape everyday social reality and normal human behaviour, see pp. 58–61.

are naturally made. Aristotle argues that a character's qualities must be appropriate to their character type: 'it should be necessary or probable that this kind of person says or does this kind of thing' (Aristotle 1996: 25). Male and female characters, for example, should exhibit different types of behaviour because, as he argues in the *Politics*, different types of behaviour are naturally appropriate for different genders: 'the temperance of a man and of a woman, or the courage and justice of a man and of a woman, are not, as Socrates maintained, the same; the courage of a man is shown in commanding, of a woman in obeying' (Aristotle 1988: 19). A character's patterns of behaviour should also be consistent. Once established, they should not alter. Aristotle criticizes playwrights whose characters develop during the action of a play. He singles out Iphigenia in Euripides's *Iphigenia at Aulis* as an example of poor characterization on the grounds that: 'when she pleads for her life to be spared she is not at all like her later self' (Aristotle 1996: 25).

Roman poet Horace argues that a character's behaviour is fundamentally determined by their social position, their gender, their age and their cultural background: '[i]t will make a great difference whether a god or a hero is speaking, a man of ripe years or a hot-headed youngster in the pride of youth, a woman of standing or an officious nurse, a roving merchant or a prosperous farmer, a Colchian or an Assyrian'. Horace agrees with Aristotle that, once an appropriate pattern of behaviour has been established for a character, it should 'remain the same all the way through as it was at the beginning' (Horace 2000: 101). The poet, who is a good citizen, correctly understands the behaviour appropriate to specific social types and will reproduce it accurately:

> The man who has learnt his duty towards his country and his friends, the kind of love he should feel for a parent, a brother, and a guest, the obligations of a senator and of a judge, and the qualities required in a general sent out to lead his armies in the field – such a man will certainly know the qualities that are appropriate to any of his characters.
>
> (Horace 2000: 107)

By linking the idea of the good citizen to an understanding of appropriate social qualities, Horace exposes a link between

appropriateness in characterization and the upholding of established social relations.

Both Aristotle's and Horace's principles of characterization
present an image of the classical world as a place in which social
roles are strictly defined and inflexible. This fixed vision of the
social subject offers little leeway for shifts in established social
relations. Roman grammarian Evanthius challenges this fixed
conception of the social subject, arguing that certain character
types no longer reflect actual behaviour within society. He praises
Roman playwright Terence for turning fixed character types on
their head; for example, through his introduction of 'prostitutes
who were not evil' (Evanthius 1974: 305). Evanthius encourages
playwrights to experiment with character types on the condition
that the character's behaviour is in accordance with 'verisimil-
itude', reflecting the ways in which people of a particular social
type differ in reality from their established theatrical character type
(Evanthius 1974: 303).

During the Renaissance, European theatre commentators
reimagined classical principles of characterization through the lens
of Christian morality. During this period, the moral character of
theatre itself was in question. In order to argue that the theatre was
a school of Christian morality, as opposed to a devilish practice
that 'enlists its adherents in the ranks of the damned', Renaissance
commentators on the *Poetics* recast playwrights as teachers of
moral conduct and their characters as instructional models (Barish
1981: 81). Italian Renaissance scholar Bartolomeo Lombardi and
philosopher Vincenzo Maggi argue that when playwrights present
'behaviour they must make exemplars of it' (quoted in Weinberg
1974: 414). Aristotle's stipulation that characters should display
'goodness' is reread as explicitly relating to moral health (Aristotle
1996: 24), taking on what literary critic Bernard Weinberg terms
a 'pedagogic utility' (Weinberg 1974: 408).[3] Good characters are
thought to instruct the audience through their good behaviour,
as Spanish Renaissance humanist Alonso Lopez Pinciano argues,
'by their honest and serious speech and by their honest and
upright actions' (Pinciano 1953: 360). Characters' fates become
determined by their moral condition. Characters are split into

---

[3] Aristotle's original definition of goodness is defined simply as the ability to make
good decisions: 'the character is good if the choice is good' (Aristotle 1996: 24).

predominantly good or bad types. The former are rewarded for their behaviour, while the latter are punished. As Pinciano observes: 'the honest, virtuous, and laudable character [...] must be given a suitable reward and the evil one punished' (Pinciano 1953: 360). Renaissance principles of characterization view the social subject through a Christian perspective, in which the social subject, in constant danger of falling into sin, should be primarily concerned with the moral condition of their soul.

In the mid-seventeenth century, a tension arose between the idea of the social subject as a moral being and the idea of the social subject as a rational being. There was a shift away from seeing characters' actions primarily in moral terms towards seeing them as the result of rational causes. Character consistency became associated with consistent motivations, rather than moral consistency. The idea of character motivation first appeared in the second half of the seventeenth century. Dryden describes 'motive' as a character's 'clear account of their purpose and design' (Dryden 1971: 43). He argues that it is the playwright's responsibility to find logical reasons for his characters' actions: 'to be sure he convinces the Audience that the motive is strong enough' (Dryden 1971: 42). This implies that audiences are now judging character behaviour on rational terms.

French playwright Pierre Corneille argues that characters can act as moral exemplars without exhibiting moral consistency because the audience can use their own powers of reason to distinguish the moral quality of a character's actions. In his 1660 *Discours*, Corneille states that characters should be admirable. Admirable characters can have both virtues and vices. They are 'outstanding and elevated whether of a virtuous temper or a criminal one'. The spectator admires the character for their desirable virtues but remains critical of their morally dubious actions: 'one simultaneously despises her actions and admires the source from which they spring' (Corneille 1991: 241–2). By the late-seventeenth century, there was a shift towards understanding the social subject as a rational being, whose actions had logical reasons and who could independently distinguish between good and bad behaviour.

By the late-eighteenth century, the preoccupation with a character's morality had given way to a preoccupation with 'tracing out the innermost workings of the soul' (Schiller 1903: vii). The benchmark of good characterization became the extent to which characters appeared to have, as English writer and philosopher William Hazlitt puts it, a 'life of their own' (Hazlitt 1998: 211). The argument for characters combining both good and bad qualities became detached from the idea of moral instruction and related to the idea that human beings have complex, contradictory personalities. German philosopher and playwright Friedrich Schiller argues that if a playwright truly wishes 'to portray men as they are', then they must endow even the most evil of men with 'good qualities, of which even the most vicious are never totally destitute' (Schiller 1903: x). Characterization thus becomes a matter of contradiction as much as of consistency. German philosopher Georg Wilhelm Friedrich Hegel argues that characters should consist of a unified set of contradictions because 'humanity is just this very paradox' (Hegel 1920: 320). Character is consistent in that it is a 'concentrated unity' (Hegel 1920: 314), but at the same time it is multifaceted, with many contradictory aspects: 'the living focus of a whole congeries of qualities and traits' (Hegel 1920: 316). The audience are imagined to empathize with characters because of their multifaceted nature: 'this wealth of content [...] creates the interest we feel in a character' (Singer 2001: 315). The character is both universal and particular at the same time. The audience recognize elements of themselves in the character, but at the same time the character is separate from them, a 'rounded and subjective unity' in itself (Hegel 1920: 316). The idea of the social subject as a moral being is replaced by the idea of the social subject as a complex and contradictory individual.

In the late-nineteenth century, there was a shift in characterization towards an understanding of human behaviour in terms of socio-psychological causation. It became increasingly necessary to consider the unique nature of the individual. English philosopher and literary critic George Henry Lewes observes that where once a play would have shown how a certain character type, 'a warmhearted man', would behave 'on suddenly receiving the news of a dear friend's death', now 'we ask *what* warm-hearted man? A hundred different men would behave in a hundred different ways on such an occasion' (Lewes 1875: 124, emphasis in original). Swedish playwright August Strindberg sees any continued use of character types as a form of political suppression that promotes 'a *bourgeois* conception of the immutability of the human soul' (Strindberg 1976: 94, emphasis in original). These 'summary judgements that authors pronounce upon people' deny the idea that the social subject is an individual with unique qualities whose character develops over time (Strindberg 1976: 95).

Naturalism advocates an understanding of character that is scientific in its approach. Zola calls for a 'psychological and physiological study' (Zola 1968a: 366) that produces 'a character whose muscles and brain function as in nature' (Zola 1968a: 363). Strindberg's interest in the 'psychological process' leads him to challenge the idea that character actions can be explained in terms of consistent motivations (Strindberg 1976: 99). Instead, he argues, characters have a 'multiplicity of motives' (Strindberg 1976: 94). A character's nature is 'wavering' and 'uncrystallized' (Strindberg 1976: 97). They are collages of contradictory elements, 'agglomerations of past and present cultures, scraps from books and newspapers' (Strindberg 1976: 95). Therefore, the human personality is impossible to pin down. Characters' actions will seem contradictory and irrational because, psychologically, characters' minds 'work irregularly, as people's do in real life' (Strindberg 1976: 99). By the end of the nineteenth century, characterization was attempting to grapple with new socio-psychological understandings of the social subject, who was no longer seen as having a fixed personality but rather as developing a personality over time in response to their experiences. At the same time, developments in psychology questioned the degree to which human behaviour could be explained in terms of rational causes.

In twentieth-century British theatre, characterization became clearly understood within the context of socio-psychological causation. Characters were positioned as both the products of their experiences and their social circumstances. Characters could transcend character type. The concept of appropriateness, however, lived on in the idea that dramatic characters should challenge social stereotypes. Noel Greig encourages playwrights to create characters 'who are not stereotypes', but he sees stereotypes as a useful starting point for this process (Greig 2005: 75). Characters should be established within the bounds of a recognizable character 'type'. This stereotype can then be subverted by adding 'shades and variations' as the play progresses to create a unique, individualized character (Greig 2005: 18). Edgar frames this process within a political context. Stereotypical characters adhere to recognizable patterns of behaviour: 'the hero behaves entirely heroically, the prince royally'. Good characterization involves a moment where the character departs from the expected stereotype and 'challenges his or her role; when the old man is brave, the lackey eloquent, the page gives sage advice'. This moment has political power because it transforms a stereotype into a living, breathing, 'three-dimensional' human being challenging preconceived notions about the behaviour of particular social groups (Edgar 2009: 58).

Motivation is framed in Stanislavskian terms as the product of desire.[4] English playwright Tim Fountain claims that 'action can only occur when a character has a goal' (Fountain 2007: 18). Dramaturg Val Taylor observes that this goal is inevitably framed as 'the fulfilment of a particular desire' (Taylor 2002: 61). Val Taylor argues that motivations logically explain why people do things, and so by extension why things happen. Audiences seek out motivations because they offer them a sense of control over their lives through presenting events as having identifiable causes: 'we want explanations because we believe this will give us control of situations through an ability to predict their occurrence' (Taylor 2002: 60).

Characters are presented as needing to be likeable in order for an audience to empathize with them and their view of the world. Ayckbourn argues that characters need to exhibit 'a certain innocence, a trust, an openness that makes us really want things to go right for them in the end' (Ayckbourn 2002: 14–15). Empathy has a political dimension. Edgar argues that it enables an audience to understand alien perspectives. By identifying and empathizing with characters who see the world differently, the audience come to a greater understanding of alien points of view: '[b]y enabling us to imagine what it is like to see the world through other eyes [...] drama develops capacities without which we cannot live together in societies at all' (Edgar 2009: 203–4). Empathetic characters promote social cohesion.[5]

Dominant approaches to characterization in contemporary British theatre represent the contemporary social subject as a unique psychological individual shaped by their social circumstances but

---

[4]For a more detailed explanation of Stanislavski's influence on playwriting, see pp. 155–6.
[5]For a further discussion of the role empathy plays in the politics of contemporary drama, see pp. 44–5.

able to transcend these circumstances through their own efforts if they so desire. At the same time, the world the social subject inhabits is presented as a rational world. Events can be explained in terms of logical causes and potentially be prevented from happening. The reasons why others see the world differently can be empathized with and rationally explained.

Over time, representations of character shift as understandings of the social subject shift. This does not necessarily mean people understand themselves better as human beings over time; it simply means they understand themselves differently.

Postdramatic/postmodern character

Hans Thies Lehmann and Elinor Fuchs both argue that socio-psychological character is in the process of being superseded by a new understanding of character that they term postdramatic or postmodern respectively. They both put forward the idea that theatre failed to enter the modernist period along with other art forms at the turn of the twentieth century and so is now in the middle of a 'modernist' break that began in the 1970s. Both present a narrative in which the linear narrative of theatrical development is in the process of breaking into a new constellation of disparate modernist practices.

Theatre researcher Hans Thies Lehmann argues that, while theatrical revolutionaries at the advent of the twentieth century question the representation of the world put forward by natural-istic forms of drama, they fail to question the seemingly essential relationship between theatre and drama. With the invention of film and television, drama moves from theatre into other mediums and it becomes clear that theatre and drama are not inter-changeable terms. If there can be drama without theatre, then there must be theatre without drama. From the 1970s onwards, Lehmann argues that a new theatrical discourse appears, that of the 'postdramatic', which explores the potential of theatre without drama. The postdramatic is most commonly associated with 'non-textual' or devised theatre practices. Lehmann argues, however, that even though 'the primacy of the text' is one of the defining features of dramatic theatre, postdramatic theatre is not necessarily non-textual (Lehmann 2006: 21). He states that 'text theatre' is 'a genuine and authentic variant of postdramatic theatre, rather than referring to something that has supposedly been overcome'. In postdramatic theatre, however, the position of the text is altered within the theatre-making process. The text is no longer the source of authority; it is considered 'as one element, one layer, or as a "material" of the scenic creation, not as its master' (Lehmann 2006: 17).

Fuchs argues that the main characterizing feature of this transitional period is a crisis of character. She positions the socio-psychological character of serious drama as an end point that can only be followed by the death of character, from which new constructions of character can then emerge, phoenix-like. Theatre scholar Susan Blattès offers four definitions of how these new conceptions of character differ from socio-psychological character. First, there is a 'lack of information available' about their background and personal details. Second, any information given about a character 'can be questioned and is frequently contradicted'. Third, '[i]t is often quite difficult or even impossible to decide on characters' motivations'. Finally, the character's actions and their dialogue lack 'coherence' (Blattès 2007: 71). What a character does contradicts what they say.

Blattès's model is problematic because it is articulated as a lack of character. The dramatic text fails to provide us with the elements from which socio-psychological character is constructed. Instead, I would argue that one specific way in which new conceptions of character differ from socio-psychological character is through a shift in focalization, from an objective to a subjective perspective. The dramatic mode of a play is traditionally seen as an objective form of representation. The audience witness a set of unmediated events happening before their eyes in the present moment. Different characters may offer subjective readings of events in an attempt to enable the audience to see them from their perspective, but the audience always have access to the objective truth because they witnessed 'what happened'. In this mode, the audience often know more about events than the characters. In contrast, the narrative mode of the novel is seen as a subjective mode, in which a narrator offers an account of a set of events that happened in the past. The reader's access to an objective truth is questionable, as they only have access to the events through the narrator's interpretation of them. Some contemporary plays attempt to offer a theatrical version of the subjective mode by presenting events through the mediating gaze of a particular character.

As character becomes more subjective, there is a shift in the representation of the social bond that defines the relationship between the individual and the collective. The subjective mode is an isolating mode; the character is trapped within their own singular perspective, conveying a sense of the social subject as increasingly isolated. This increasing individuation raises a need to redefine the nature of the collective experience. There is a tension between these two contradictory impulses, the one drawing the social subject into deeper isolation, the other branching out to re-establish a sense of the collective. This expresses an idea of the social subject under the forces of global financial capitalism as simultaneously more isolated from and more connected to the communities in which they live.

Realism

Neilson claims he sees the world as a place in which 'there are no permanent truths' (Neilson 2008a). In several recent plays, he has attempted to reflect this by shifting from an objective to a subjective mode of representation. Rather than situating his protagonists as driving the action of a drama taking place in an external dramatic world, he moves the dramatic action inside the internal landscape of his protagonists' heads. From the subjective viewpoint of the protagonists' internal landscape, there is no access to permanent truths. There is only the truth of the world as the character sees it.

Realism (National Theatre of Scotland/Edinburgh International Festival 2006) explores the internal landscape of an average, 'healthy', white Scottish man, Stuart (Neilson 2007a). The play presents a day in Stuart's life from the inside of Stuart's head. On the Saturday in question, Stuart has decided to 'do nothing' (Neilson 2007b: 97). He spends the day regretting his decision to split up with his girlfriend, Angie. In the external world, '[f]uck all' happens (Neilson 2007b: 156). The inside of Stuart's head, however, is packed full of action.

In the original production, Stuart's internal landscape was visualized as a Daliesque desert into the middle of which the entire contents of Stuart's flat had been inexplicably dumped. The action within this landscape is baffling and disorientating as the play gives exactly the same weight in representational terms to dreams, memories, fantasies and external reality itself. At times, Stuart's head is a 'wild delirious trip', an 'all-singing, all-dancing show' (Gardner 2006). At other times, it is a place of deep anxiety, guilt, insecurity and loneliness. Everything worries Stuart. He suffers from hypochondria as a result of his psyche's terrifying diagnoses of minor symptoms. Stuart's 'funny' left eye, constant 'cramps' and sensation of feeling 'thirsty a lot' must be diabetes (Neilson 2007b: 103). An '*itching*' birthmark on Stuart's shoulder must be cancer (Neilson 2007b: 95). In his dreams, Stuart is constantly under threat. In one, the sky is full of Israeli bombers. In another, a squirrel Stuart once squashed angrily demands that Stuart pay to put his guts back in.

The women inside Stuart's head make him feel guilty. His mother appears whenever Stuart is doing something he knows is wrong. Her voice emanates from the washing machine, berating him for not checking the pockets of his trousers before putting them in. She materializes in the middle of a masturbatory fantasy in which Stuart's two ex-girlfriends, Laura and Angie, are having sex, infecting it with questions about Christmas presents and the size of her bottom:

Mother What do you want for your Christmas?

Laura Oh God, that's good – rub my little cunt!

Mother I've got a bum like a baby elephant's.

Mother slaps her bottom. The rhythm falls into time with Stuart's spanking of Angie.

Angie Spank my big elephant bum!

Laura What do you want for your Christmas?

Mother What do you want for your Christmas?

Angie What do you want for your Christmas, then?

Furious, Stuart gives up.

(Neilson 2007b: 118)

Stuart's mother takes on a prohibitive role in Stuart's psyche and this role is extended to the other women in his life. He accuses Laura of trying to turn him into a 'leaf-eating, non-smoking, rice-eating wank' when she tells him off for choosing a microwaved prawn curry for his dinner (Neilson 2007b: 142). Angie scolds him for scraping toast into the sink and spoiling the cat.

The men in Stuart's head make him feel insecure. His childhood friend Mullet hurls insults at him: 'fucking knob' (Neilson 2007b: 101); 'fat fucking shite' (Neilson 2007b: 102). He bullies Stuart, making him hop like a rabbit, chasing him with shit on a stick and forcing him to eat crayons. Stuart's sense of self-worth is further eroded by the dismissive behaviour of his cat, Galloway. At Stuart's imaginary funeral, Galloway undermines all the positive things other characters have said about him with his single-sentence eulogy: 'He was a prick' (Neilson 2007b: 151).

Stuart's anxieties, guilt and insecurities are further heightened by his inability to keep his thoughts within the bounds of what society considers acceptable. Stuart's thoughts perform their greatest transgression when, in response to an outrageous gas bill, they conjure up the Black and White Minstrels:

> *He becomes involved in a song-and-dance routine. The lyrics consist only of the words 'What a bunch of cunts' and sometimes 'What a bunch of fucking cunts' for variety's sake.*
> *Male dancers join in – they are blacked up, like Al Jolson.*

> (Neilson 2007b: 120)

When he challenges the blacked-up dancers for being a 'bit fucking racist', they blame him for imagining them in the first place (Neilson 2007b: 121). Stuart finds himself labelled a racist by his own imaginative world. A similar situation arises later, as he remembers a conversation with Angie in which she accused him of being racist and homophobic. In his attempt to prove that he is neither of these things, Stuart convicts himself of both. He expresses disgust at the idea of gay male sex: 'I say that if you're a heterosexual man – regardless of how enlightened you are – you find the thought of, you know –' (Neilson 2007b: 134). When he tries to explain why he is not a racist, he can only do it in racist terms:

Stuart Yes – if an Asian shopkeeper gives me change, I always make a point of just making slight contact with his hand.

Angie What's that supposed to prove?

Stuart Well. You know – just to make sure he knows I don't think I'll get the Paki touch or something.

(Neilson 2007b: 135)

Stuart is in a conundrum in his head. While he does not believe he is a racist or a homophobe, he is fully aware that society would read his thoughts as both racist and homophobic. Gardner interprets Stuart's frequent bursts of political incorrectness as suggesting that 'the thought police can't control what goes on inside our heads' (Gardner 2006). The thought police, however, are very much inside Stuart's head. His mind is peopled with characters who are on hand to punish him for socially unacceptable thoughts, if he does not punish himself for them first.

Stuart's dreams, memories and fantasies reveal him to be lonely. In reality, he actively pushes people who care about him away. He dumps Angie and rejects his best friend Paul's repeated offers of company. Holed up in his flat, he is like the castle his mother sees in the tea leaves, surrounded by a moat 'to keep the folk from getting in' (Neilson 2007b: 100). The women in his life may be prohibitive figures, but he longs for female company. He spends a page of dialogue trying to work out what he could say in a phone message to persuade Angie to call him. He both remembers his mother fondly and needs her desperately. Some cheap aftershave she once gave him is the first thing he would save in a fire: 'I wouldn't save my CDs first or my iPod or anything; the first thing I'd save would be that aftershave' (Neilson 2007b: 118). After her death, he imagines her as an angel and asks for her heavenly intercession to help him win Angie back.

Stuart has a fantasy about his own death, allowing him to gather all the people he misses at his funeral. The eulogies he imagines these people giving express his loneliness and isolation through images of separation but togetherness. Laura remembers how once, after they had fallen out, it snowed and Stuart wrote '"I love you Laura". Everywhere you could see' (Neilson 2007b: 150). Angie remembers how if 'he had to leave before me in the morning, he'd always put one of my teddy bears in bed beside me, with its little arm over me' (Neilson 2007b: 151). In these images, Stuart's love is present but Stuart is physically absent. He expresses great love for others but is unable to express it to them directly.

Stuart has one desire. He wants Angie to ring him. This desire is fundamentally self-defeating because it relies on another person taking action. By dramatizing the inside of Stuart's head, Neilson is able to show us the anxieties that generate this self-defeating want and prevent him from actively pursuing his desire to be with Angie. He longs for Angie, but he feels that women undermine him. He is racked by insecurities about his physical appearance and his moral character. He still harbours feelings for Laura, his first love. He has inherited the idea from his mother that love should be unachievably perfect: 'Don't you settle for less than love, than true love, do you hear me?' (Neilson 2007b: 140). The doubts that rattle inside Stuart's head make it easy to understand the difficulty he has in taking action.

Stuart's actual actions in the external world seem random and disconnected. For example, at the beginning of act three, Stuart takes a ready meal out of the fridge, puts it in the microwave, watches it cook and says, 'You can't put a price on a dream house.' The dialogue seems unrelated to the action. Inside Stuart's head, however, the scene plays out differently. Laura scolds Stuart for eating bad food and asks what will happen to all the animals they are planning to have if he dies. Stuart points out that, if they are going to have that many animals, they will need to buy a house on the scale of 'Blofeld's fucking secret complex'. At which point Laura points out that: 'You can't put a price on a dream house!' (Neilson 2007b: 143). In this version, the action and dialogue make sense. *Realism* suggests that though our actions in real life seem random and unmotivated, they are the logical outcome of complex, contradictory thought processes.

The self-defeating nature of Stuart's objective and the seeming randomness of his external actions suggest apathy. Mullet berates Stuart for becoming apathetic: 'You were going to be an astronaut. What's happened to that guy? What's happened to the guy who was going to build a rocket and fly to fucking Mars?' (Neilson 2007b: 103). The dreams Mullet invokes are childish ones, but they imply a capacity for action that the middle-aged Stuart has lost. He is too 'knackered' to play football or even go for a pint

(Neilson 2007b: 97). That Stuart has the capacity for action is clear from his internal landscape. In his imagination, his 'stunningly lucid intervention' in a radio debate on the Scottish smoking ban incites a riot (Neilson 2007b: 112). This triumph, within the frame of his internal landscape, fills Stuart with enough self-confidence to consider what he might actually say to Angie. This impetus to action, however, never translates into real action. He does not call Angie. He needs Angie to call him.

The social subject's retreat into imagination seems logical if, like Stuart, their capacity for effective action in their internal and external worlds differs greatly. Psychoanalyst Sigmund Freud argues, however, that to live out the desire to be 'great' purely through the imagination leads to political passiveness. It allows the social subject to 'blow off steam' but diminishes their capacity to take the action needed to instigate change in the external world (Freud 1997: 88).

Stuart, it appears, has given up on the external world. At the end of the original production, the audience were given a glimpse of Stuart's external life. A grey kitchen was flown in, contained within a small, sealed box. In comparison to the colourful expansiveness of Stuart's imagination, his external world is represented as a bland space of separation and confinement. Stuart enters the kitchen, '*then proceeds to make himself, in real time and with little fuss, a cup of tea. This done, he sits at the kitchen table*' (Neilson 2007b: 156). Stuart's external world is unbearably mundane in comparison to the exciting, whirling world inside his head.

Neilson claims he is interested in subjective characterization because it offers a way to challenge serious drama's representation of the social subject as being driven by clear objectives and able to take effective action: 'A long held maxim has always been that drama differs from life because, in drama, you know what everyone wants. But that constant contradiction – the ability to want and both not want the same thing – is a fundamental part of the human character [...] The greatest oppositional forces facing normal people come from within' (Neilson 2007a). Through the character of Stuart, Neilson proposes that the internal landscape of the social subject and the reasons for their actions are more complex than socio-psychological causation can express. Consequently, it is more difficult for the social subject to take action in the external world than the structures of serious drama suggest.

Pornography

Like *Realism*, Simon Stephens's *Pornography* (Deutsches Schauspielhaus, Hamburg 2007; Traverse/Birmingham Rep, UK Tour 2008) offers an image of an isolated social subject through a subjective mode of representation. *Pornography* tells the story of eight characters in the days leading up to the London bombings on 7 July 2005. The play consists of four monologues, two duologues and a final verbatim section, which lists personal details about the fifty-two victims of the bombing. Monologues dominate the play reflecting what Lehmann sees as an increasing shift towards the narrative mode in contemporary theatre.

Dramatic character is traditionally rooted in the idea of action. While Aristotle links character to the possession of certain qualities 'that in respect of which we say that the agent is of a certain kind', he states that character is primarily expressed through action: 'character is included along with and on account of the actions' (Aristotle 1996: 11). *Pornography* challenges this idea. Four of the play's characters describe their stories rather than enacting them. As Lehmann observes, the audience's interest in these monologues is located more in 'the peculiar act of the *personal* memory/ narration' than in the question of what will happen next (Lehmann 2006: 109, emphasis in original). The narrators exist in two simultaneous moments of time. They are involved in the moment of the past event they are recounting and they are in the present moment constructing their version of events. This double representation of time highlights the process of self-determination through self-writing that is taking place in front of us. The narrator becomes both protagonist and author.

Fuchs explores the idea of theatre as writing in *The Death of Character*. She argues that, while some contemporary theatre practitioners continue to follow French dramatist and director Antonin Artaud's call for a theatre of absolute presence, 'the proliferation of reproducible culture has made the attribution of "presence" suspect' (Fuchs 1996: 90). Therefore many theatre practitioners have abandoned the search for 'the "aura" of theatrical presence', shifting their focus onto exploring the process of reproduction itself (Fuchs 1996: 72). Their interest has moved from the spoken to the written. Whereas speech is associated with the idea of presence, writing is associated with a gap between presence and representation. As literary theorist and philosopher Chris Norris states:

> In speaking one is able to experience (supposedly) an intimate link between sound and sense, an inward and immediate realization of meaning which yields itself up without reserve to perfect, transparent understanding. Writing on the contrary destroys this ideal of pure self-presence. It obtrudes an alien, depersonalized medium, a deceiving shadow which falls between intent and meaning, between utterance and understanding.
>
> (Norris 2003: 28)

Dramatic writing aims to create the illusion of spontaneous speech, but this speech is written. When Brecht calls for a theatre of 'complex seeing', he is asking for a theatre that can be both read and reread and seen as written and rewritten (Brecht 1964: 44). Through the use of the narrative mode, theatre breaks with the illusion that it is occurring in a spontaneous present and declares its written-ness. The characters write as they speak. Events can only be experienced through words. The world itself is no longer ontologically present. It is distanced and can only be experienced as language. It is 'world-as-text' (Fuchs 1996: 81).

Pfister argues that a heavy use of monologue implies a 'disruption of communication and the isolation and alienation of the individual' (Pfister 1988: 134). *Pornography* abounds with images of such isolated individuals: 'Lone drivers with no passengers' (Stephens 2008: 38); 'The tube is full of people and nearly all of them nowadays have iPods' (Stephens 2008: 6). Stephens links this isolation to increasing mechanization. The cars and iPods act as barriers shielding us from 'the fucking horror' of other people (Stephens 2008: 57). Machines now service us instead of other human beings: 'On some tube lines now you don't even get drivers. The machines have started to run themselves' (Stephens 2008: 56). Even the most intimate human relationship becomes devoid of human connection, as sexual fulfilment is delivered online twenty-four hours a day.

There is an emphasis on absence in the characters' accounts of their lives; the absence of a meaningful connection to another human being. The widow's absent husband is ever present in her thoughts. She sees him in other men in the street: 'I see one man. He does look like my husband. Just for a second I was thrown' (Stephens 2008: 61). The mother's husband may be physically present in her life, but he is absent in every other way. She can only describe him in terms of his external appearance: 'He's windswept when he comes back' (Stephens 2008: 5); 'His hair is clean. And his skin. He's had a shave' (Stephens 2008: 7). This absence generates desire. This is not presented as desire for someone, but rather as an impossible desire to be the object of someone else's desire. The widow masturbates in her dead husband's robe as if this makes him present in the act (Stephens 2008: 58). The mother longs for her distant husband to touch her: 'Just rest his hand on my neck and stroke the back of my hair' (Stephens 2008: 6). The need for a connection to others is expressed through a yearning to be the object of sexual desire, but the characters cannot make themselves into an object of desire. The power to do that resides within the subject not the object. Like Stuart in *Realism*, the narrators have created self-defeating objectives for themselves. Bauman identifies such self-defeating objectives as a feature of liquid modernity and a way in which global financial capitalism perpetuates desire in a world of instantaneous gratification: 'the motivating powers of desire [are] invested in its unfulfilment' (Bauman 2012: 158).

The use of the narrative mode increases the sense of the narrators as isolated individuals. The other characters in their stories are distant and only glimpsed in fragments. The schoolboy constructs the character of his teacher piece by piece. At first she is a 'grey skirt', then a name, 'Lisa', a 'smile' (Stephens 2008: 12) and a brand of cigarettes, 'Marlboro Lights' (Stephens 2008: 14). When other characters speak, the audience can only hear their words through the narrator's interpretation of them. Speech is reported, not spontaneous. There is a question as to whether the other character meant their words to mean what the narrator interprets them as meaning. Jason takes Lisa's words 'I have no idea Jason, you tell me' as an expression of interest in him, rather than a teacher's dismissal of a disruptive student (Stephens 2008: 12). When other characters act, the narrator ascribes meaning to their actions. Jason interprets Lisa's conversation with a male teacher as a sexual advance: 'she starts talking to the head of maths. It makes me want to cut his throat open' (Stephens 2008: 15). The narrator presents the audience with 'reported character'. There is no alternative representation of the other character available to compare the narrator's report of them against. The actual nature of the reported character is unknowable. There is an impression of wholeness and individualization through the use of detail, but there is no ontological core.

In the narrative mode, the narrator is not only the author of events, but a character in those events. The narrator writes themselves. They are both subject and object. They are the 'I' who narrates and the character that is narrated. Stephens's play is full of images of the self as simultaneously both subject and object. The mother's work colleague has a picture of himself on his desk. This double sense of self is presented as uncanny. The widow warns that: 'If you stare long enough into a mirror, of course, you begin to hallucinate' (Stephens 2008: 57).

This double sense creates a gap within the self. Characters are as distanced from themselves as they are from others. The mother describes the actions that she takes to leak a confidential report in a detached manner: 'I go to the fax machine. I find the number of Catigar Jones. Fax/Start. Set.' She does not explain them or emotionally engage with them. She is only forced to own these as her actions because she 'was the only person in the office on Tuesday night' (Stephens 2008: 9). The schoolboy is dislocated from his voice. Jason reports his own words in conversations:

Are you worried about losing your job?

Am I what?

Because teachers and students aren't really meant to fall in love with each other. I'd look after you though. If you did?

Jason, what on earth are you talking about?

(Stephens 2008: 16)

The widow is dislocated from her body. She lacks a sense of its physical needs: 'Sometimes I forget if I've eaten or not' (Stephens 2008: 57). Characters are dislocated from their emotions. Tears become something that happen to you. The widow observes: 'there are tears pouring down the sides of my face. This makes absolutely no sense to me at all' (Stephens 2008: 63). The characters are disconnected not only from others but from themselves.

Release from isolation and disconnection becomes imagined as something that can only be achieved through violent means. The schoolboy expresses his frustrated desire for an intimate connection with his teacher through violent sexual images: 'I would cut out her cunt with a fork. I would scrape off her tits' (Stephens 2008: 17). The suicide bomber sees violence as generative. It will rip through the isolation and disconnection, freeing the 'bewigged, myopic, prurient, sexless, dead' people he sees around him (Stephens 2008: 40). He believes the bomb will release people from a state of passivity and propel them back into action: 'from now on you can do, you have it in you to do whatever it is that you want to do' (Stephens 2008: 38). Philosopher René Girard argues that acts of violence can be generative under certain conditions. A single act of ritualized violence can enable a community to escape from a seemingly endless cycle of reciprocal violence. The acts of violence in *Pornography* are not generative, even on Girard's terms. Girard states that in order for an act of violence to be generative, it must be 'unanimous' (Girard 1977: 151). The whole community must believe that the sacrifice will be beneficial to them. The suicide bomber's act of violence is not unanimous. He forces it on the community, selfishly satisfying his own desires. The violence he unleashes is pornographic, not generative.

A productive solution to isolation and disconnection is articulated through the play's collective monologue form. In *Postdramatic Theatre*, Lehmann argues that Pfister's reading of the monologue as an expression of isolation can easily be turned on its head. Though the speaker of a monologue may fail to communicate effectively with other characters onstage, they do succeed in communicating effectively with the audience. Rather than enacting a failure of communication, 'a speech that has the audience as its addressee intensifies communication' (Lehmann 2006: 128). The monologue draws the audience into an intimate relationship with the character speaking. In the form of the soliloquy, it can allow them direct access to the character's innermost thoughts. They no longer have to decipher them from the character's actions, as in the dramatic mode. The monologue conveys a sense of connection to others, as opposed to isolation from them: 'closeness within distance, not the distancing of that which is close' (Lehmann 2006: 110).

This sense of closeness within distance is reflected in the form of the collective monologue. Psychologist Jean Piaget defines 'collective monologue' (Piaget 1932: 9) as when 'every one talks about himself without listening to others' (Piaget 1932: 14). Young children, he observes, have a tendency to soliloquize in front of each other while playing, thinking perhaps that they are interesting others in their actions and thoughts. Psychologist Lev Vygotsky argues that the collective monologue is actually a form of socialized speech. He argues this on three premises. First, the collective monologue is a form of speech that only occurs in the presence of others: 'it accompanies the child's activity in the collective [...] but not when the child is by himself'. Second, there has to be an 'illusion of understanding'. When children are placed in the presence of deaf children or children who speak different languages, they do not voice a collective monologue. Finally, the words in a collective monologue are voiced rather than whispered inaudibly, which suggests that these utterances are meant to be heard (Vygotsky 1987: 263). He concludes that the collective monologue is a mixed form of speech. It exists on the borderline between 'speech for oneself' and 'speech for others' (Vygotsky 1987: 266). In *The Division of Labour*, Emile Durkheim identifies a dialectical tension between isolation and connection in capitalist society. He observes that within societies based on the division of labour the social subject is 'at once more individual and more solidary' (Durkheim 1960: 37). The collective monologue offers a form of communication that reflects this seeming contradiction. It articulates what psychiatrist David Cooper terms a 'viable dialectic between solitude and being with others' (Cooper 1971: 44).

Though the speakers in *Pornography* narrate their thoughts individually, together they articulate a collective monologue. They form one body. This is articulated not only through their mode of speech, but also in the underlying structure of the play, which is based on Shakespeare's seven ages of man. In the first monologue, the mother's baby stands for 'the infant, / mewling and puking in the nurse's arms'. The second is spoken by a 'whining school-boy'. The duologue between the incestuous brother and sister presents a pair of lovers. Next comes the monologue of a modern-day soldier, the suicide bomber. The affluent academic in the duologue that follows is 'the justice / in fair round belly'. The widow in the final monologue is 'slipper'd' like Shakespeare's pantaloon. Finally, the list of the bombing's victims represents the final stage of life, 'mere oblivion' (Shakespeare 1975, II: ii, 143–66). The characters are individuals but together they represent the course of a single life.

Through its representation of community, *Pornography* articulates a viable dialectic between solitude and being with others. The four bombers are separated isolated figures, but they feel a strong sense of connection. They are ever present to each other. Standing on the station platform, they 'wait at four different points, staring in four different directions' (Stephens 2008: 41). Though isolated, they are connected: 'We don't need to check that each other are here. We trust one another. We're here' (Stephens 2008: 39). It is not only the bombers, however, who experience this form of solidarity. The other characters in the play may articulate values, experiences and desires that oppose those of the bombers, but they share a similar bond. The form of the collective monologue enables the expression of this sense of connection. The characters may not be speaking to each other but they are speaking in the same direction. They all express the same desire to be the object of another's desire. They all share the experience of the bombings. They are all disturbed in its wake. They hold the same core values. Stephens represents this sense of community through the sharing of food. During her long walk home after the bombings, the widow knocks on a stranger's door and asks for some of the chicken she can smell cooking. The stranger shares her chicken with her. This Durkheimian sense of community, as something that is simultaneously collective and comprised of individuals, is represented through this act as one that nourishes.

Shoot/Get Treasure/Repeat

Ravenhill's cycle of short plays *Shoot/Get Treasure/Repeat* (Paines Plough, Edinburgh 2007) presents a more unsettling image of a community that is both more individual and more solidary. The cycle depicts events taking place during a long, non-specific war on terror and includes several short plays that feature a chorus, who address the audience directly. In 'Women of Troy', four women plead with the terrorists who bomb their city, begging them to stop. In 'War of the Worlds', the chorus express their sympathy for and then revulsion at the inhabitants of a bombed city. In the 'Odyssey', a group of soldiers bid farewell to the city they have been occupying. In 'Birth of a Nation', a chorus of artists encourage the people of a shattered city to heal through art.

These choruses articulate a collective monologue. Each chorus is made up of individuals, each of whom is a 'good person' (Ravenhill 2008: 14). Collectively they are the 'good people' (Ravenhill 2008: 7). A dialectic between solitude and being with others is articulated through the personal pronouns they use. When the chorus speaks for their community as a whole, the subject of their sentences becomes 'we': 'We want to ask you this' (Ravenhill 2008: 7); 'we accept, we celebrate' (Ravenhill 2008: 10). At other times, characters speak out as individuals within the group: they want 'to talk about me' (Ravenhill 2008: 7). At this point 'I' dominates: 'I work for the good of our society' (Ravenhill 2008: 8); 'I care' (Ravenhill 2008: 14). The chorus can speak for other individuals, who belong to the community, but who are not present or cannot speak. A woman in the chorus speaks on behalf of her absent lover: 'My lover feels the grief that I feel' (Ravenhill 2008: 121). In these moments, the chorus becomes representative of a wider community that extends beyond the stage.

The speakers in these choruses are not identified by character names. Their lines of dialogue float anonymously on the page. Although the chorus form one body onstage and on the page, the idea of the individual remains present. The chorus refer to individuals by name: 'Zachery' (Ravenhill 2008: 7), 'Alex' (Ravenhill 2008: 14). They build pictures of these individuals: 'I call him three-shot Thomas because … well, because' (Ravenhill 2008: 121); 'Zac – your paintings on the fridge that I'm so proud of' (Ravenhill 2008: 14). At the same time they build pictures of themselves as individuals: 'I have a buzz job amongst the buzz people' (Ravenhill 2008: 125); 'I take fruit and I put it in the blender and I make smoothies for my family' (Ravenhill 2008: 7). Although none of the speakers is named, some of them appear to be characters from other plays in Ravenhill's cycle. One of the speakers is the wife of Thomas and the mother of Zachery and has a juicing obsession like the character of Helen in 'Intolerance'. Another speaker has a son called Alex and lives in a gated community like Olivia in 'Fear and Misery'. Individual speakers contribute their own thoughts but together these voices become one voice because they voice similar opinions. The individuals do not speak to each other but they speak in the same direction.

Fischer-Lichte argues that in the 1960s and 1970s 'forms of choric theatre represented, propagated and even partly brought about a self-organizing community that allowed for a shared communal experience' (Fischer-Lichte 2009: 239). In more recent forms of choric theatre, however, what 'seems to be a community is actually revealed to be a group of self-alienated conformists' (Fischer-Lichte 2009: 241). Ravenhill presents us with figures that represent lifestyle choices as opposed to individuals. They describe their lives as based on the idea of individual freedom, but the only freedom they articulate is the freedom to shop: 'We have so much choice. Who will provide my electricity? Who will deliver my groceries?' (Ravenhill 2008: 180). Their descriptions of themselves sound like advertising copy: 'I only eat good food. Ethical food. Because I believe that good choices should be made when you're shopping' (Ravenhill 2008: 8). Any illusion of community is 'nothing but a clever marketing strategy promising the consumer that the market will fulfil his desire for solidarity, his yearning for a community, for communal experience' (Fischer-Lichte 2009: 41).

Ravenhill's chorus is problematic, not only in terms of its positioning of community as a marketing strategy, but also in terms of its consensus on a single set of core values. Lehmann suggests that the contemporary chorus articulates an '*excessive consensus*' (Lehmann 2006: 129, emphasis in original). The speakers are in agreement with each other, rather than being in conflict, as conventional dramatic wisdom dictates they should be. Their consensus is excessive because it prevents the expression of dialogue. The chorus aim to put an end to the war by imposing a single worldview on the whole of humanity. The chorus believe that their 'core values are everything because they are humanity's core values' (Ravenhill 2008: 180). Their mission is to bring 'freedom and democracy' to the whole world, and they intend to use military force to impose it (Ravenhill 2008: 8): their 'flaming sword will roam the globe until everywhere is filled with the goodness of good people' (Ravenhill 2008: 17).

There is no space for dialogue with those who disagree. The excessive consensus of the chorus blocks out any expression of an alternative viewpoint. The only voices allowed to speak are those that speak in consensus with the chorus. In the 'Odyssey', the former dictator of an invaded country is allowed to speak, but only because his words now support those of the chorus: 'My evil was great. I did not believe in democracy. I did not believe in freedom. I did not believe in choice.' A boy from the invaded country is also permitted to speak, as his voice adds to the consensus: 'I am happy. I am learning the core values – freedom and democracy. I think they are very good' (Ravenhill 2008: 187). The repetitive phrasing and the simple sentence construction in the language of both the dictator and the boy indicate that they are repeating phrases learnt by rote, rather than speaking their own words. They have been taught how to join the collective monologue, but a question remains as to whether the views they express are their own.

At the end of 'Birth of a Nation', a blind woman is brought on stage. When she opens her mouth to speak, it is revealed that she has no tongue. The woman is physically prevented from expressing her own views. The chorus of artists encourage her to express her feelings through painting, writing, dance and performance art. They hand her a paintbrush and a pen. They move her body for her as if she is dancing. The woman can only express her horror and suffering through a scream. Her body is thrown into convulsions, which the artists translate as a form of dance. The chorus read her actions as supporting their project as opposed to challenging it. They congratulate themselves on another success for their healing through art programme.

The excessive consensus onstage alters the nature of dramatic conflict in the choral plays. Conflict is absent from the stage and is shifted instead from the intra-scenic axis to the theatron axis. The conflict is now located between the chorus and the audience. The audience find themselves positioned as what German director Einar Schleef terms 'the enemy-chorus' (Fischer-Lichte 2009: 245). Ravenhill explicitly attributes an oppositional stance to the audience in the play's text. The audience are positioned as the Other; they are 'strange', 'so different' and 'the opposite' of the chorus (Ravenhill 2008: 11). They are terrorists. They are the inhabitants of a bombed city, of an occupied city. They are the unwilling beneficiaries of healing through art. They are 'the bad people' that the chorus are addressing (Ravenhill 2008: 15). The audience threaten to break the chorus's consensus on the core values. There is no room for dialogue between the chorus and the audience. The audience are addressed but are given no space to respond. The excessive consensus of the chorus prevents the resolution of this conflict through discussion. There is only thesis. Antithesis is banished from the stage, and with it the hope of any synthesis. The chorus demand that the audience join their consensus. They offer the audience the hope of rebirth, but only on their terms: 'As we want you to be reborn' (Ravenhill 2008: 197).

Although Ravenhill's chorus's use of collective monologue presents a disturbing picture of global financial capitalism as monologic, dehumanized and aggressive, this representation has a positive function. Out of the conflict between the chorus and the audience, a sense of community is born. Fischer-Lichte articulates the idea of an 'ephemeral community'. This is a community that exists only 'for the time span in which [...] common actions were performed and the same experiences shared' (Fischer-Lichte 2009: 227–8). The audience are united under the attack from the chorus. As Schleef observes, the audience form 'a whole against the chorus, which hopes to defeat them successfully' (Fischer-Lichte 2009: 245). An ephemeral community is created within the audience, through their opposition to the chorus and its core values.

This use of chorus has the potential to produce what philosopher Jacques Rancière terms 'an emancipated spectator' (Rancière 2007: 271). An emancipated spectator has 'the power to translate in their own way what they are looking at' (Rancière 2007: 278). The chorus offer no antithesis to their thesis, so instead the audience must actively build their own argument in opposition to the argument presented onstage. Here, Ravenhill acts in the manner of philosopher Joseph Jacotot's 'ignorant master', who does not teach his pupils but rather 'commands them to venture forth in the forest, to report what they see, what they think of what they have seen, to verify it, and so on' (Rancière 2007: 270). Each individual member of the audience constructs their own alternative viewpoint. This process, Rancière observes, is one that is both individual and solidary. Each individual audience member's response may be different, but the power to provide their own answers unites them: '[i]t is the power to connect with the intellectual adventure that makes them similar to any other insofar as his path looks unlike any other. The common power is the power of the equality of intelligences' (Rancière 2007: 278). A sense of community that articulates a viable dialectic between solitude and being with others is brought into being through the action of the chorus and their collective monologue.

In structuralist terms, narratives consist of characters whose ability to act is limited by the character role they play and the sphere of possible actions defined by that role. The spheres of character actions that are assigned to dramatic characters shift over time and reflect shifts in our understanding of the nature of the social subject. Serious drama's socio-psychological approach to characterization is not the end of character, but merely the most recent understanding of character in a long line of different understandings of character.

Fuchs argues that a crisis of character in contemporary theatre is producing new imaginings of the social subject through new approaches to characterization. In contemporary British plays, new conceptions of character often involve a shift in focalization, from an objective to a subjective perspective. In *Realism*, Neilson offers a subjective view of the world from the inside of his protagonist's head and explores the complex network of causes that prevent the contemporary social subject from taking effective action. In *Pornography*, Stephens presents us with characters who self-determine themselves through the narrative mode, becoming simultaneously the subject and object of their own stories. Stephens's use of collective monologue presents these characters as simultaneously increasingly isolated from and increasingly connected to others, so articulating an idea of contemporary community as a dialectic between solitude and being with others. In *Shoot/Get Treasure/Repeat*, Ravenhill uses an enemy chorus voicing a collective monologue to unite his audience into an ephemeral community. Rather than imagining the social subject produced by financial capitalism as isolated and unable to take action, these representations of networked communities of individual agents imagine new forms of connection and offer the possibility of finding new ways to take effective political action.

Conclusion

Even the most sublime work of artwork takes up a determining attitude to empirical reality by stepping outside of the constraining spell it casts, not once and for all, but ever and again, concretely, unconsciously polemical towards this spell at each historical moment.

ADORNO 2004: 6

When serious drama is examined from the perspective of Jameson's three levels of textual analysis, its political character is contradictory. The politics of its content and the politics of its form within the social and historical context for which it was originally developed articulate a progressive socialist politics. The politics of its class origins in a middle-class campaign to free late-nineteenth-century theatre of its melodramatic and working-class character and its politics of form within the context of the liquid nature of contemporary British society, however, are more reactionary in their character.

The structures of serious drama reproduce structures that are associated with solid modernity and as such they are inadequate to capture the complex and ever-shifting social structures of liquid modernity. Serious drama can offer a critique of current political issues in its content and offer imaginary resolutions to these problems through dialectical discussion, but by reproducing rational representations of social structures through its dramaturgy, serious drama misrepresents the complex mechanisms that underlie the processes of thinking, planning and taking action in a globalized society. Its representation of social structures perpetuates the idea that British society continues to operate on the basis of understanding time as linear, objective and measurable; space as concrete and discrete; causation as a linear mechanical chain of cause and effect; and the nature of the social subject as shaped by socio-psychological causation. This produces a gap between the representation of social reality (the ways in which it is understood to operate) and the lived experience of social reality (the ways in which it is experienced as operating). This gap makes it difficult for the social subject to take effective action, as their map for action no longer matches the actual landscape in which they are attempting to effect change.

The liquid dramaturgies discussed in this book produce dramatic structures which attempt to capture more effectively the increasingly liquid nature of lived experience under the pressures of global financial capitalism. Temporal structures shift away from the axis of succession and towards the axis of simultaneity. Spatial structures become more virtual and layered, with multiple contradictory spaces existing simultaneously, enfolded into each other. Causation becomes less mechanical and increasingly indeterminate, offering a network of possible and equally valid causal connections that produce multiple shifting interpretations of events. Finally, understandings of the nature of the social subject shift from an objective to a subjective viewpoint, in which both the world and the social subject themselves can only be viewed through the eyes of a specific individual whose perspective authors events. This in turn forces a rethinking of the conception of community, not as a united collective, but as a dialectic between solitude and being with others. These shifts are reflective of and potentially produce new understandings of both the nature of the world and the social subject within the context of liquid modernity. As cultural theorist Stuart Hall notes, '"new times" are both "out there", changing our conditions of life, and "in here" working on us' (Hall 1996: 225).

These liquid dramaturgies can be argued to articulate a progressive politics as they enable the social subject to understand more clearly the changed nature of the political landscape in which they are operating, so enabling them to imagine new and more effective strategies for political action. Bauman suggests that any 'safety' that can hope to be found within the shifting structures of liquid modernity 'depends not on fighting the endemic contingency and uncertainty of the human condition, but on recognizing it and facing its consequences point-blank' (Bauman 2012: 213). Any rethinking of representations of social structures that better enables the social subject to understand how to have political agency within the complex mechanisms of a globalized society is a political act as it provides the social subject with a more accurate 'overall map of how these power relations connect and of their resistances' (Hall 1996: 233). As Bauman argues: '[t]o work in the world (as distinct from being 'worked out and about' by it) one needs to know how the world works' (Bauman 2012: 212). Within this context, a play with its ability to tangibly articulate the web of social structures that underlie a particular version of the world through its dramaturgical structures becomes, in literary theorist I. A. Richards's terms, an effective 'machine to think with' (Richards 1960: 1).

In keeping with the nature of the politics of the structures I have described in this book, however, I want to end on a contradictory and cautionary note. While the liquid dramaturgies of the contemporary British plays explored in this book may better enable the social subject of liquid modernity to understand how to take political action in a changing political landscape, they may also reinforce the very structures whose nature they seek to reveal. By reproducing the liquid social structures produced by the rise of global financial capitalism within their dramatic structure, these plays may actually reaffirm them, so articulating a progressive but capitalist politics, rather than the progressive socialist stance that is imagined in this book.

Bibliography

Adams, T. (2009), '"I Hate to be Told Somewhere is Out of Bounds for Women." Enter Enron ...', *Guardian*, http://www.theguardian.com/stage/2009/jul/05/lucy-prebble-playwright-interview-enron [accessed 30 January 2016].

Adorno, T. W. (2004), *Aesthetic Theory*, London: Continuum.

Adorno, T. W. (2007), 'Commitment', in R.Taylor (ed.), *Aesthetics and Politics*, London: Verso.

Allen, R. E. (ed.) (1990), *The Concise Oxford Dictionary*, 8th edn, Oxford: Clarendon Press.

Althusser, L. and Balibar, É. (2009), *Reading Capital*, London: Verso.

Anon. (1658), 'An Excellent Ballad of George Barnwel an Apprentice of London, Who was undone by a Strumpet', printed for F. Coles, T. Vere and W. Gilbertson, http://ballads.bodleian.ox.ac.uk/view/edition/719 [accessed 19 July 2015].

Anon. (2010), 'Outrage as Brewery Advertises "Cold Lech" Beer next to Tomb of Polish President Lech Kaczynski', *Daily Mail,* http://www.dailymail.co.uk/news/article-1299911/Outrage-brewery-advertises-Cold-Lech-beer-tomb-Polish-President-Lech-Kaczynski.html [accessed 29 July 2015].

Archer, C. (1931), *William Archer: Life, Work, and Friendships*, New Haven, CT: Yale University Press.

Archer, W. (1882), *English Dramatists of Today*, London: Low, Marston, Serle and Revington.

Archer, W. (1886), *About the Theatre*, London: T. Fisher Unwin.

Archer, W. (1929), *The Old Drama and the New*, New York: Dodd, Mead and Company.

Aristotle (1961), *Aristotle's Physics*, Lincoln: University of Nebraska Press.

Aristotle (1987), *The Poetics of Aristotle: Translation and Commentary*, Chapel Hill: University of North Carolina Press.

Aristotle (1988), *The Politics*, Cambridge: Cambridge University Press.

Aristotle (1996), *Poetics*, London: Penguin.

Aristotle (1999), *Poetics*, London: Nick Hern.

Aristotle (2009), *The Nicomachean Ethics*, Oxford: Oxford University Press.

Augier, É. (1877), *Théâtre complet: Volume 2*, Paris: Calmann Lévy.

Ayckbourn, A. (2002), *The Crafty Art of Playmaking*, London: Faber and Faber.

Bakhtin, M. M. (1984), *Rabelais and His World*, Bloomington: Indiana University Press.

Barish, J. A. (1981), *The Antitheatrical Prejudice*, Berkeley: University of California Press.

Barthes, R. (1977), *Image, Music, Text*, London: Fontana Press.

Bartlett, M. (2008), *Contractions*, London: Methuen.

Bassett, K. (2007), 'Generations', *Independent,* http://www. independent.co.uk/arts-entertainment/theatre-dance/reviews/ equus-gielgud-londonbrgenerations-young-vic-londonbrthe-eleventh-capital-royal-court-upstairs-london-438823.html [accessed 7 August 2011].

Bassett, K. (2008a), 'Relocated, Royal Court Upstairs, London; ... Sisters, Gate, London; 2,000 Feet Away, Bush Theatre, London', *Independent,* http://www.independent.co.uk/arts-entertainment/ theatre-dance/reviews/relocated-royal-court-upstairs-londonbrsisters-gate-londonbr(2000-feet-away-bush-theatre-london-851863),html [accessed 10 July 2015].

Bassett, K. (2008b), 'Six Characters in Search of an Author', *Independent,* http://www.independent.co.uk/arts-entertainment/theatre-dance/ reviews/six-characters-in-search-of-an-author-minerva-chichesterbr-free-outgoing-royal-court-downstairs-londonbr-the-frontline-shakespeares-globe-london-866238.html [accessed 15 October 2009].

Bauman, Z. (2007), *Liquid Times: Living in an Age of Uncertainty*, Cambridge: Polity Press.

Bauman, Z. (2012), *Liquid Modernity*, Cambridge: Polity Press.

Beaumarchais, P.-A. C. de (1991), 'Essay on the Serious Genre of Drama', in M. J. Sidnell (ed.), *Sources of Dramatic Theory: Volume 2, Voltaire to Hugo*, Cambridge: Cambridge University Press.

Berkowitz, G. (2005), 'Incomplete and Random Acts of Kindness', *The Stage,* http://www.thestage.co.uk/reviews/review.php/7850/incomplete-and-random-acts-of-kindness [accessed 26 May 2011].

Berkowitz, G. (2007), 'Generations', *The Stage,* http://www.thestage. co.uk/reviews/review.php/16087/generations [accessed 7 August 2011].

Billingham, P. (2007), *At the Sharp End: Uncovering the Work of Five Contemporary Dramatists*, London: Methuen.

Billington, M. (1995), 'The Good Fairies Desert the Court's Theatre of the Absurd', *Guardian*, 20 January, p. 22.

Billington, M. (2001a), 'Blasted', *Guardian,* http://www.guardian.co.uk/ stage/2001/apr/05/theatre.artsfeatures?INTCMP=SRCH [accessed 10 September 2011].

Billington, M. (2001b), 'Humble Boy', *Guardian*, http://www.
theguardian.com/stage/2001/aug/10/theatre.artsfeatures3 [accessed 28
January 2016].

Billington, M. (2008a), '2000 Feet Away', *Guardian*, http://www.
guardian.co.uk/stage/2008/jun/17/theatre.reviews2 [accessed 6
October 2008].

Billington, M. (2008b), 'Follow the Banned', *Whats on Stage*, http://
blogs.whatsonstage.com/2008/07/04/follow-the-banned/#more-370
[accessed 6 October 2008].

Billington, M. (2008c), 'Relocated', *Guardian*, http://www.guardian.
co.uk/stage/2008/jun/18/theatre.reviews [accessed 6 October 2008].

Billington, M. (2008d), 'The City', *Guardian*, http://www.guardian.
co.uk/stage/2008/apr/30/theatre2 [accessed 28 October 2009].

Billington, M. (2009), 'Time and the Conways', *Guardian*, https://www.
theguardian.com/stage/2009/may/06/time-conways-review-priestley
[accessed 2 July 2016].

Billington, M. (2012), 'Love and Information', *Guardian*, http://www.
theguardian.com/stage/2012/sep/15/love-and-information-royal-court-
review [accessed 29 January 2016].

Blattès, S. (2007), 'Is the Concept of "Character" Still Relevant in
Contemporary Drama?', *Contemporary Drama in English* 14: 69–81.

Booth, M. (1964), *Hiss the Villain*, London: Eyre & Spottiswoode.

Bottoms, S. (2009), 'Authorizing the Audience', *Performance Research*
14 (1): 65–76.

Bourdieu, P. (1977), *Outline of a Theory of Practice*, Cambridge:
Cambridge University Press.

Bowers, J. P. (2002), 'The Composition that All the World Can See:
Gertrude Stein's Theater Landscapes', in E. Fuchs and U. Chaudhuri
(eds), *Land/Scape/Theater*, Ann Arbor: University of Michigan Press.

Brecht, B. (1964), *Brecht on Theatre*, London: Methuen.

Brenton, H. and Hare, D. (1985), *Pravda*, London: Methuen.

Brooks, P. (1985), *Melodramatic Imagination: Balzac, Henry James,
Melodrama and the Mode of Excess*, New York: Columbia University
Press.

Brooks, P. (1994), 'The Melodramatic Imagination', in D. Hollier (ed.),
A New History of French Literature, Cambridge, MA: Harvard
University Press.

Browning, C. R. (2001), *Ordinary Men: Reserve Police Battalion 11 and
the Final Solution in Poland*, London: Penguin.

Calhoun, C. (1982), *The Question of Class Struggle*, Oxford: Blackwell.

Carlson, M. (2002), 'After Stein: Traveling the American Theatrical
"Lang-scape"', in E. Fuchs and U. Chaudhuri (eds), *Land/Scape/
Theater*, Ann Arbor: University of Michigan Press.

Carney, S. (2005), *Brecht and Critical Theory*, London: Routledge.

Castelvetro, L. (1984), *Castelvetro on the Art of Poetry*, Binghampton, NY: Medieval & Renaissance Texts and Studies.

Caughie, J. (2000), *Television Drama: Realism, Modernism, and British Culture*, Oxford: Oxford University Press.

Cave, R. A. (2009), 'Body Language in Pinter's Plays', in P. Raby (ed.), *The Cambridge Companion to Harold Pinter*, Cambridge: Cambridge University Press.

Cavendish, D. (2015), 'Widowers' Houses', *Telegraph*, http://www.telegraph.co.uk/culture/theatre/theatre-reviews/11324059/Widowers-Houses-Orange-Tree-Theatre-review.html [accessed 20 July 2015].

Churchill, C. (1960), 'Not Ordinary, Not Safe', *The Twentieth Century* 168: 443–51.

Churchill, C. (2008), *Plays: Four*, London: Nick Hern.

Churchill, C. (2012), *Love and Information*, London: Nick Hern.

Cibber, T. (1968), *The Lives of the Poets of Great Britain and Ireland*, Hildesheim, Germany: Georg Olms Verlagsbuchhandlung.

Cohn, R. (1991), *Retreats from Realism in Recent English Drama*, Cambridge: Cambridge University Press.

Collini, S. (2004), 'On Variousness; and on Persuasion', *New Left Review* 27: 65–97.

Collins, D. (1994), *Time and the Priestleys: The Story of a Friendship*, Stroud: Sutton Publishing Ltd.

Cooper, D. (1971), *The Death of the Family*, London: Vintage Books.

Corneille, P. (1991), 'On the Purpose and Parts of a Play', in M. J. Sidnell (ed.), *Sources of Dramatic Theory: Volume 1, Plato to Congreve*, Cambridge: Cambridge University Press.

Costa, M. (2012), 'Playwright Nick Payne: Master of the Multiverse', *Guardian*, http://www.theguardian.com/stage/2012/nov/02/nick-payne-playwright-constellations [accessed 18 November 2015].

Crimp, M. (2008), *The City*, London: Faber and Faber.

Crouch, T. (2009), *The Author*, London: Oberon.

Culler, J. (1981), *The Pursuit of Signs: Semiotics, Literature, Deconstruction*, Ithaca, NY: Cornell University Press.

Curteis, I. (2002), *The Falklands Play*, BBC.

Derrida, J. (1988), *Limited Inc*, Evanston, IL: Northwestern University Press.

Diderot, D. (1757), *Le Fils naturel*, http://www.theatre-classique.fr/pages/programmes/edition.php?t=../documents/DIDEROT_FILSNATUREL.xml [accessed 1 August 2016].

Diderot, D. (1991a), 'Conversations on *The Natural Son*', in M. J. Sidnell (ed.), *Sources of Dramatic Theory: Volume 2, Voltaire to Hugo*, Cambridge: Cambridge University Press.

Diderot, D. (1991b), 'Discourse on Dramatic Poetry', in M. J. Sidnell (ed.), *Sources of Dramatic Theory: Volume 2, Voltaire to Hugo*, Cambridge: Cambridge University Press.

Dollimore, J. and Sinfield, A. (1994), *Political Shakespeare: Essays in Cultural Materialism*, Manchester: Manchester University Press.

Dryden, J. (1971), 'An Essay on Dramatick Poesie', in A. Roper (ed.), *The Works of John Dryden: Volume XVII, Prose 1668–1691*, Berkeley: University of California Press.

Dryden, J. (1975), *All for Love*, London: A&C Black.

Dunne, J. W. (1927), *An Experiment with Time*, London: A&C Black.

Durkheim, E. (1960), *The Division of Labour in Society*, Glencoe, IL: The Free Press of Glencoe.

Edgar, D. (1987), *Plays 1*, London: Methuen.

Edgar, D. (1990), *The Shape of the Table*, London: Nick Hern.

Edgar, D. (1991), *Plays 3*, London: Methuen.

Edgar, D. (1999), *State of Play: Playwrights on Playwriting*, London: Faber and Faber.

Edgar, D. (2000), 'In Defence of Evil', *Observer*, http://www.guardian.co.uk/theobserver/2000/apr/30/featuresreview.review2 [accessed 21 September 2009].

Edgar, D. (2001), 'Making Drama Out of Crisis', *Guardian*, http://www.guardian.co.uk/education/(2001/jul/07/socialsciences.highereducation [accessed 24 April 2009].

Edgar, D. (2003), 'Secret Lives', *Guardian*, http://www.guardian.co.uk/stage/(2003/apr/19/theatre.artsfeatures [accessed 24 April 2009].

Edgar, D. (2005), 'Rules of Engagement', *Guardian*, http://www.guardian.co.uk/stage/(2005/oct/22/theatre.fiction [accessed 24 April 2009].

Edgar, D. (2008), 'Doc and Dram', *Guardian*, http://www.guardian.co.uk/stage/2008/sep/27/theatre.davidedgar [accessed 28 September 2008].

Edgar, D. (2009), *How Plays Work: A Practical Guide to Playwriting*, London: Nick Hern.

Elam, K. (2002), *The Semiotics of Theatre and Drama*, London: Routledge.

Eldridge, D. (2005), *Incomplete and Random Acts of Kindness*, London: Methuen.

Engels, F. (1987), *The Condition of the Working Class in England*, London: Penguin.

Esslin, M. (2000), *Pinter the Playwright*, London: Methuen.

Etkind, A. et al. (2012), *Remembering Katyn*, Cambridge: Polity Press.

Euripides (2005), *The Bacchae and Other Plays*, London: Penguin.

Evanthius (1974), 'On Drama', in O. B. Hardison, K. Kerrane and A. Preminger (eds), *Classical and Medieval Literary Criticism: Translations and Interpretations*, New York: Frederick Ungar.

Fisher, M. (2013), 'Time and the Conways', *Guardian,* https://www.
theguardian.com/stage/2013/mar/11/time-and-the-conways-review
[accessed 2 July 2016].

Fischer-Lichte, E. (2009), *Theatre, Sacrifice, Ritual: Exploring Forms of
Political Theatre*, London and New York: Routledge.

Forster, E. M. (2005), *Aspects of the Novel*, London: Penguin.

Foucault, M. (1991), *Discipline and Punish: The Birth of the Prison*,
London: Penguin.

Foucault, M. (2011), 'Of Other Spaces', *Foucault, Info,* http://foucault.
info/documents/heteroTopia/foucault.heteroTopia.en.html [accessed 23
May 2011].

Fountain, T. (2007), *So You Want to Be a Playwright?*, London: Nick
Hern.

Freud, S. (1997), *Writings on Art and Literature*, W. Hamacher and
D. E. Wellbery (eds), Stanford, CT: Stanford University Press.

Fuchs, E. (1996), *The Death of Character: Perspectives on Theater After
Modernism*, Bloomington: Indiana University Press.

Fuchs, E. (2004), 'EF's Visit to a Small Planet: Some Questions to Ask a
Play', *Theater* 34 (2): 4–9.

Gardner, L. (2006), 'Realism', *Guardian,* http://www.guardian.co.uk/
stage/2006/aug/17/theatre.edinburgh2006 [accessed 24 April 2009].

Gardner, L. (2007), 'Generations', *Guardian,* http://www.guardian.co.uk/
stage/2007/mar/01/theatre2 [accessed 7 August 2011].

Gardner, L. (2009), 'The Author', *Guardian,* http://www.guardian.co.uk/
stage/2009/sep/30/the-author-review [accessed 14 September 2011].

Gibson, M. D. (2006), '1979 and All That: Periodization in Postwar
British Theatre History', *Theatre Survey*, 47(1): 33–50.

Girard, R. (1977), *Violence and the Sacred*, Baltimore, MD and London:
Johns Hopkins University Press.

Gooch, S. (2004), *Writing a Play*, London: A&C Black.

Gramsci, A. (1971), *Prison Notebooks*, Q. Hoare and G. Nowell-Smith
(eds), London: Lawrence & Wishart Ltd.

Greene, B. (2000), *The Elegant Universe: Superstrings, Hidden
Dimensions and the Quest for the Ultimate Theory*, London:
Vintage.

Greig, D. (2003), 'Edinburgh preview: David Greig', *Observer,* http://
www.guardian.co.uk/culture/2003/jul/27/edinburghfestival2003.
features4 [accessed 20 August 2011].

Greig, D. (2010), *Selected Plays (1999–2009)*, London: Faber and
Faber.

Greig, N. (2005), *Playwriting: A Practical Guide*, London: Routledge.

Greimas, A. J. (1983), *Structural Semantics: An Attempt at Method*,
Lincoln and London: University of Nebraska Press.

Griffiths, T. (1975), *Through the Night*, BBC.

Grimes, C. (2006), *Harold Pinter's Politics*, Madison, WI: Fairleigh Dickinson University Press.

Gurvitch, G. (1964), *The Spectrum of Social Time*, Dordrecht, Netherlands: D. Reidel.

Hall, E. T. (1966), *The Hidden Dimension*, New York: Doubleday.

Hall, S. (1996), 'The Meaning of New Times', in D. Morley and K.-H. Chen (eds), *Stuart Hall: Critical Dialogues in Cultural Studies*, London and New York: Routledge.

Handke, P. (1997), *Plays: 1*, London: Methuen.

Hare, D. (1990), *Racing Demon*, London: Faber and Faber.

Hare, D. (1991), *Murmuring Judges*, London: Faber and Faber.

Hare, D. (1993a), *Asking Around*, London: Faber and Faber.

Hare, D. (1993b), *The Absence of War*, London: Faber and Faber.

Harvey, D. (1990), *The Condition of Postmodernity*, Oxford: Blackwell.

Harvey, D. (2010), *The Enigma of Capital and the Crises of Capitalism*, London: Profile.

Hazlitt, W. (1998), *The Selected Writings of William Hazlitt*, D. Wu (ed.), London: Pickering & Chatto.

Hegel, G. W. F. (1920), *The Philosophy of Fine Art*, London: Bell.

Hewison, R. (2008), 'The City', *Times,* http://entertainment.timesonline.co.uk/tol/arts_and_entertainment/stage/theatre/article3850262.ece [accessed 28 October 2009].

Hilliard, R. L. (2014), *Writing for Television, Radio, and New Media*, Stamford, CT: Cengage Learning.

Holcroft, S. (2011), *Edgar and Annabel*, in *Double Feature: Volume One*, London: Nick Hern.

Holderness, G. (1992), 'Introduction', in G. Holderness (ed.), *The Politics of Theatre and Drama*, London: Macmillan.

Horace (2000), 'The Art of Poetry', in P. Murray and T. S. Dorsch (trans.), *Classical Literary Criticism*, London: Penguin.

Howarth, W. D. (1997), *French Theatre in the Neo-Classical Era, 1550–1789*, Cambridge: Cambridge University Press.

Hutcheon, L. (2012), *A Theory of Adaptation*, London: Routledge.

Ibsen, H. (2002), *Hedda Gabler*, London: Methuen.

Innes, C. (1992), *Modern British Drama 1890–1990*, Cambridge: Cambridge University Press.

Jameson, F. (1971), *Marxism and Form: Twentieth-Century Dialectical Theories of Literature*, Princeton, NJ: Princeton University Press.

Jameson, F. (1983), *The Political Unconscious*, London: Routledge.

Johnston, B. (1992), *The Ibsen Cycle: The Design of the Plays from*

Pillars of Society to When We Dead Awaken, University Park: Pennsylvania Press.

Jones, C. (2001), *Humble Boy*, London: Faber and Faber.

Kane, S. (2001), *Complete Plays*, London: Methuen.

Kelleher, J. (2009), *Theatre and Politics*, Basingstoke: Palgrave Macmillan.

Kershaw, B. (1992), *The Politics of Performance: Radical Theatre as Cultural Intervention*, London: Routledge.

Kot, W. (2007), 'Krzyk Katynia', *Wprost,* https://www.wprost.pl/113932/Krzyk-Katynia [accessed 23 July 2016].

Kritzer, A. H. (2008), *Political Theatre in Post-Thatcher Britain: New Writing: 1995–2005*, Basingstoke: Palgrave Macmillan.

Lacan, J. (1992), *The Seminar. Book VII: The Ethics of Psychoanalysis, 1959–1960*, London: Routledge.

Lash, S. and Urry, J. (1987), *The End of Organized Capitalism*, Cambridge: Polity Press.

Lefebvre, H. (1991), *The Production of Space*, Oxford: Blackwell.

Lehmann, H.-T. (2006), *Postdramatic Theatre*, London: Routledge.

Lessing, G. E. (1962), *Hamburg Dramaturgy*, New York: Dover Publications Inc.

Lewes, G. H. (1875), *On Actors and the Art of Acting*, London: Smith, Elder & Co.

Lillo, G. (1965), *The London Merchant*, W. H. McBurney (ed.), London: Edward Arnold.

Lucas, F. L. (1927), *Tragedy: In Relation to Aristotle's Poetics*, London: Hogarth Press.

Luckhurst, M. (2002), 'Contemporary English Theatre: Why Realism?', *Contemporary Drama in English* 9: 73–84.

Luckhurst, M. (2009), 'Speaking Out: Harold Pinter and Freedom of Expression', in P. Raby (ed.), *The Cambridge Companion to Harold Pinter*, Cambridge: Cambridge University Press.

Lyotard, J.-F. (1984), *The Postmodern Condition: A Report on Knowledge*, Manchester: Manchester University Press.

Marlowe, C. (1999), *The Complete Plays*, London: Dent.

Martin, R. (2002), *Financialization of Daily Life*, Philadelphia, PA: Temple University Press.

Marx, K. (2008), *Capital: An Abridged Edition*, D. McLellan (ed.), Oxford: Oxford University Press.

Matthews, B. (1906), *The Development of the Drama*, New York: Charles Scribner's Sons, https://archive.org/stream/developmentdram00mattgoog#page/n10/mode/2up [accessed 8 January 2016].

Mayer, D. (2004), 'Encountering Melodrama', in K. Powell (ed.),

The Cambridge Companion to Victorian and Edwardian Theatre, Cambridge: Cambridge University Press.

Meyer, M. (1971), *Henrik Ibsen: The Farewell to Poetry 1864–1882*, London: Rupert Hart-Davis.

Miller, A. G., Gordon, A. K. and Buddie, A. M. (1999), 'Accounting for Evil and Cruelty: Is to Explain to Condone?', *Personality and Social Psychology Review* 3 (3): 254–68.

Moi, T. (2006), *Henrik Ibsen: Art, Theater, Philosophy*, Oxford: Oxford University Press.

La Motte, A. H. de (1754), *Oeuvres*, Paris.

Neilson, A. (2007a), 'Foreword', in *The Wonderful World of Dissocia and Realism*, London: Methuen.

Neilson, A. (2007b), *The Wonderful World of Dissocia and Realism*, London: Methuen.

Neilson, A. (2008a), 'Last Word: Anthony Neilson on Relocated', *Guardian*, http://arts.guardian.co.uk/theatre/drama/story/0,,2287274,00.html [accessed 24 April 2009].

Neilson, A. (2008b), *Relocated*, unpublished manuscript.

Neipris, J. (2005), *To Be a Playwright*, Abingdon: Routledge.

Newey, K. and Richards, J. (2010), *John Ruskin and the Victorian Theatre*, Basingstoke and New York: Palgrave Macmillan.

Norris, C. (2003), *Deconstruction: Theory and Practice*, London: Routledge.

Osborne, J. (1957), *Look Back in Anger*, London: Faber and Faber.

Paget, D. (1992), 'Oh What a Lovely Post-modern War', in G. Holderness (ed.), *The Politics of Theatre and Drama*, London: Macmillan.

Patterson, M. (2003), *Strategies of Political Theatre: Post-War British Playwrights*, Cambridge: Cambridge University Press.

Payne, N. (2012), *Constellations*, London: Faber and Faber.

Pfister, M. (1988), *The Theory and Analysis of Drama*, Cambridge: Cambridge University Press.

Piaget, J. (1932), *The Language and Thought of the Child*, London: Kegan Paul Trench, Trubner & Co. Ltd.

Pinciano, L. (1953), *Philosophía Antigua Poética*, Madrid: Instituto 'Miguel de Cervantes'.

Pinero, A. W. (1995), *Trelawny of the Wells and Other Plays*, Oxford: Oxford University Press.

Pinter, H. (2005), *Plays: 4*, London: Faber and Faber.

Pirandello, L. (1925), 'Pirandello Confesses …', *The Virginia Quarterly Review* 1(1), http://www.vqronline.org/essay/pirandello-confesses [accessed 14 January 2016].

Pirandello, L. (2008), *Six Characters in Search of an Author*, London: Nick Hern.

Prebble, L. (2009), *ENRON*, London: Methuen.

Priestley, J. B. (1937), 'Introduction', in *Two Time Plays*, London: William Heinemann.

Priestley, J. B. (2000), *An Inspector Calls and Other Plays*, London: Penguin.

Propp, V. (1968), *Morphology of the Folktale*, Austin: University of Texas Press.

Rabey, D. I. (2003), *English Drama Since 1940*, London: Routledge.

Radosavljević, D. (2012), 'Sarah Kane's Illyria as the Land of Violent Love: A Balkan Reading of Blasted', *Contemporary Theatre Review* 22 (4): 499–511.

Radosavljević, D. (2013), *Theatre-Making: Interplay Between Text and Performance in the 21st Century*, Basingstoke: Palgrave Macmillan.

Rancière, J. (2007), 'The Emancipated Spectator', *Art Forum* (March): 270–81.

Ravenhill, M. (2008), *Shoot/Get Treasure/Repeat*, London: Methuen.

Ravenhill, M. (2013), *Plays 3*, London: Methuen.

Rebellato, D. (2009), *Theatre and Globalization*, Basingstoke: Palgrave Macmillan.

Richards, I. A. (1960), *Principles of Literary Criticism*, London: Routledge and Kegan Paul.

Richardson, B. (2007), 'Plot after Postmodernism', *Contemporary Drama in English* 14: 55–67.

Robertson, R. (1992), *Globalization: Social Theory and Global Culture*, London: Sage.

Robinson, M. (1997), *The Other American Drama*, Baltimore, MD and London: Johns Hopkins University Press.

Saunders, G. (2002), *Love Me or Kill Me: Sarah Kane and the Theatre of Extremes*, Manchester: Manchester University Press.

Schiller, F. (1903), *The Robbers, Fiesco, Love and Intrigue*, London: John C. Nimmo Ltd.

Searle, J. R. (1996), *The Construction of Social Reality*, London: Penguin.

Shakespeare, W. (1975), *As You Like It*, A. Latham (ed.), London and New York: Routledge.

Shaw, G. B. (1884), *A Manifesto*, London: Geo. Standring.

Shaw, G. B. (1887), *The True Radical Programme*, London: Geo. Standring.

Shaw, G. B. (1946), *Plays Unpleasant*, London: Penguin.

Shaw, G. B. (1986), *Major Critical Essays*, London: Penguin.

Shaw, G. B. (1993), *The Complete Prefaces: Volume 1 1889–1913*, D. H. Lawrence and D. J. Leary (eds), London: Allen Lane.

Shepherd, S. and Womack, P. (1996), *English Drama: A Cultural History*, Oxford: Blackwell.

Shklovsky, V. (1990), *Theory of Prose*, Elmwood Park, IL: Dalkey Archive Press.

Sidney, S. P. (1994), *Sir Philip Sidney: A Selection of His Finest Poems*, Oxford: Oxford University Press.

Sierz, A. (2000), *In-Yer-Face Theatre: British Drama Today*, London: Faber and Faber.

Sierz, A. (2011), *Rewriting the Nation: British Theatre Today*, London: Methuen.

Singer, P. (2001), *Hegel: A Very Short Introduction*, Oxford: Oxford University Press.

Smith, A. (1817), *The Theory of Moral Sentiments*, Philadelphia, PA: Anthony Finley.

Smith, I. (2006), *Pinter in the Theatre*, London: Nick Hern.

Sophocles (1986), *Plays 1*, London: Methuen.

Souriau, É. (1950), *Les Deux cent mille situations dramatiques*, Paris: Flammarion Editeur.

Spencer, C. (2009), 'Enron', *Telegraph,* http://www.telegraph.co.uk/journalists/charles-spencer/5893217/Enron-at-Minerva-Theatre-in-Chichester-review.html [accessed 30 January 2016].

Spencer, C. (2012), 'Love and Information', *Telegraph,* http://www.telegraph.co.uk/culture/theatre/theatre-reviews/9547878/Love-and-Information-Royal-Court-Theatre-review.html [accessed 30 January 2016].

Stafford-Clark, M. (1997), *Letters to George: The Account of a Rehearsal*, London: Nick Hern.

Stanislavski, K. (1988), *An Actor Prepares*, London: Methuen.

Stein, G. (1949), *Last Operas and Plays*, New York: Rinehart & Co.

Stein, G. (2004), *Look at Me Now and Here I am: Writing and Lectures, 1909–45*, London and Chester Springs, PA: Peter Owen Ltd.

Stephens, S. (2006), *Motortown*, London: Methuen.

Stephens, S. (2008), *Pornography*, London: Methuen.

Stoppard, T. (2010), *The Real Thing*, London: Faber and Faber.

Strindberg, A. (1976), *Strindberg Plays 1*, London: Methuen.

Szondi, P. (1987), *Theory of the Modern Drama*, Cambridge: Polity.

Taylor, J. R. (1969), *Anger and After: A Guide to the New British Drama*, London: Methuen.

Taylor, P. (2005), 'Incomplete and Random Acts of Kindness', *Independent,* http://www.independent.co.uk/arts-entertainment/theatre-dance/reviews/incomplete-and-random-acts-of-kindness-royal-court-491922.html [accessed 26 May 2011].

Taylor, P. (2008), 'The City', *Independent,* http://www.independent.co.uk/

arts-entertainment/theatre-dance/reviews/the-city-royal-court-london-818719.html [accessed 28 October 2009].

Taylor, P. (2012), 'Love and Information', *Independent*, http://www.independent.co.uk/arts-entertainment/theatre-dance/reviews/love-and-information-royal-court-london-8144232.html [accessed 30 January 2016].

Taylor, V. (2002), *Stage Writing: A Practical Guide*, Malborough: The Crowood Press Ltd.

Toffler, A. (1970), *Future Shock*, New York: Random House.

Trueman, M. (2011), 'Edgar and Annabel', *Matt Trueman*, http://matttrueman.co.uk/2011/08/review-edgar-and-annabel-double-feature-national-theatre.html [accessed 22 January 2016].

tucker green, debbie (2005), *Trade and Generations*, London: Nick Hern.

Urban, K. (2001), 'An Ethics of Catastrophe: The Theatre of Sarah Kane', *PAJ: A Journal of Performance and Art* 23 (3): 36–46.

Vizetelly, E. A. (1904), *Émile Zola: Novelist and Reformer*, London and New York: John Lane.

Vygotsky, L. S. (1987), *The Collected Works of L.S. Vygotsky*, R. W. Rieber and A. S. Carton (eds), New York and London: Plenum Press.

Wade, L. (2005), *Breathing Corpses*, London: Oberon.

Walker, J. (1969), *The Factory Lad*, in M. R. Booth (ed.), *English Plays of the Nineteenth Century: Dramas 1800–1850*, Oxford: Clarendon Press.

Waters, S. (2010), *The Secret Life of Plays*, London: Nick Hern.

Weber, M. (2011), *The Protestant Ethic and the Spirit of Capitalism*, New York: Oxford University Press.

Weigh, A. (2008), *2000 Feet Away*, London: Faber and Faber.

Weinberg, B. (1974), *A History of Literary Criticism in the Italian Renaissance*, Chicago: University of Chicago Press.

Whitman, R. F. (1977), *Shaw and the Play of Ideas*, London: Cornell University Press.

Wilder, T. (1992), *Conversations with Thornton Wilder*, J. R. Bryer (ed.), Jackson: University Press of Mississippi.

Wiles, D. (2014), *Theatre and Time*, Basingstoke: Palgrave Macmillan.

Williams, R. (2001), *The Raymond Williams Reader*, J. Higgins (ed.), Oxford: Blackwell.

Wimsatt, W. K. and Beardsley, M. C. (1970), 'The Intentional Fallacy', in *The Verbal Icon: Studies in the Meaning of Poetry*, London: Methuen.

Wood, C. (1988), *Tumbledown*, BBC.

Wu, D. (2000), *Making Plays: Interviews with Contemporary British Dramatists and Their Directors*, Basingstoke: Palgrave Macmillan.

Žižek, S. (2006), 'Why are Laibach and the Neue Slowenische Kunst not Fascists?', in R. Butler and S. Stephens (eds), *The Universal Exception: Selected Writings Volume Two*, London: Continuum.

Zola, É. (1968a), 'Naturalism in the Theatre', in E. Bentley (ed.), *The Theory of the Modern Stage*, Harmondsworth: Penguin.

Zola, É. (1968b), *Œuvres Complètes*, Paris: Cercle du Livre Précieux.

INDEX